A FORK IN THE ROAD

A FORK IN THE ROAD

FROM SINGLE PARTNER TO LARGEST LEGAL PRACTICE IN THE WORLD

ROGER LANE-SMITH

ICON

Published in the UK in 2014 by
Icon Books Ltd, Omnibus Business Centre,
39–41 North Road, London N7 9DP
email: info@iconbooks.com
www.iconbooks.com

Sold in the UK, Europe and Asia
by Faber & Faber Ltd, Bloomsbury House,
74–77 Great Russell Street,
London WC1B 3DA or their agents

Distributed in the UK, Europe and Asia
by TBS Ltd, TBS Distribution Centre, Colchester Road,
Frating Green, Colchester CO7 7DW

Distributed in Australia and New Zealand
by Allen & Unwin Pty Ltd,
PO Box 8500, 83 Alexander Street,
Crows Nest, NSW 2065

Distributed in Canada by
Penguin Books Canada,
90 Eglinton Avenue East, Suite 700,
Toronto, Ontario M4P 2Y3

Distributed in South Africa by
Jonathan Ball, Office B4, The District,
41 Sir Lowry Road, Woodstock 7925

Distributed in India by Penguin Books India,
11 Community Centre, Panchsheel Park,
New Delhi 110017

ISBN: 978-184831-797-0

Typeset in Bembo by Marie Doherty

Printed and bound in the UK by Clays Ltd, St Ives plc

To Harry and Dorothy, my parents, who set me on the right road; and to Pamela who kept me on it!

About the author

Roger Lane-Smith was born in 1945 at Adlington Hall in Cheshire, England.

He qualified as a lawyer in 1969 and in 1977 started his own single-partner law firm in Manchester, intent on creating from scratch the world's largest law firm. Thirty-three years later he achieved this ambition with the firm of DLA Piper, now the world's largest with in excess of 4,500 fee-earners across 87 offices in 32 countries with revenues of £1.5bn. He retired as Senior Partner in 2005, although he continues as Senior Consultant to the firm.

Roger has been married for 45 years to Pamela and they live in Cheshire and in Provence. They have two adult children, Zoë and Jonathan, and a grandson, Logan.

Roger's passions outside the law include golf, shooting and fine wine.

Contents

List of Illustrations

Author's note

This book is a book about my life. It is not a book about the history of DLA. The views that I express are obviously very much my own personal views and therefore obviously do not necessarily reflect the formal views of DLA Piper or any of its partners. I try to tell the story in as honest a way as I can and in doing so I have perhaps stepped over the mark in views concerning personal relationships, but in a book such as this it is inevitable. As a lawyer I am happy (because I cannot be sued) that nothing in this book is defamatory. I have done my best and hope that you find it as enjoyable to read as I did to write.

The profession of practising law involves very strict ethical standards, particularly regarding client confidentiality. I take this extremely seriously and for that reason there is nothing in this book that reveals even a hint of the huge reservoir of client confidences that have built up in my head over the 50 years or so.

Foreword

by John Timpson

It's foolish to make generalisations and I was certainly way off the mark when I thought that corporate lawyers were pedantic, process-driven and somewhat serious. That was before I met Roger Lane-Smith.

In fact my wife, Alex, met Roger before I did. We were at one of those charity dinners where you would willingly give twice the ticket price not to attend. While I was struggling with small talk at my end of the table Alex was sitting next to Roger.

On the way home we compared notes. My companions discussed holidays, gardening and local pubs, but Roger just wanted to talk to Alex about business. It was 1982 and I was the Managing Director running Timpson, which was a subsidiary of the UDS Group (alongside John Collier and Richard Shops). 'I didn't really know what this guy Roger was talking about', said Alex, 'but I think you should see him. He said he will ring you on Monday morning.'

On Tuesday Roger was in my office telling me what a management buyout was and how we could go about it. Within eight weeks he had buyout specialist Candover fronting the funding and fifteen months later I bought back our business. By that time I was getting to know Roger pretty well.

I discovered Roger isn't fazed by anything or anyone. UDS were taken over and we found we were negotiating with Hanson Trust. Undaunted by their tough reputation, Roger went straight to the top. On the back of a two-minute chat at a cocktail party in New York, Roger telephoned Chief Executive Sir Gordon White and on a transatlantic call fixed for us to talk about a deal while Sir Gordon was over in London for Ascot.

When Roger masterminded the exchange of contracts in September 1983 he orchestrated fourteen sets of London lawyers and a couple from Scotland. There was no hint that, at that time, he was leading a modest Manchester practice with only five partners.

Since then I've witnessed Roger's direct determination in many more deals. While he created one of the world's biggest legal firms he helped me grow our business many times over.

For over 30 years Roger has been one of my non-executive directors, his mind perhaps wandering while we talked about watch repairs and warehousing but always fully focused whenever there's the slightest hint of developing another deal.

I love Roger's 'do it now' attitude. Not many lawyers live life holding a glass that is always much more than half full. While others argue petty points of detail, Roger looks for the simple way to get the deal done. I have seen his frustration when dramatic deals unnecessarily drag on through the night. Roger doesn't let the tussle of legal wrangling get in the way of common sense. His route one approach to deal-making did me an enormous favour when he exchanged and completed the purchase of our house within six days. Alex and I have lived there very happily for over 27 years.

Despite Roger's dislike of drawn-out deals we inevitably spent many nights in London waiting for the other side to shuffle the paperwork. It gave Roger the chance to introduce me to some excellent restaurants, lots of fine wine and his fascinating fund of stories. Roger's enthusiasm and individual character can also be seen on the golf course, where he's an unpredictable performer, capable of driving the ball 325 yards on one hole and 35 yards on the next. I am never surprised when he comes up with a birdie or takes a mobile phone call in the middle of the fairway.

When I first met Roger it was quite clear he was ambitious but I didn't realise how far his constant pursuit of success would take him. I am lucky that several times he swept me along with his relentless optimism. I spent eight years stalking one major competitor and even longer trying to buy another. They were both long shots, but not to Roger who kept urging me to chase each deal by saying, 'Don't worry, we will get them one day', which we did. He brought the same attitude to the many twists that have made DLA a worldwide success. I look forward to reading the stories he has to tell about such a fascinating journey.

Roger sets a standard for other lawyers to follow. His highest accolade came from Alex, who once told me: 'If we ever have a divorce I'm having Roger acting on my side.'

Introduction

by Sir Nigel Knowles

I became Managing Partner of a law firm called Dibb Lupton Broomhead on 1 January 1996, completely unaware that in only a few months I would merge 'my' firm with 'Roger's' firm (Alsop Wilkinson) and forge a relationship with a man I am proud to now count as one of my closest friends. In 1996, Dibb Lupton Broomhead consisted of 600 lawyers in six offices. The firm was largely without a vision or a strategy and didn't have the right sort of reputation in relation to the way it dealt with its people and clients. We wanted, however, to be a truly national firm. To achieve this, we needed more good people and a bigger critical mass. As Managing Partner, I soon realised I had a lot on my plate! Alsop Wilkinson was about half the size of Dibb Lupton Broomhead and soon emerged as a possible merger candidate. (Roger was the Chairman of that firm.)

Roger's book gives an account of his very colourful and interesting professional life. I am not sure the merger of two medium-sized law firms in 1996 qualified as one of the most 'colourful' parts of his professional journey, but it certainly was a highlight for him – the merger of these two firms was one of the events that ultimately created the world's largest law firm – DLA Piper.

From a business perspective, in the 1996/97 financial year, Dibb Lupton Broomhead had set an income budget of £68m and Alsop Wilkinson had set a budget of £32m. In a single stroke, following a 'merger meeting' lasting only three hours one Saturday morning, we became a £100m revenue law firm. When Dibb Lupton Alsop was 'born' on 1 October 1996, it was the largest merger of two UK law firms. Roger subsequently became Senior Partner and I remained as Managing Partner. We, of course, had a great team around us and our success then and for almost a decade since, is due to a great many partners – not all of whom can be mentioned in the pages of this book, and some of whom have joined the firm since Roger's retirement.

Roger's tale of his life, both before and after that 1996 merger, is a remarkable story of his vision and determination to create the world's largest law firm. Roger is a natural leader, has infinite amounts of energy and determination and is a person who never gives up. He is larger than life (in every way), is a lateral thinker and as you will read, is both eloquent and amusing.

Occasionally he wanted to depart from the path we'd all agreed, but only because he thought he could make the firm better and usually it did. Shortly after the creation of DLA Piper on 1 January 2005, Roger stepped down as Senior Partner leaving me and the team to firm up on the detail and make it work!

Along the way, Roger and I have shared so many exciting times and had plenty of laughs together (along with some stress, of course). Roger was a hugely popular guy in the firm, whose after-dinner speeches at Partners' conferences became legendary! I shall never forget his final speech as Senior Partner at a Partners' conference in Paris. The speech was hilarious (as always) and heartfelt and every partner rose to a standing ovation which seemed never-ending.

In the pages that follow Roger will tell you his story of his professional life. He's a great guy, with a lot of stories to tell and a remarkable way of telling them, and I'm sure you will enjoy reading this book.

Monetary Values

Money and its value is always a problem when writing about a period that stretches over a number of years, particularly when parts of that period have included some years of very high inflation. Furthermore, establishing a yardstick for measuring the change in the value of money is not easy either. Do we take the external value of the pound or what it will buy in the average (whatever that may be) weekly shopping basket? Do we relate it to the average manual wage? As we know, while prices in general might rise, and have done so in this country every year since the Second World War, the prices of certain products might fall. However, we are writing about a business, and money and its value crop up on almost every page. We therefore have to make some judgements. We can only generalise, and I think the best yardstick is probably the average working wage.

Taking this as the benchmark, here is a measure of the pound sterling relative to its value in 2014.

Apart from wartime, prices were stable for 250 years, but began to rise in the run-up to the First World War.

1665–1900   multiply by 120
1900–1914   multiply by 110

1918–39	multiply by 60
1945–50	multiply by 35
1950–60	multiply by 30
1960–70	multiply by 25
1970–74	multiply by 20
1975–77	multiply by 15
1978–80	multiply by 8
1980–87	multiply by 5
1987–91	multiply by 2.5
1991–97	multiply by 1.5

Since 1997, the rate of inflation has been very low by the standards of most of the 20th century, averaging until very recently less than the government's originally stated aim of 2.5 per cent (since reduced to 2 per cent). Some things – such as telephone charges and many items made in the Far East, notably China – have gone down in price while others, such as houses, moved up very sharply from 1997 to 2008 before falling back in the financial crisis. In 2011, on the back of sharply rising commodity and food prices, inflation accelerated again to reach 5 per cent per annum. However, as commodity prices fell back and much of the world suffered very low growth, the rate of inflation began to subside again in 2012 and 2013 and, by the middle of 2014, was falling to rates where the authorities started to worry about the harmful effects of deflation.

CHAPTER 1

A Moment in Time

It is late June 2011 and at 4.30 in the afternoon I'm sitting on the terrace of our home in Provence. It is 37° in the shade with butterflies and bees fluttering and flitting through the mass of lavender. There are wonderful Provencal smells, the pool is at 27° and the sky is a perfect blue with a gentle breeze rustling through the palms.

The time has come. I must gather my thoughts and memories to look back over the last 65 years and start to put together the story. Ever since I can remember I have had a burning desire to achieve something in my life and to one day look back and know that I had done so.

People have many and various ambitions and in my early days I had my fair share – airline pilot, rock star, prime minister, most of the usual suspects – except that mine firmed up fairly early at about the age of fifteen. I don't remember the precise moment but as ever I was being pressed to decide which path to take in life. I made one big, sudden decision – I wanted to be a lawyer. I think that I enjoyed arguing, being in control, sorting out difficult problems and finding a way through. Becoming a lawyer seemed to offer me the chance to do just that.

As it turned out, I ended up being involved with some of

the greatest deals, acting for some of the most famous people in the world and meeting many more along the way. All this began with just me and a secretary, going on to create the world's largest law firm with over 90 offices, covering every continent, with 5,000 or more lawyers and 10,000 or more jobs. They are a collection of some of the finest legal talent and the greatest clients in the world.

It is a story I am ready to tell and, like every would-be autobiographer, I suppose I am wondering quite where to start. As I look back over the years I can see that there were a limited number of moments that truly were a fork in the road. Sometimes I made a deliberate decision to follow one route, never then knowing what another may have led to, and sometimes it was a sheer matter of chance and luck that one road opened up as another petered out ahead of me.

This surely happens to everyone. You see a new face at a party – you can seek them out and find that through them your life changes, for better or worse, forever. Or you simply turn to a familiar face and relax in your comfort zone.

I have had several forks in the road that I know made a vast difference to my life. So I'll start with one day, 1 October 1977.

I was just eighteen days away from my 32nd birthday. Having married at 23, I had two children, aged six and four, a big home, a big mortgage, and a brand new £10,000 (£150,000 in today's money) bank loan facility to start my own law firm. I had just walked out pretty acrimoniously from another firm that I had joined as partner at the age of 27. The previous four years had been quite stressful and, as you will see, very eventful, but in the end the truth was that I had one burning ambition, which was to do my own thing.

It had been raining hard for most of the day, which is not an uncommon feature of early autumn days in Manchester.

After months spent fighting over every last penny with my former partners, I was ready to go to my new little office suite at 20 Kennedy Street in the heart of the city, only 300 yards from where my old firm was located on Cross Street. I had a favourite chair at my old desk, orthopaedic for my perennially bad back, and I went to pick it up to take it with me as I left the old office and my soon to be former partners for, I hoped, the last time.

'Have you paid us for that chair?' chirped up one of the deadbeats. The chair had seen plenty of wear and tear and would not have sold for 10p in a car boot sale.

'No. How much for this then?' I said through gritted teeth.

'£20.' (£300 in today's money.)

I paid up.

My back was killing me and as I walked out into the pouring rain I upended the chair and put it on top of my head to shield me from the torrents. I then staggered the 300 yards to my new nest and up one floor into my little eyrie.

I was soaking wet and I plonked the chair down behind my smart little newly bought antique partner's desk. I grabbed a large cut glass and filled it full of ice cubes (a fridge is a must in a busy lawyer's office!). The Gordon's gin and slimline tonic quickly followed the ice into the glass with a slice of lime. I had prepared for this moment! I let the ice-cold nectar slip down my throat and breathed out an enormous sigh of relief, heavily tinged I'm sure with more than a large element of trepidation.

'I've done it!' the Outer Man exclaimed.

'Yes – but what exactly have you done and just what are you now going to do?' the Inner Man needled.

I looked out of the window – rainy Manchester in

October. The Outer Man had to get together with the Inner Man to create a partnership, a way forward for both of them.

'No point in aiming low and missing,' said the Inner Man, chiding the Outer Man. 'You're only going to do this if you are single-minded, with a clear unwavering mission and ambition that you can hang on to every day from now on!'

'I don't see why I can't create from these small, in fact infinitesimal, beginnings the best and finest law firm the World has ever seen.' The Outer Man had his chest puffed out now and the second gin and tonic was starting to have its effect.

'I'm up for that,' confided the Inner Man. I suppose the first wave of G and T had hit him too by this time.

And so they embraced each other and the union was formed, its motto being: From this day onwards let it be known that I will endlessly strive and not rest until such time as it shall be declared that, officially, this is the largest law firm the World has ever seen.

And so it was written. Only one small thing now – how to pull it off?

CHAPTER 2

The Early Days

As you will soon learn, a lot of my teens, and quite a lot of the rest of my life in moments of leisure, have been consumed by music, specifically rock music.

Sometime in the late 1990s we had a big Christmas party for the clients and partners of the firm at a wonderful venue – Adlington Hall in Cheshire. I had hired a group, The Prestons; a band of lawyers, Queen's Counsel in fact, who enjoyed playing 1960s rock and roll music. On the keyboard was my old pal, Peter Birkett QC, leader of the Northern Circuit of the Bar, raconteur *extraordinaire* and general good egg.

I was going to play in the band that night. I had a limited edition, gold-fretted Fender Stratocaster as made for Dave Gilmour of Pink Floyd on loan to me from his mate and mine Ronnie Stratton. I banged right in on rhythm guitar with 'I Saw Her Standing There', one of the greatest rock songs Paul McCartney ever penned. The room was rocking. At the end of that first song I took the microphone. I thanked the band for having me and the audience for putting up with me. I pointed out that this was my second public appearance at Adlington Hall and that it had been over 50 years since my first, in a room on the first floor of the Hall on 19 October 1945.

Adlington Hall is set in over 2,000 acres in Cheshire.

A certain Earl Edwin owned the estate in the 11th century until one William the Conqueror came along and unceremoniously turfed him out on his ear and gave the estate to one of his favourites, Hugh Lupus.

Obviously, the Lupus family were pretty grateful and proceeded to remain on the estate for the next seven generations. However, in 1221, when the last surviving male descendant of Hugh Lupus passed on, he failed to leave a male heir behind him and so the estate reverted to the Crown. At some point thereafter Henry III gave the estate to one of his followers, Hugh de Corona, whose granddaughter Ellen married one John de Legh. They produced a son Robert (1308–70) to whom the estate was given.

The Great Hall at Adlington was constructed between 1480 and 1505 around the original base of two great oak trees whose roots remain today supporting the east end of the Great Hall. The Legh family remain the owners of the estate today, having held it now for almost 700 years.

The reader will no doubt now be wondering what all this has to do with me. My last name is not Legh, although my wife's maiden name was Leigh. Notwithstanding that fact I entered the world on 19 October 1945 in that wonderful building and so have always simply been able to give my place of birth as Adlington Hall, Cheshire, England. During the latter stages of the Second World War the Hall was used as a maternity hospital. There were a total of 999 babies born there and I must have been 900 and something.

My father Harry was a Flight Lieutenant in the Royal Air Force. He met my mother, Dorothy Shuttleworth, at a dance in a church hall near Stockport in 1942 (what would have happened if he hadn't taken the trouble to ask Dorothy for a dance? No me!).

They married in 1943. My father had qualified as a pilot

but because pilots didn't have much of a survival rate it was decided that he would teach others to fly instead. He also qualified as an engineer which provided him, and therefore me, with some financial wherewithal in life. My father had made a good friend of a French airman called Roger and so, when I came along, I was called Roger. That was my first French connection! I recently told this story to a French friend who coyly observed that it is just as well my father did not know Bleriot – I am not so sure as Bleriot seems like a rather dashing first name to me!

Whenever I read autobiographies I often wonder why anyone would be interested in the early years of the subject, for example who their relations were – unless they were famous or interesting – what street they lived on and all sorts of other details that seem to me to add little to the sum of human knowledge. For that reason I do not intend to dwell on my early years, at least until some facts emerge which I judge are likely to interest the reader.

My father's family were originally from Kent but moved north as the railways were being constructed in the early 19th century. They moved to work on the building of the railways, as far as I can see. I don't believe that any of my ancestors, on either my father's or my mother's side, had ever had a career in the law, although my father used to tell me that my grandfather, or great-grandfather, was related (I think a cousin) to one F.E. Smith who became a celebrated lawyer and politician in the early years of the 20th century.

F.E., as he came to be known, was from the north-west of England and became a barrister and later King's Counsel in London. He became a close friend and cohort of the young Winston Churchill and did so well that eventually he was ennobled as Lord Birkenhead.

F.E. clearly had a sense of fun and an acerbic tongue.

Once he was appearing before a judge whom he intensely disliked, and the sentiment was mutual. At some point the judge lost his control and said to F.E.: 'Mr Smith – you are being very offensive.'

F.E. responded quick as a flash, 'As a matter of fact my Lord we both are. The difference is that I'm trying to be, but you can't help it!'

He also knew all the tricks of the trade as an accomplished advocate. Once he was acting for an insurance company defending a personal injury claim by a young man who claimed to have been injured so badly in an accident with a tram that his right arm was permanently damaged and so he could not perform any manual work. He could not earn a living and so was claiming massive damages.

F.E. got him in the box. He told him how much he empathised with his predicament, how dreadful it must be for him and how the judge needed to understand just how disabling the injury was.

He said, 'Would you please show the judge how high you can lift your arm now?'

The man struggled and gradually lifted his arm to around 30 degrees. He was very stiff and apparently in some considerable discomfort.

'You poor man,' said F.E. 'Now can you show the judge how high you could lift your arm before the accident?'

The man's arm shot straight up in the air to 180 degrees. You could hear a pin drop in the courtroom. Then the expression on the man's face turned from helpful triumphalism to one of abject resignation as he realised his claim was irreparably holed below the water line.

I have no idea if F.E. was indeed in any way part of my genes, but if he was I'm eternally grateful and hope that a little bit of his magic and allure rubbed off on me.

CHAPTER 3

Elvis

L ike most of us, I don't remember much of any signifi-cance before the age of four.

During those four years up to 1949 we lived in a small house on the outskirts of Stockport, overlooking a munici-pal park and very close to Stockport County Football Club. After a couple of years, my sister Hazel came along and my father was getting his engineering business, Haverhill Engineering, going. I never asked my father why he named his business after a place in Suffolk.

In 1949 we moved to a leafy suburb of Manchester called Cheadle Hulme. I do remember my first day at school, Queens Road Primary, and generally I had a pretty happy if not particularly memorable time there. The highlight was probably leaving to move on to senior school at the age of eleven.

What was Britain like in the late 1940s and early 1950s?

I cannot improve on what the masterly David Kynaston wrote in his *Austerity Britain 1945–51*:

Britain in 1945. No supermarkets, no motorways, no tea-bags, no sliced bread, no frozen food, no flavoured crisps, no lager, no microwaves, no dishwashers, no Formica, no vinyl, no CDs, no computers, no mobiles, no duvets, no Pill, no trainers, no hoodies, no Starbucks. Four Indian restaurants. Shops on every corner, pubs on every corner, cinemas in every high street, red telephone boxes, Lyons Corner Houses, trams, trolleybuses, steam trains. Woodbines, Craven 'A', Senior Service, smoke, smog, Vapex inhalant. No launderettes, no automatic washing machines, wash day every Monday, clothes boiled in a tub, scrubbed on the draining board, rinsed in the sink, put through the mangle, hung out to dry. Central heating rare, coke boilers, water geysers, the coal fire, the hearth, the home, chilblains common. Abortion illegal, homosexual relationships illegal, suicide illegal, capital punishment legal. White faces everywhere. Back-to-backs, narrow cobble streets, Victorian terraces, no high-rises. Arterial roads, suburban semis, the march of the pylon. Austin Sevens, Ford Eights, no seat belts, Triumph motorcycles with sidecars. A Bakelite wireless in the home, *Housewives' Choice* or *Workers' Playtime* or *ITMA* on the air, televisions almost unknown, no programmes to watch, the family eating together. Milk of Magnesia, Vicks Vapour Rub, Friar's Balsam, Fynnon Salts, Eno's, Germolene. Suits and hats, dresses and hats, cloth caps and mufflers, no leisurewear, no 'teenagers'. Heavy coins, heavy shoes, heavy suitcases, heavy tweed coats, heavy leather footballs, no unbearable lightness of being. Meat rationed, butter rationed, lard rationed, margarine rationed, sugar rationed, tea rationed, cheese rationed, jam rationed, eggs rationed, sweets rationed, soap rationed, clothes rationed. Make do and mend.

In terms of government, to many people's surprise, in the summer of 1945 the voters rejected the Conservatives and their leader Winston Churchill and gave a landslide victory to the Labour party. Led by Clement Attlee, who had been privately educated at Haileybury and ISC but was nevertheless a supporter of socialism, the next five years proved to be one of the most reforming periods in the UK of the whole 20th century. Whereas the attitude in 1918 had been one of trying to return to the golden pre-war era, in 1945 few wanted to return to the 1930s and there were great changes as many industries were nationalised; coal and the Bank of England in 1946, electricity in 1947, the railways in 1948, gas in 1949 and iron and steel in 1951.

In 1957 one of my friends had a guitar and we had all learnt the three basic chords of E, A and B7. Equipped with that, we could play most songs of the time but particularly 'Heartbreak Hotel' by Elvis Presley. Elvis was just coming to the attention of the world and was our god. Little did I know that twenty years later as a lawyer I would be representing his estate after his untimely death.

We planned a 'goodbye concert' for the end of term. I can't remember what I did wrong but somehow I managed to get banned from participating in the concert other than cheering on from the back of the hall.

So in summary, the years 1945 to 1957 were, as far as I can remember, happy and relatively uneventful.

In September 1957, having failed my eleven-plus exam – which I was forced to take despite having a heavy bout of influenza – through the strenuous efforts of my parents I took and passed the entrance examination for Stockport Grammar School, which had been founded in 1485, and was one of the oldest schools in the country. At about the same time that I was due to start at Stockport Grammar we moved house again; this time to a larger but still suburban detached home on the borders of Bramhall, another suburb of South

Manchester. This move, as the reader will see, eventually had a particularly helpful effect on my early musical career.

Everything kicked off fairly well at the grammar school. My classmates seemed like a reasonable bunch and, despite the occasional bullying which seems ingrained at most schools, early progress seemed to be made. I got a paper round which brought in useful cash and, furthermore, it was a choice round, delivering to some very large houses that gave good tips at Christmas. Caddying at Bramhall Park Golf Club bought more early financial, albeit meagre, rewards which were ploughed back into golf lessons with Mr Goodchild, the professional. Thus was born my love of golf which endures to this day.

I loved Buddy Holly and Eddie Cochran, and was very upset when they died in tragic accidents at an early age.

I messed around with one or two musical instruments; the violin, which was a disaster, and the trumpet which, if possible, was an even bigger, and certainly noisier, disaster. I ended up taking piano lessons. Even before my first lesson I had figured out how chords worked and I had a very attractive piano teacher. I was fascinated by her white painted fingernails. She was a very elegant lady. However, I soon tired of the piano which was a definite failing on my part. It was then on to classical guitar. After having some weekly lessons I was hooked. I had a Spanish guitar from Segovia and I loved it.

At school I had a classmate called Malcolm Swann. He also played Spanish guitar and the group to follow was The Shadows. Hank B. Marvin was our hero. My interest was starting to move over from classical/Spanish guitar to pop. The Shadows played a concert in Stockport and a mate joined me at the stage door to catch the band as they went into rehearsal. Hank Marvin and Bruce Welch arrived and wanted us to show them the way to a restaurant where they could get a curry. I spent the next hour with my hero!

Malcolm and I messed around a little and had the makings of a group at school. At about the same time, my mother wanted me to take dancing lessons, which meant quickstep and waltz, not ballet, at a dance class in Bramhall. I was horrified by this until I realised that it was just a great way to meet the opposite sex which, at fourteen or fifteen years of age, was a challenge. To be cool in front of the girls I would go along with a few pals, but started taking my acoustic guitar along slung over my back Bob Dylan-style and trying to look mean and moody.

There is a classic story of when John Lennon first met Paul McCartney in the days of the Quarrymen about this same time. John asked Paul what tunes he knew and Paul knocked off 'Twenty Flight Rock' by Eddie Cochran. John was particularly impressed that Paul could play the guitar solo in the song.

One night, outside the front steps of the big shed where the weekly dancing lessons took place, I bumped into another guy with a guitar. He wore horn-rimmed glasses à la Buddy Holly. We were sizing each other up, mates and girls watching.

'What do you know?' he said.

I moved straight into 'Twenty Flight Rock'. He was with me in a heartbeat and so was born a beautiful friendship. Ian Curley, 'Curls' as he would always be called, and I had collided in life and things were now about to hot up.

CHAPTER 4

Trailblazers

You will recall the hackneyed saying that if you could remember the 1960s, you weren't there!

It must have been sometime early in 1960 that Curls and I met and sure enough everything seemed to accelerate away; my memories of what happened next are, as a result, a little hazy. We had to form a group. We had another mate, Geoff Ford, who is still a good friend today, who could sing a bit. We picked up a drummer, Albert, from somewhere. When we discovered, and he accepted, that Geoff couldn't really sing, we found Nigel Thompson, who had a great voice. I desperately needed a proper electric guitar. My old acoustic was not going to cut it even with an electric pickup fitted.

The summer holidays of 1960 found me working at the Co-op department store in Stockport to save enough money – £45 – to buy a Hofner Sunburst Guitar. A decent salary then was £20 (£500 in today's money) a week so that puts £45 into perspective.

By September 1960, guitar bought, group in practice, we needed a uniform and we needed a name. One day we all went into Manchester and went to Austin Reed, the men's tailor. We found a sand-coloured zip-up jacket called a 'Trailblazer'. We loved the colour and we loved the double entendre of a jacket that one wore on the trail, and as we would be blazing a trail to success and fortune, the Trailblazers it was.

White shirts and red bow ties (ugh!) completed the look. We were the Trailblazers!

We played a rather esoteric set of music mixing Cliff Richard and the Shadows, the Everly Brothers, Buddy Holly and Elvis. We couldn't write a song to save our lives, and really that fact sealed our fate. However, two things then happened to change everything we did.

First, I was still messing around with a band at school with Malc Swann and others. We played a few concerts there to entertain the school dances that were held with girls from the next-door convent school.

One day, after a school concert, another sixth former came up to me with an LP under his arm. 'Your band's OK but you're playing crap music,' he said. 'Get playing some of this stuff instead.'

With that he stuck the LP under my arm and walked off. The LP was *A Fistful of Berries* by Chuck Berry. It was a complete revelation and we couldn't stop playing 'Johnny B. Goode', 'Sweet Little Sixteen' and scores more!

At about the same time we bumped into a new face at the dancing class. He was called Rod Mayall, but he liked to be called Stan Mayall – don't ask! Stan was a pretty natty dresser, very unconventional for those days. He used to wear the most amazing socks of the brightest hue. When challenged at school by a master who said, 'Mayall – why are you wearing those bright green socks?', Stan's response was, 'Cos my luminous pink ones are in the wash, Sir!'

Stan was 'sort of' into the music scene and he asked Curls and me to his home, which was just across the fields at the back of my house. Stan's home was unusual. It was a bungalow but somehow a little strange, as were his parents, and in the garden was a very large tree in which was contained a commodious treehouse in which lived Stan's elder brother.

Stan's brother was called John – John Mayall. At the time that meant nothing to Curls and me. We would spend hours and days on end up in the treehouse with John and Stan as John taught us about 'the Blues'.

John had an amazing collection of records of the Deep South Blues artists – Big Bill Broonzy, Sonny Boy Williamson, Howlin' Wolf and on and on. John taught us to play hard-driving rhythm and blues music until it was riveted deep down in our souls. Curls and I were transported and hooked.

John was just forming his own band – the Blues Breakers. We weren't good enough (students still) to make the cut. Some guy called Eric Clapton beat me to the punch!

Now we were rocking. The Trailblazers' first big public appearance had been at a Scoutatoo (a fête to raise money for the Scouts) at Bramhall Hall on 2 September 1961. We weren't bad but we weren't great. We needed to hit the bigger venues, but we were only sixteen going on seventeen and too young to play in the Manchester clubs where everything was really starting to erupt.

We used to bump into Freddie and the Dreamers, Wayne Fontana and the Jets (soon to change their name to the Mindbenders), and we kept seeing a group coming over from Liverpool and doing well in the Manchester clubs, the Beatles.

We wanted so much to get into the concerts but we were just too young. We found a bass guitarist, Albert bought some drums, but still it wasn't happening. We were approached to form the backbone of a new group to be formed around a great singer called Cliff Bowes. Inevitably the backing group was going to be called – yes reader you've got it – the Arrows! We went for the audition and had to back Cliff singing Gene Vincent's 'Be Bop a Lula'. I was on lead guitar, Curls on rhythm, Albert on drums. We had a tight sound and we were good. Job done. The Trailblazers were no more and the world saw the birth of Cliff Bowes and the Arrows.

I suppose I should pause at this point since the intelligent reader will be thinking about two things. He already knows that Cliff Bowes and the Arrows did not go on to dominate the charts and the headlines in the 1960s. He wants to know, 'You're 17, still at school, A levels are coming up so what are you doing about education and what is happening about the opposite sex?'

On education my mind was focused on rock and roll but, fear not, also on GIRLS! The reader has a pretty good idea about the music side. A good hard-driving rock and roll band, who can't write a song, moving into the era where John Lennon, Paul McCartney and George Harrison are seriously about to rev up a gear. I haven't forgotten Ringo Starr but he couldn't write music.

Girls had been on my mind for at least two years by now and I had a steady girlfriend called Christine. Blonde, with a good figure, she had just left school and was starting a job. On the education front I had got seven O levels and was taking History, English and French Literature at A level. At least I knew, or thought I knew, what I would do if I couldn't make it as a rock star. I would be a solicitor!

It was the Beatles who finally convinced me. In October 1962 out came 'Love Me Do' – and on the B side – 'PS I Love You'. I played it so much I wore it thin! In 1963, having passed my driving test, I persuaded my father to let me borrow his grand Rover 90 Saloon to take four friends to a concert at the Pavilion Gardens in Buxton to see live … the Beatles.

We got there around 7.00pm and got into the hall. The capacity was probably about 400 but it seemed like there were twice that many people there. We were up at the front by a pillar which would prevent us from being crushed to death if the army of girls all advanced at the same time.

The tension built, the room was at fever point, the curtains came back and there were the Beatles who went straight into 'Too Much Monkey Business' by Chuck Berry. John Lennon squared up to the microphone with his legs planted apart and let his body bounce on his knees with the beat. Paul and George shared the other microphone. Ringo hit the back beat on the drums that penetrated your very soul.

Never, before or since, have I heard such a sound that made the hairs on the back of my neck stand on end. They swept everything away in front of them and we all knew that we were experiencing first-hand the band to end all bands. It was at that moment that I decided that we could never compete with this and that my future lay in the law, not in rock and roll.

CHAPTER 5

The Law

B ack in the early 1960s there were two ways of becoming a solicitor. The first was to go to university and get a degree, preferably, but not necessarily, in law, then go on to work with a firm of solicitors as a trainee for two and a half years before taking the Law Society Final Exams. In those days a trainee was called an articled clerk. The alternative was to go straight from school into a solicitor's firm and sign up to Articles of Clerkship for five years. Since the only university I was interested in going to was Cambridge, and I wasn't prepared to work hard enough to get in there, it would have to be the 'five year route'.

At this point I haven't told you much about my parents. My father was a totally straightforward hardworking man who loved his family and my mother was the same, plus she was not used to taking 'no' for an answer. One day she came home and announced that she had got me an interview. She had walked straight into a solicitor's office in Stockport, asked to see the senior partner, got an audience and then announced that her son was in the market for Articles and that if they knew what was good for them they would see me, and if they did they would definitely take me on!

This full-frontal approach must have worked because a

few days later I walked into the offices of Barlow Parkin and Co., an old-established firm in Stockport with a Manchester branch office, to meet the partners.

Peter Barlow, the son of the founder, was a true gentleman of the old school. He had the 'corner office', the largest room with the best view, and his office looked completely chaotic. He had suffered from shell shock in the 1939–45 war and as a result always seemed somewhat detached and absent-minded. The next partner was Gordon Hand, a tough scrapper, a fighter who handled all the court work and litigation. Then came Henry Clixby, another quiet gentleman who had suffered badly at the hands of the Japanese as a prisoner of war in Burma. Finally, Peter Wilkinson was the progressive youngster who ran the Manchester office.

They took me on and I signed a five-year commitment with Henry Clixby as my 'Principal'. For the first year there was to be no pay as they were teaching me, but after that I would get £1 per week (£25 in today's money). I had got my foot on the very bottom rung of the legal profession ladder and was ready to start the climb.

Without being at all pompous it seems to me that the role of an autobiographer is not only to tell of how he or she achieved what they did, or did not, but also to give some sense of how the world was at the time the story is told. That way if this book is read in 2050, or even 2150, the reader will know something of how things really were all those years ago.

What was Britain, Great Britain or even the United Kingdom doing in the 1960s? It was doing three things. Socially, it was breaking out from the class and age straitjacket of the 1950s or even, if you like, of the Victorian era. Politically, it was about to try a new form of government, having grown tired of the old Conservative regime which it saw as increasingly incompetent and complacent. Economically, it was waking up to the fact that the world was suddenly a competitive place.

First, socially it was an era of personal liberation or, as Kenneth O. Morgan put it in the book *From Blitz to Blair*:

In the view of some critics one of moral anarchy. The popular consumer culture of the Beatles, Mary Quant and Carnaby Street was allied to the sexual freedom provided by the pill. The Wilson years were seen by the world as a time of 'permissiveness', no doubt with exaggeration (after all, only 9 per cent of single women took the pill in 1970). The children of the post-war baby-boomers trampled over the remains of Victorian puritanism and inhibition. Working-class young people in full employment embraced the pop music and fashion of the new consumerism. The middle-class young went to university on full grants, often in a new mood of rebellious liberation. The anguished response of the critics like Mrs Mary Whitehouse suggested that Britain faced a cultural crisis. In an age of relativism, its moral climate would never be the same.

The government did not create the mood of libertarianism. But it did try to respond to it as best it could, without losing touch with the respectable conservatism of the silent majority. The main legislative response came during, and in part from, Roy Jenkins's time at the Home Office between 1965 and 1967. During this period, the old censorship of the Lord Chamberlain and others over the arts, symbolised in the Crown's prosecution of the publishers of *Lady Chatterley's Lover* back in 1959, disappeared ... Other kinds of freedom were also given tacit encouragement. Homosexuals, the victims of intolerance and persecution since the days of Oscar Wilde, won partial liberation in 1967. A private member's bill … decriminalised homosexual relations in private by consenting adults. Another private member's bill by the Liberal David Steel to allow the abortion of unwanted pregnancies also went through. It was greeted with dismay by the Roman Catholic Church, for which it was clearly a severe defeat. In 1969 the government allowed amendment of the divorce laws, which many had long seen as intrusive and inhuman. It also supported penal reform in decisive fashion. Sydney Silverman's bill for ending capital punishment was passed in 1965; the change was made permanent under Callaghan in 1969. The Wilson years therefore saw a disappearance of the brutality of the rope from British history.

As we have already seen, it is not possible to write about Britain in the 1960s without mentioning the Beatles and the transformation that they represented. From the Cavern in Liverpool, a wonderful city in the nineteenth century but not yet greatly admired by the 1960s, the Beatles broke on to the national and, indeed, the international stage in 1963. Arthur Marwick in his book, *The Sixties*, put it well, writing:

A year of hit records and television appearances in Britain, together with a performance at Sunday Night at the London Palladium on 13 October 1963, led to the emergence of 'Beatlemania' among the group's adoring pre-teen and teenage fans. The Beatles' conquest of Great Britain was ratified by their appearance at a Royal Command Performance at the Prince of Wales Theatre, London. The sight of screaming fans, and the Beatles themselves, telegenic and always ready with laconic and wittily debunking remarks, delivered in broad Liverpudlian accents, became one of the early sixties 'spectacles' ...

There is no point in pretending that the Beatles captivated everyone; but their significance was acknowledged by pretty well everybody who paid attention to the news, and within their own constituency they topped the polls, perhaps in part because they still had the power to annoy the staid and middle-aged.

Economically, by 1963 the UK was still doing reasonably well if not growing at the pace of its rivals in Europe. Furthermore the French president, Charles de Gaulle, had vetoed the UK's belated attempt to join France, Germany, Italy and the Netherlands in the Common Market. Harold Wilson had just been elected as leader of the Labour party and in March 1963 Labour were running no less than 17 per cent ahead of the Conservatives in the polls.

Nevertheless, the ever-confident prime minister, Harold Macmillan, popularly known as 'Supermac', was confident that his chancellor of the exchequer, Reginald Maudling, would deliver an expansionist budget and the Conservatives would claw back Labour's lead.

Suddenly in early June, one of Macmillan's ministers, the war minister, John Profumo, resigned. Married to the well-known actress, Valerie Hobson, he had been having an affair with Christine Keeler who coincidentally had also been seeing Captain Yevgeny Ivanov, a Soviet diplomat, who turned out to be a spy working for Soviet military intelligence. The scandal exploded and Macmillan's hopes for an improvement in the polls were shattered. The Conservatives were now 20 per cent behind Labour and Macmillan became the most unpopular leader since Neville Chamberlain in 1939.

Macmillan became ill in the autumn and resigned in the October. This led to a contest between Rab Butler, favourite at 6 to 4 on, Lord Hailsham at 7-4, Reginald Maudling at 6–1 and Sir Alec Douglas-Home at 10–1. To most people's surprise Douglas-Home won and became prime minister.

He was to receive an early shock on 23 November 1963 when it was announced that the president of the United States, John F. Kennedy, had been assassinated in Dallas, Texas. With the Cold War with the Soviet Union at its height this was a severe shock to the whole world, particularly to the UK, as the USA was its closest and most powerful ally.

In 1964 the prime minister had to hold a general election as it was five years since the one the Conservatives had won in 1959. Sir Alec Douglas-Home delayed it as long as he could and he was fortunate as the Conservatives' popularity improved during the summer.

However, the populist newspaper, the *Sun*, showed what it felt was the mood of the voters when it publicised these quotes in the run-up to the 1964 general election:

Why I am voting Labour
Voter 1: Because I believe a vast amount of talent and energy, especially among the young, will be released if we give Labour a chance to make a new Britain.

Voter 2: Britain of the future shall be a classless one where all petty snobbisms of accent, dress, education will be defunct ... a society which seeks to harness the talents of all in the best possible manner.

Labour's new leader, Harold Wilson, had addressed his party's annual conference in October a year earlier and concluded that socialism should be recast 'in terms of scientific revolution':

> But that revolution cannot become a reality unless we are prepared to make far-reaching changes in economic and social attitudes which permeate our whole system of society.
>
> The Britain that is going to be forged in the white heat of this revolution will be no place for restrictive practices or for outdated methods on either side of industry … In the Cabinet and the boardroom alike, those charged with the control of our affairs must be ready to think and speak in the language of our scientific age.

It caught the mood of the moment.

In the event the election, on Thursday 15 October 1964, was extremely close but Labour just won and Harold Wilson became prime minister. He had promised 'the ending of economic privilege, the abolition of poverty in the midst of plenty, and the creation of real equality of opportunity'. He also had promised that 'the British will again become the go-ahead people with a sense of national purpose'.

Wilson, with James Callaghan as his chancellor of the exchequer, soon found that the general economic scene in Britain was not as rosy as the Conservatives had been painting it and in 1966 came yet another strike, this time by the National Union of Seamen (NUS). It was complicated but in essence the seamen were refusing to work on Saturdays and Sundays unless those days were treated as overtime. If this demand was met it would create an effective pay rise of 17 per cent, well above the 3.5 per cent allowed by the voluntary incomes policy which had been demanded by the Americans when they bailed out the pound in 1965.

In spite of being summoned to 10 Downing Street by the prime minister, Harold Wilson, the seamen went on strike on 16 May 1966. The pound immediately came under pressure. Wilson stepped up the pressure, accusing the NUS leaders of being a 'tightly knit group of politically motivated men' or, in other words, communists. The strike was eventually called off but by July, in spite of England's victory in the World Cup, the pound was under severe pressure and, at the end of July after much discussion about devaluation of the pound, the alternative, a deflationary package, was announced to a shocked House of Commons by Wilson. It included cuts of £100 million to the overseas aid budget and £150 million to public investment; a limit of £50 for MPs' travel overseas; a 10 per cent increase in excise and petrol duties; another 10 per cent increase in surtax; heavy hire purchase restrictions and to cap it all, a mandatory freeze on all wages and prices for six months.

The new policy worked but only for a short period and, by the autumn of 1967, the pound came under severe pressure again. This time, rather than yet more cuts, devaluation was considered and, after consultation with the Americans, it was agreed that the pound should be devalued from $2.80 to the pound to $2.40.

The announcement was made just after 9.00pm on Saturday 18 November 1967. More cuts had to be made, including £400 million from the expected rate of growth of public spending. The bank rate was raised from 6.5 to 8 per cent, more hire-purchase restrictions were imposed as well as higher Corporation Tax.

Having been arguing for three years that devaluation would be a national defeat, 'the economic equivalent of a plague or war,' Wilson announced to the nation that it was a victory, saying:

Our decision to devalue attacks our problem at the root and that is why the international monetary community have rallied round with a display of formidable strength to back the operation.

Tonight we must face the new situation. First, what this means. For now the pound abroad is worth 14 per cent or so less in terms of currencies. That does not mean, of course, that the pound here in Britain, in your pocket or purse or in your bank, has been devalued. What it does mean is that we shall now be able to sell more goods abroad on a competitive basis. This is a tremendous opportunity for all our exporters, and for many who have not yet started to sell their goods overseas. But it will also mean that the goods that we buy from abroad will be dearer, and so for many of these goods it will be cheaper to buy British.

Meanwhile, in September 1964, when I signed up to my five years of training in the law, I signed a parchment-type document called an engrossment of a deed, which recited what my firm would do for me, which was teach me the law, and what I would do for them, which was keep my nose to the grindstone.

Traditionally, new 'articled clerks' were not paid by the solicitor's firm, at least not to start with. In fact to get 'articles' at any sort of reasonable firm it had been the custom to pay *them* a 'premium', which was a lump sum of money for them to accept the chore of training a new would-be lawyer. In 1964 that practice had all but stopped but still I was to be paid nothing for the first year, then £1 per week with periodic reviews over the five-year period.

For £1 I could put four gallons of petrol in my 1937 Austin Seven Ruby Cabriolet (which my father had bought for £45) or I could go to the pub and buy five to six pints of bitter. [In 2014 four gallons of petrol would cost about £24 and five to six pints of bitter £15 to £20.]

A good working man's salary was £1,000 a year (£25,000 in today's money), a reasonable detached home could be bought for £5,000 and the car that every young man dreamed of owning one day – a Jaguar E-type convertible which had just come out – could be bought new for just £2,000.

I think my parents gave me an allowance of £3–£4 per week plus the occasional subs on top.

Barlow Parkin and Co. were one of the established firms in Stockport, a large town about seven miles south of the centre of Manchester, but really just part of a large industrial conurbation, and a pretty drab one at that. Manchester had gone from being the thrusting powerhouse of the Industrial Revolution, the home of the first railway and birthplace of the modern computer (thanks to Alan Turing), to a city that, following the move of textile manufacture to Asia and elsewhere, seemed to be down on its luck. The whole conurbation out to other surrounding areas like Bolton (England's biggest 'town'), Oldham, Wigan, Bury and on and on were left with hundreds of textile mills, massive structures that more often than not stood empty and decaying.

Still, despite all this, there was a growing feeling that everything was about to change. The years after the end of the Second World War in 1945 had been memorable mainly for rationing and austerity. We had got by, first with a Labour government led by Clement Attlee until 1951 and then a number of Conservative governments led by Sir Winston Churchill, Anthony Eden, Harold Macmillan (Supermac – who told us all that we'd never had it so good!) and finally the charming but anachronistic aristocrat, Sir Alec Douglas-Home.

Then along came Harold Wilson and his Labour party promising that they would propel the country out of its torpor through 'the white heat of the technological revolution'. It didn't really matter that nobody (including Wilson) really knew what that meant. It sounded very encouraging and Wilson was elected.

By 1964 the Beatles really were starting to take the world by storm. Up until then it was really only Elvis Presley who had caused a sensation in the late 1950s but now even he was swept away by the tide of the Beatles. Suddenly we thought differently and wore our hair, dressed, talked and thought outside the box. Our generation was about to take control and nothing would ever be the same again.

The law back then was enshrined in mystery to the man in the street.

I was allocated a rather large office of my own, overlooking a car park, but with a large mahogany square table which was somehow more impressive than a desk. My immediate workmates in the two adjoining rooms were two old-style legal executives or 'managing clerks', Bill Frost and Bert Gibbons. I suppose they were both in their late fifties.

Bill was mainly engaged in liquor licensing (off licences, new pubs, bars, restaurants and special premises for late night 'music and dancing') with a bit of general litigation thrown in. Bert was a property man. A chain smoker, his office looked as though a team of people had walked in laden with title deeds, books and hundreds of files, up-ended the lot in a great pile and then walked away. Bert loved it that way.

In the age before electric typewriters, let alone word processors, everything had to be written out in longhand. Bert would sit crouched over his desk for hours on end writing out enormous 'Abstracts of Title' in pencil, which in due course Phyllis in the typing pool would attempt to decipher on a manual typewriter. Bert's idea of relaxation was to wander into my office, short and stocky in his heavy three-piece suit, plant himself in front of the window staring over the car park, light a cigarette and then recite 'what is this life if full of care – we have no time to stand and stare'. Always the same!

There really was no formal training of the kind that law firms provide today. I sat with Bill and Bert and they explained what they were doing and why, and eventually I started to help them. The partners were the same; decent, kind, intelligent men who took the time to show me what they were doing and why.

Gordon Hand undertook prosecution work for the police in the local magistrates' courts and soon my job was to read all the witness statements and prepare for Gordon a summary of the basic facts and highlight the strengths and weaknesses of the case. I then sat behind him in court and fed him the papers and the lines. Gordon also taught me the ropes on general litigation, court rules, engaging barristers and generally how to give the opposition a hard time.

Peter Barlow had the best office as his father Ernest had founded the firm and had clearly been very bright and successful. Peter was immersed in wills, probates and trusts and quickly got me involved in seeing clients and understanding the issues. I also acted as his unofficial chauffeur, as he wasn't good at driving following shell shock in the war. Henry Clixby was the main real estate man and a total gentleman, and he showed infinite patience in teaching me the intricacies of the arcane world of real estate law.

All in all, I was pretty fortunate. I had a good gang of pals picked up over the teenage years from school and the 'rock and roll' set. There were probably about ten of us who were as thick as thieves plus a steady female gang adjacent in the form of six to seven girls who normally were 'with' one or more of us. We just had fun and laughs hanging out.

As I related earlier, my father had bought me my first car, a 1937 Austin Seven Ruby Cabriolet. It was a well preserved little car, a four-seater with a hood/rag-top in black and burgundy and a steady little engine. Not satisfied with that I took it to my father's engineering works and got the mechanics to shave the cylinder head to 'soup up' the engine, repainted it sky blue with black and white 'chequer flag' tape all over it so it looked, I thought, very cool.

It didn't last long. One snowy day in winter I was driving up a long hill when I realised something was wrong. First flames started to lick out of the side of the engine compartment and then I was overtaken by a cyclist! Before the top of the hill the engine exploded and the car died. My tolerant father forgave me and bought, for £50, a lovely black 1936 Morris Eight Saloon with three forward gears, and a top speed of about 65mph, which I polished until you could see your face in it.

By 1966 it was time to go off to law school to a one-year 'crammer' which would end up with me sitting the Law Society Part I Examinations. The place to go was the College of Law in Guildford in Surrey, a prosperous town close to London that felt a million miles away from Stockport.

On a 'recce' down there with one of my pals, Chris Ecclestone, I ended up in a pub where we got pretty drunk in the company of one Richard, a mystery man already at law school. He was a most remarkable character. He owned a vast Austin Westminster car with a hugely powerful engine that he drove flat out everywhere, with his hand pressed hard down on a custom-made horn that emitted an ear-splitting three-tone siren. No one could ever seemingly get to the bottom of where Richard came from or who his family were, nor why he apparently had endless supplies of cash and never really did any work but at the same time charmed everyone.

He lived in a pub called the Sanford Arms on the Epsom Road in Guildford with the pub landlady. That is to say he occupied the spare room, helped in the bar, entertained the customers and had a large breakfast cooked for him every morning by the landlady. She was a typical pub landlady type in her sixties, who enjoyed a large gin and tonic and once a week went greyhound racing.

Richard was leaving so I inherited his slot at the Sanford Arms. He disappeared for a while, leaving me in charge of his enormous car, only to return briefly, resume possession of the car and disappear forever, never to be seen or heard of again. He either made a fortune as a diamond smuggler or, probably more likely, got caught and locked away at Her Majesty's pleasure for a long time. Nevertheless he was such fun!

The days at Guildford passed by easily. By now I had realised that the law was no longer a means to an end. I actually loved it. I felt intellectually stimulated and just loved unravelling complex and knotty problems. I did well on all my tests and made some new friends. My sojourn at the Sanford Arms was quite enjoyable but the landlady obviously thought that I should be spending more time behind the bar serving and entertaining the customers, like Richard had, rather than studying law. At the end of the first term she told me, fairly abruptly, not to bother coming back.

In the meantime I had hooked up with two others in my class, Ken Greenall and Martin Cavanagh, and we managed to find a very nice apartment above a home in a quiet road in Shalford just outside town. Ken was from South Manchester and Martin from Bath. We got on fine. I cooked, Ken washed up and Martin cleaned the flat.

The owner of the house was a very attractive single woman with two daughters who were both about our age and drop-dead gorgeous. They were friends with 'pop star' Jonathan ('Everyone's Gone to the Moon') King and very friendly to us, though unfortunately in an entirely platonic way!

By now, again with my dad's help, I was the proud owner of a 1958 MGA Roadster which was white with wire wheels.

I also met up with another inmate from law school called Ian Burton. Ian was also from Manchester with a wealthy father who could be relied upon to keep Ian in good cars and ample pocket money.

Ian and I became good friends. Over the years later he became, and remains, not only one of my very closest friends but also the leading fraud and general Mr Fix-it lawyer in London, with a glittering client list from the movers and shakers of the day to some very wealthy Russians.

The days and weeks positively rolled by in a blur of study, laughs, endless hours with Iris the barmaid at the Jolly Farmer in Guildford, and a rare victory for England against Germany at football in the 1966 World Cup final.

Meanwhile, the 'Swinging Sixties' continued on their mercurial way. In London, as well as all the fashionable boutiques on Carnaby Street, the most successful boutique, Biba, opened in the more sedate Kensington. The famous model, Twiggy, described it as 'like no shop I had ever seen, with clothes hanging off wooden hat stands and wicker baskets filled with tee-shirts like vests with shoe-lace necks. Nor were there any shop assistants, just young girls with long blonde hair wandering about.'

Nevertheless, it was enormously successful, though its success did not last as long as that of Laura Ashley which had also opened in Kensington in 1967. The latter was more restrained and that allowed it to survive through the cut-throat atmosphere of the 1970s and 1980s.

With the fall of the Conservative government, a revolutionary new era was ushered in with wide-reaching social repercussions. The deb season became unimportant, the classless classes emerged and the Selective Employment Tax and other socialist legislation made life increasingly difficult for the old guard, an increasing number of whom went into exile for tax purposes. The success of the Beatles and the Rolling Stones coincided with the arrival of a youth-oriented culture and a new pop aristocracy of actors, artists, singers, fashion photographers, interior decorators and men's outfitters from a wide mixture of social backgrounds. The rigid standards of the past were relaxed. Kenneth Tynan said 'fuck' on television, homosexuality between consenting adults was legalised and vast quantities of mind-bending drugs were consumed. In this new environment, media people seemed to be the leading lights and David Frost confirmed this impression when on 7 January 1966, the Prime Minister Harold Wilson, the Earl of Longford and Dr John Robinson, Bishop of Woolwich paid court to him at a breakfast at the Connaught Hotel. It was not long before socially active aristocrats such as the Earl of Lichfield shed their titles and joined in the swim. In apparent contrast to these goings-on was the resolution of the young Lord Strathnaver, great-nephew of the late Duke of Sutherland, to become a policeman. The anachronistic activities of the young Earl of Lucan and his friends at the Clermont Club also struck a different note. However, by the end of the decade, the new pop aristocracy had also shown a measure of respect for old-fashioned British values by acquiring stately homes, Rolls-Royces and even flats in Mayfair's Albany.

CHAPTER 6

I Meet My Wife

Eventually I was back in the office in Stockport where by now I was starting to feel like a proper lawyer. I saw clients on my own, handled cases, and just became more and more confident. We had our fair share of unusual clients. One woman came to see me with some cock and bull story about being blackmailed by Winston Churchill. She was as mad as a hatter. Rather disconcertingly this woman wore a wig. Underneath the wig she was totally bald and her head was very shiny and polished. In a meeting, she had a habit of moving her head vigorously to accentuate a point; an affirmative produced a violent nodding of the head and a negative a similarly violent shake from side to side. The problem was that her head was so highly polished that the wig itself did not move at all – only her head – so a nod meant that her forehead disappeared and reappeared frequently during a vigorous nod!

I ended up doing a bit of a number on matrimonial cases. At one point I had a 'quadruple' where in a row of four detached houses the wife of the first went off with the husband in the second and so on up the row, and the one on the end went off with the first in the row. It meant four fees based almost entirely on the same set of facts and it only being necessary to change the names and addresses in each petition! At the same time I continued to help Gordon Hand with the police prosecution work, doing more and more myself. The minute I qualified I would take this over entirely as I was now able to do the advocacy myself.

It really wasn't very difficult to be a prosecutor in the Stockport magistrates' court. The chief magistrate was the local butcher. I think he owned the slaughterhouse. He was a massive man with a very large and very red face who instilled instant fear in all but the most resolute accused. His standard line gave the game away. When the accused was arraigned in the dock and the charges read out, they were then given the usual choice of pleading 'Guilty' or 'Not Guilty'. If the unfortunate accused said 'Not Guilty' the response from the Butcher was invariably: 'If you're not guilty then why are you here?' At which point all one can do as a prosecutor is to make a grimace at the Butcher which implies 'Exactly – Your Worship!' and leave matters to his (un)tender mercy.

1967 was an important year for another reason and this was of a personal nature. On the girlfriend front things were not too bad, and anyway I was only 22 years old. Then one evening at a party at the house of Geoff Leigh-Ford, the first singer in our Trailblazers, I saw this beautiful girl sitting on the knee of one of my other close friends, Rodney Hylton-Potts, who did a good number as an Elvis lookalike and was also a trainee lawyer. I learnt her name was Pamela Leigh and I was pretty smitten, but she was with Rodney.

The Rodney/Pamela relationship didn't last long so I saw an opening through which I attempted to slip. She came as my guest to a black tie Masonic ball (my father was a Provincial Grand Steward) or some such thing and Pamela looked wonderful. She managed to politely duck my advances in the cab on the way home but we became friends. Soon afterwards she took off with a girlfriend, Rosie, to cook in Arosa in the Swiss mountains but she was back for her 21st birthday at home on 27 June 1967. It was a splendid black tie affair at her parents' home and I bought her the *Sergeant Pepper's Lonely Hearts Club Band* LP as a 21st present. But then she was off again.

Her younger brother Geoffrey became one of my gang of drinking companions and one Sunday lunchtime Geoff brought Pamela along (she was by that time working as a PA at Cadbury Schweppes in London). I went round to her home that night – guitar in hand – and after two or three hours that was that. We were an item and remained so from then on.

By now I was starting to plan for my next and final stint at Guildford Law School. I rented a lovely cottage in Shamley Green outside Guildford with two of my law school buddies and Pamela gave up her job in London (her flatmate Rosie married Richard Jones, an Australian submariner), got a job helping to organise the Surrey County Show and we moved in together. Her mother didn't know!

I was doing well at law school and so started to think ahead to what we should do when I qualified which, if everything went to plan, would be on 1 October 1969. Pamela and I both had the wanderlust. I really could not face settling down to life as a Stockport solicitor. There was that memorable moment in July 1969 on a starlit night in Shamley Green when I stood in the garden looking up at the moon knowing that minutes before a human being had landed on it. Surely anything was possible now?

We talked for hours about where we would go – Perth in Australia, Asia, Vancouver, the Caribbean. One of the great benefits of our having had the world's largest Empire is that vast tracts of the globe are regulated by what is basically

English common law. The world was, I believed, truly my oyster.

I passed my final exams, we got married in September and by 1 October 1969 I was duly admitted as a solicitor of the Supreme Court of Judicature in England and Wales. Now we were ready to get going!

CHAPTER 7

The Foreign Advocate

When we got married, Peter Barlow very kindly offered to rent us a little farmhouse he owned, called Stanley Hall Farm, a black and white Cheshire 'magpie' dating from about the sixteenth century. He let us have it for £5 per week and by this stage the firm was paying me £20 (£400 in today's money) per week. I had told the firm that we wanted to work abroad and as ever they were very understanding. If I wanted to stay they were happy to have me. If I wanted to satisfy my wanderlust then that was fine too.

At work now I could appear in court (County court, magistrates' court, etc.) as an advocate under my own steam. I took over most of the police prosecution work from Gordon and also the liquor and general licensing work. As part of this, I was instructed by a local club in Stockport called the Coco a Poco. It was a fairly dubious eating and drinking venue where live acts, a sort of cabaret, appeared and everyone got pretty drunk. They wanted an extension to their licence to permit what they described in their instructions as a 'Ladies' Dancing Troupe' or some such elaborate label for what actually I detected was to be an upmarket strip show. I presented the facts in the very best possible light, though it was obvious from the outset that the chairman of the licensing bench smelt a rat.

I had done my homework and made sure I covered all the technical bases. The police didn't put up any objection. Perhaps they were looking forward to the show as much as the rest of the punters. In any event the chairman came to his conclusion. He said they had listened very carefully to the arguments that I had put forward and reluctantly come to the conclusion that they had no other option than to accede to my request. The chairman looked straight at me and said:

> Mr Lane-Smith, you therefore have succeeded in your application – although I have a strong feeling that in reality there's going to be a lot more Poco than Coco!

In another case I was prosecuting a motorist for obstruction on the A6. The basic facts were that a Volkswagen camper van driver and the accused had had some altercation and had both pulled up to argue the toss. The camper van was in front and at some point that driver thought the argument was going nowhere, so he decided he was going to drive off. The accused stood in front of the camper van with his back on the flat front and spread-eagled his arms thus preventing the other driver from leaving the scene – hence obstruction. In the court the 'accused' box was located on a raised dais four to five feet above the well of the courtroom. It was accessed by a flight of steps at the rear.

In cross-examination I took the accused through the facts and then asked him to demonstrate to the magistrates the manner in which he had 'leant' on the camper van. He spread-eagled his arms and leant firmly on the side of the box … which then promptly fell apart and the accused dropped about five feet into the well of the court, flat on his back. At this, in a fairly crowded courtroom, one could hear a pin drop although everyone, including me, was stifling a huge belly laugh – he wasn't hurt.

To his eternal credit he picked himself up and brushed himself down. Somehow he managed to pick up, in complete silence from the onlookers, all three sides of the witness box, remount the steps, resume the stand with his arms precariously now holding all three sides up and together.

He then looked me straight in the eye and said, 'I'm sorry. What was your question again?' What a star – that was one case I was happy to lose!

Pamela and I were getting down to the serious business of choosing our future. I had sent letters out to law firms throughout the British Commonwealth and the old Empire. This included Australia, the Far East, Canada, Africa and the Caribbean and thankfully I received a good number of positive responses. One exception was from British Columbia where the Law Society in Vancouver took the view that they could take no cognisance of the fact that I was a fully qualified solicitor in England (the mother country in terms of their own legal system) and wanted me to spend three years at university in Vancouver, two years at their law school and then a sixth and last year with a local law firm before I could be admitted to practise law there. In other words they were saying that they were protecting their own and could struggle by without my help for the foreseeable future!

One day I got a letter from one Sir Anthony Lousada. He was the retired senior partner but still consultant to an old-time London firm called Stephenson Harwood. The letter said that he had been asked to respond to a letter I had sent to Johnson, Stokes and Master, the top local law firm in Hong Kong, and a very powerful force throughout Asia. He wanted to see me. In short, he was a delightful fellow, truly 'old school', chairman of the board of trustees of the Tate Gallery and had other distinguished appointments. He told me that Johnson, Stokes and Master ('JSM' as they were always called) needed an associate to one of their main shipping lawyer partners, an expatriate Brit who had been in Hong Kong for some years. I knew nothing about mercantile law but was perfectly capable of mugging up on it with the right textbooks.

In short, Sir Anthony and I got on like a house on fire. Within a few days he got back to me to say that JSM had accepted his recommendation and wanted to hire me on an initial three-year contract at an attractive salary and good fringe benefits. Could we be ready to go to Hong Kong in a couple of months' time?

You bet we could! We started planning our tropical wardrobe which meant lightweight clothing for the very humid summer months. I got some information on apartments in the mid-levels below Victoria Peak and I studied some mercantile and marine textbooks and became very well-informed.

About a month before we were due to leave I got a call from Sir Anthony. The partner, for whom I would be working, was about to visit his family home in the Lake District with his new fiancée and could Pamela and I pop up to join them for lunch and a 'get to know you' session. Of course we could – but little did I know that we were about to encounter another major fork in the road.

Shortly afterwards, on one sunny autumn Saturday in 1970, Pamela and I drove up to the Lakes and the house of the parents of my new boss. We arrived on time at about noon. He was very convivial and I liked him at once. He introduced us to his fiancée, a very attractive Hong Kong Chinese lady who also seemed very friendly and receptive.

We kicked off well over pre-lunch gin and tonics. His fiancée went off, I assumed to check on the progress of lunch. We had another G and T and were close to going in for lunch. I needed a 'comfort break' after a longish drive and enquired as to the location of the facilities. He directed me to the half-landing on the staircase. I went up and opened the unlocked door, only to find the fiancée seated on the loo. Our eyes stayed locked in horror for perhaps three to five seconds and I muttered the customary apology.

In later years I came to understand the 'Chinese mind' very well as you will see but one of the most important concepts is 'face'. That is to say you *never*, never ever, cause loss of face to the Chinese.

Through no fault of mine exactly that had just happened. She obviously thought that for all the time we would be bumping into each other in Hong Kong neither of us would ever forget those five seconds. It truly was a stroke of fate – a fork in the road.

We got through lunch and obviously neither Pamela nor he knew what had happened until after we left. We shook hands and he told me how much he looked forward to seeing us in Hong Kong in a few weeks' time.

Three days later came the expected call from Sir Anthony. He was obviously very embarrassed and clearly didn't know what had happened. He simply said that the problem was 'the chemistry wasn't right' – so reluctantly JSM would be withdrawing their offer. It was the hand of fate. But for that moment, we would have been in Hong Kong weeks later and could well have spent our working career in that fabulous city. However, it had been snatched away.

We had other offers. One was a small practice in Hong Kong who wanted me to be an advocate in the courts and another was a firm in Kitwe in the copper belt in Zambia.

Then came an offer to meet one of the partners in a Jamaican firm called Dunn, Cox and Orrett. This was the top firm in Jamaica and their partner was to be in London the following week. Pamela and I went down to meet him and his wife, a charming couple, in a serviced apartment just off Sloane Square. The practice seemed first rate, they had a top-flight (for Jamaica) client list and they really wanted a new associate.

My enduring memory of the meeting is a long discussion of the respective merits of whether when hanging clothes in a wardrobe it was preferable to have the hooks on the coat hanger facing forwards or backwards. I think we worked out that one or the other would be easier to remove in a hurry. It is curious the trivia that often engages the human mind. In short they offered me the job. We were ready to start in a matter of weeks and at least we had the lightweight clothing that we had bought for the abortive Hong Kong assignment.

The next two to three weeks were a flurry of activity. The partners at Barlow Parkin were wonderful. Peter Barlow was happy to let my pal Chris Ecclestone and his new wife Sue take over the tenancy at the farmhouse and they would also take on the car. Going-away parties were held with a band organised to play such classics as 'Jamaica Farewell' (it should have been 'Jamaica Hello') and 'Yellow Bird' ('up high in banana tree') and so on. It was all very emotional and it felt like we were going to the other end of the earth, but bear in mind that the furthest Pamela and I had ever travelled was Corfu for our honeymoon!

We booked our flight to go via Bermuda to see Ian Curley's sister Sheilagh (remember Curls from the Trailblazers?) who had married Pete, an American TWA airline pilot, whom she met when she was a TWA hostess. After two or three days there we would fly on to Kingston,

Jamaica to start our new life in the tropics. After some tearful farewells we set off and spent a very pleasant two or three days in Bermuda. It was then, and still is today, a stunning island. Part of the old Empire, a Crown colony with a governor, the capital Hamilton is a beautiful town and the whole island seemed almost picture-postcard perfect.

Despite all that we very clearly felt some simmering resentment from the local black population. It felt like trouble was brewing which unfortunately it was, since not that long afterwards there was a mini uprising and the governor was assassinated.

So we got on the flight to the island of Jamaica full of anticipation. Almost three hours later we started our descent into Kingston over the Blue Mountains. It all looked very green, lush and beautiful from the air. Twenty minutes later we were on the ground in Kingston and, 30 minutes after that, were in a cab en route to the hotel we had been told to head for. The immediate environs of the airport looked pretty depressing, not unusual in most parts of the world, but it seemed as we got closer to the centre of Kingston that things weren't improving that much.

I don't think we were naive enough to suppose that the route to our hotel would be bedecked with tropical flowers and happy waving people who had turned out specifically to welcome us to their island paradise, but this was a long way from that.

We got to the hotel. We had a bungalow in the densely vegetated tropical garden, and there was a good bar and decent restaurant which we piled into. On going back to our bungalow after dinner, we came across a toad the size of a dog planted firmly on our doorstep and reluctant to move to give way to our bungalow.

Welcome to Jamaica!

CHAPTER 8

Island in the Sun

A few words to set the historic backdrop to Jamaica in early 1970 would be instructive, since not all readers will have that information readily to hand. I will try to keep it short but it is in reality the early history of the British Empire – I love history as well as the law. One learns so much from what has passed before.

The very first enduring colony that England (Britain) ever established was in Jamestown, Virginia in 1607. A century earlier in 1509 the Spanish had settled in Jamaica, founding Spanish Town in 1523. Although discovered earlier, the first meaningful English settlement was of Barbados in 1627 (Barbados was uninhabited at that time). Activity gradually moved up through Antigua to Jamaica which in 1655 was taken by the English from the Spanish and went on to become (with Barbados) one of the great money-spinners of the nascent Empire, mainly based on sugar cane.

It is beyond doubt that the great wealth created by the sugar barons in the West Indies had been achieved at the price of a massive relocation of native Africans to the new colonies through the slave trade.

The British expatriates who came to Jamaica to settle it enjoyed mixed fortunes. Some became rum-sodden wrecks while at the other end of the spectrum others became hugely wealthy on the back of the sugar trade, when sugar had become almost as precious and valuable a commodity as gold. Families such as the Drakes and Townsends made huge fortunes and bought magnificent estates back in Britain.

Then, like all good things, it came to an end. Sugar beet could produce similar commodities and there was a massive adverse reaction to the slave trade, which was abolished in the Empire in 1808. Without cheap labour the sugar trade had no real viable future. The sugar price eventually collapsed in 1922.

Jamaica attained its independence to become a member of the Commonwealth on 6 August 1962. In truth Kingston in 1970 felt like a powder keg that was about to explode. The city itself had a Wild West feel to it and there seemed to be a great deal of violence. The main problem seemed to be not a black/white issue but a split between the two main political parties; the Jamaica Labour Party, who had just come to power under Edward Seaga, and the People's National Party led by Michael Manley.

The partners in Dunn, Cox and Orrett were generally a fairly congenial bunch. They all seemed to have their houses in the foothills of the Blue Mountains which were heavily fortified and guarded. The other lawyers, clerks and so on in the office were generally a friendly crowd, although I think they were bemused as to why we had left England to come to make our home in Kingston. As they pointed out, it was normally the other way round! Even getting to and from the office seemed a major challenge each day. We were told to be very careful even going from the office to our vehicle in the firm's car park. The joke in the office was that there was only a 50/50 chance of making it to the vehicle without being knifed!

Pamela and I felt a quickly growing sense of unease about this whole enterprise. We were starting to get in deeper, the firm was about to buy me a car and we were shown a small villa that they intended to rent as our home for the next three years. It certainly didn't seem to be in a particularly safe neighbourhood. Pamela wasn't allowed to have a work permit so quite what she would do all day was also a real concern.

I had to bite the bullet and organise a meeting with a couple of the senior partners, including the one who had hired me. It was not an easy meeting, particularly when our main message was that we thought their home town was about the most dangerous place we had ever seen. They tried to understand. The firm had another office in Montego Bay at the other end of the island which was more of a resort area and would we drive up there to see what we thought of living and working there?

We said we were very willing to give it a try and so set off the next morning to drive up there. Jamaica is a wildly beautiful island and the drive up took us through some amazing tropical countryside. We stayed the night at Ochos Rios on the north coast, but even there, once out of the hotel, there was a very uneasy feel. It was just constantly edgy.

The next day we arrived in Montego Bay. Around the beaches were some pretty nice hotels but immediately off the main beat it felt just like Kingston again. I could feel another fork in the road coming up.

Having decided that Montego Bay and therefore, in reality, Jamaica and our whole new life was not going to work out, we were feeling pretty depressed and honestly rather foolish. We went down to Doctor's Cave Beach to have a day of reflection on our future. We quickly fell into conversation with our near neighbours on the beach. On the one side was a lovely lady, probably in her early sixties, who lived in the Cayman Islands, an hour's flight away. On the other side was a nice young couple from New York. We told our neighbours the whole story and that we were definitely at a fork in the road.

Our new friends from New York were adamant that we go with them to New York and stay with them for a while. I would get a job with one of the big New York law firms as a 'British liaison' and then study for my New York bar exams and become dual qualified.

The lady from George Town, Grand Cayman said we must return with her and she would put us up. Grand Cayman was a Crown colony. Their law was English law and the whole place was about to open up and boom as a financial centre and tax haven. Our timing could not be better because we would be in on the ground floor.

The day passed with us swaying between the twin attractions of New York or the Caymans or the third prospect, return to the UK with our tails between our legs with the goodbye parties and 'Yellow Bird' calypso still ringing in our ears. One thing we were sure of – it was 'Jamaica Farewell'.

CHAPTER 9

A Country Practice

Forty-eight hours later we were sitting on an aeroplane over the Atlantic, en route back to the United Kingdom. I can reflect back now on how our lives might have changed if we had chosen a different fork in the road. Had we gone to Grand Cayman with our 'nice lady' there is no doubt our timing would have been perfect. The island was still a British Crown colony, there had never been any slavery (no plantations) so no problems between blacks and whites, and the island was just about to pass new laws that would make it one of the most attractive tax havens in the world. I came to know other solicitors who went out in the early 1970s and almost every one of them made a great deal of money (tax free!) and mostly retired by the age of 50. Equally, had we decided to go to New York with our new American friends I am sure we would have settled long enough for me to take the New York State bar examinations and become dual qualified, which would have been a huge asset as law firms started to become international in the late 1970s.

However, there are no regrets. The fork we chose led down a road that became immensely fulfilling.

Back in England in September 1970 we felt pretty silly. None of our parents, friends or work colleagues could believe the Jamaican adventure was over in just over three weeks. It was time to get a job quickly and move on. Fortunately, at that time there were 'only' about 20,000 qualified solicitors in England and Wales (in 2012 there were 120,000 and that's another story). The result was that there were plenty of opportunities available to a young solicitor, so we borrowed a car from my father and drove round the country for interviews.

After about three weeks we found what we thought we wanted. Before we were married we had once been to a May Ball at Oxford University (the bands that night were Cream – featuring Eric Clapton – and the Nashville Teens). The morning after the ball we had drifted off west of Oxford and ended up in the Cotswolds, which we had thought just about the most beautiful part of England that we had ever seen.

I had an interview with a true country practice, a firm called Farrant and Sinden in Chipping Norton with 'branch offices' in Moreton-in-Marsh and Charlbury. The views from the rear of the period building the firm occupied were out over the rolling hills of the Cotswolds. It was so different from Manchester and the north-west and there seemed to be an almost permanent 'diffused light' in the pretty countryside and the stunning small towns and villages.

This was it – a place we could put down our roots. I took the job as an assistant solicitor on the grand salary, the going market rate, of £2,000 per annum (£40,000 in today's money). Our immediate short-term home was a very pleasant room in the Red Lion pub in the little hamlet of Little Compton, a couple of miles outside Chipping Norton.

The firm itself had three partners. Kenneth Meaby, who was the senior partner, had spent some time in the army and was the epitome of a distinguished country solicitor. He had the best room on the ground floor of the building with a full picture window looking out over the Cotswold Hills, a full-size partner's desk and a fireplace with a fire going in the winter days, in front of which lay his dog which came in with him each day.

The next partner was Colin Smith, who had really wanted to be an architect but had flunked his architecture exams (we later saw why when he designed his own house!) and the young partner was Howard Lapsley, a larger rather untidy fellow in his mid-thirties who I think instinctively saw me as a challenge!

Colin's office was on the second floor (overlooking the hills) and above him was Howard on the top floor, also with the 'country view'! My office was on the top floor at the front of the building. My first slight shock was to find out that my secretary was a rather dapper little man in his late sixties who took shorthand. The work was a mixed bag of a typical country practice. There was some conveyancing, probate and wills, small-scale litigation and some magistrates' court advocacy. This was all the sort of work I'd been involved in as an articled clerk so I didn't find it at all difficult.

I tended to pick up work off all the partners – I was the only assistant – and so tended to deal with anything and everything. My enduring early memory is that of defending a man for 'duck rustling', a little known offence not that common even in those rural parts. I also handled the defence of a man who was accused of attempting to drive a vehicle under the influence of drink. The car had broken down in the late afternoon and the man tried in vain to get it going. After a while he gave up, went into the local pub and there proceeded to attempt to drink the pub dry! Some three hours later he returned to the car, forgetting that it had broken down, and was trying in vain to get it going when the police turned up.

There was no doubt at all that my client was completely paralytic – no breathalyser in those days, but I doubt if he could have *seen* a white line let alone walk along it in a straight line! My defence involved an argument that it was not possible to commit an offence if someone was attempting to do the impossible. If it was technically not possible to start the car (this was the fact – it never ran again) then it was not possible to convict him of attempting to drive a vehicle that would never again start. He was acquitted!

In truth the work was not in the slightest bit demanding. I took more and more work off the partners, who I felt were either plodding or lazy and in the end I thought that I could have done all the work in the office before lunchtime and the partners could have stayed at home and left me to it. That was the arrogance of youth!

On the domestic front we had found a delightful house called 'Windrush Vale' in the village of Naunton, not far from Stow-on-the-Wold. It was a typical Cotswold honey-coloured stone house with a garden running down to the River Windrush. It was idyllic. It was owned by a delightful couple by the name of Charles Dickens and his wife Pinkie. Charles had a wholesaler business in Cheltenham and had found a large country home that he could take a ten-year lease on. We snapped it up. We had quickly made friends with locals, in part through our time at the bar in the evenings at the Red Lion pub, including Peter and Sally Green who farmed the local estate at Little Rollright Manor close to Chipping Norton. Peter and Sally remain very good friends to this day.

Soon afterwards, we moved into Windrush Vale where we found out that Pamela was pregnant with what was to be our firstborn, Zoë, who must have been conceived in the Red Lion pub as she was born about nine months later on 21 June (the longest day) 1971 in the cottage hospital at Moreton-in-Marsh.

However, practising law in Chipping Norton was really not going to satisfy my ambition. It drove me crazy and most of the work was mind-numbingly dull. Once a week I was sent off to the branch office in Charlbury, a delightful little town, where I would make myself available to clients in the back room of the local greengrocer's shop. On another day each week I was sent to man the firm's other outpost, a single room above a sweet shop in Moreton-in-Marsh. Looking back now I really can't recall anybody ever coming into either of these offices which seemed to me to be a complete waste of time. I was bored to death at the office but we loved living in Naunton and were in no rush to move. Naunton was only five miles or so from Cheltenham which, although hardly a very large town, was by comparison with Chipping Norton a veritable metropolis!

I started to cast my net around there and came across a small firm by the name of Bailey and Bailey who were look-ing for an assistant solicitor. I went to meet the owner, an eccentric man named Major Bailey, who had a large mous-tache and a military bearing. He had started the practice after leaving the army about fifteen years earlier. I asked him what happened to the other Mr Bailey. The Major told me that he was entirely fictional, but he had called the business Bailey and Bailey since it seemed to him that that would convey an impression of being long-established. I suppose it had worked.

The office was in a pretty Regency street in the heart of Cheltenham. Bailey himself said he was tired of working and wanted someone to take over his office and clients while he 'popped in' now and then. He had another 'partner', a man in his fifties, very dapper with a small moustache, who was called Noel Cameron-Smith and only practised criminal law. Noel kept about 40 per cent of whatever he billed and collected and the other 60 per cent came into the office revenue.

There was one other employee, a legal executive (solicitor's clerk) called David who was only slightly older than me. He walked with a pronounced limp and chain-smoked cigarettes. All in all it was something of an odd setup but in essence the Major was going to let me run the business and that was attractive. I told the partners at Farrant and Sinden that I didn't think they had enough work to justify my being there and so I was moving on. I would miss some things about Chipping Norton, not least the local pub/hotel which was owned by Keith Moon, the crazy drummer in The Who – who rolled up most weekends in a pink Rolls-Royce and then played a leading role in late-night drinking sessions at his establishment.

I also would miss Colin Smith whom I rather liked. He was the would-be architect. He had designed and built his own dream house in the local village of Oddington where the picture window in the kitchen had a cinemascope view of the brick garage wall two feet away, the staircase failed to interconnect with the landing, to the bemusement of the local builders, and the French windows in the dining room opened directly onto the swimming pool. Unfortunately there was only a twelve-inch gap between the dining room exterior wall and the pool so, more than once, throwing open the windows at night led to guests stepping out on to the terrace and falling directly into the pool! Colin was fortunately a better solicitor than architect.

By July 1971, I had moved on to Cheltenham and had a very pleasant office on the first floor of a Regency terrace (10 Regent Street if I remember correctly). It was immediately behind the local upmarket House of Fraser department store.

The business was not in bad shape but needed some proper organisation. The client base was almost exclusively private clients, conveyancing, wills and probate and some knockabout litigation, with Noel Cameron-Smith hanging about in the local magistrates' court hoping for something juicy (ideally a good murder) to fall into his lap. Now and then it did. Cheltenham was, and I am sure still is, a very pleasant town. There were some decent local solicitors and I started putting myself about the local business community to drum up further work.

In the office I now actually had a female secretary as opposed to the 60-odd-year-old boy in Chipping Norton – a rather severe 50-plus-year-old Mrs Talmage. I don't think I ever established her Christian name.

David, the legal executive, was quite good at putting himself around the local estate agents to get conveyancing work. To dub him as a sort of Uriah Heep is probably slightly unfair but not too far from the mark. His mother seemed to rule his life with an iron rod. She seemed to have decided to make it her business to find out all about my personal affairs and she had an alarming way of going about it. Her technique was to talk to David in my presence as though I was not in fact present. She would say to David, 'Does he have any children yet?', or 'How much did he pay for that home in Naunton where he lives?'

It was an odd feeling to be present with David's mother. It was rather like being a fly on the wall at the inquest on one's own death in mysterious circumstances! Overall though I rather liked the setup, being in effect my own boss, and certainly we loved the life of the Cotswolds with our lovely village house and its garden running down to the Windrush stream, and a feeling of Ambridge except that the pub was the Black Horse rather than the Bull and everybody was called 'Hanks' rather than 'Archer' – but there was probably a lot of inbreeding!

Major Bailey would drop by once a week to see how things were and collect some money. After six months or so the Major called me in for what he called a 'serious chat'. He told me that he liked what he saw of me and for that reason was prepared to consider selling the business to me and retiring. He suggested I give it some thought and let him know what sort of offer I could make to him. I did think it over and decided that the thing to do was to talk to our own bank manager at NatWest in Cheltenham to see if he would lend me the money to buy the Major out. I sat down with him, went through the accounts of the business and worked up a figure which I thought would be fair and attractive to the Major. I then arranged to have a meeting with Major Bailey the following week to make him an offer.

I sat down with Major Bailey and told him the process I had been through, and that I had spoken to the bank manager and felt confident that I could finance the offer I was putting forward. He asked me what information I had given to the bank. I told him the historic accounts, management accounts, etc., as well as my own plans for how I would grow the business. The Major looked aghast.

'You showed *our* bank manager the accounts without asking me first?'

'Yes,' I replied. 'He is *our* bank manager and it's odd to see how this could be a legitimate breach of confidence.'

The Major then proceeded to rant and rage. I should never have done what I did, now the bank manager knew everything. I assumed he pretty much knew anyway, as he could read the office account bank statement after all. There was no rationality to the Major's position. He thought I was guilty of some sort of betrayal. I pointed out that it was *he* who had approached *me* to buy the practice, not the other way round.

All this did was convince me of something that I had suspected from the beginning (and Pamela had told me after she met the Major for the first and only time), namely that he was ever so slightly 'round the bend', and I also got the strong feeling that there was something in his past that he was desperate to keep hidden from view. In any event our relationship, such as it was, was at an end. He thought I had betrayed him and I thought that he was off his head! A pity, but it was another fork in the road so it was time to rethink.

All this happened in the early spring of 1972. Fortunately at that time the legal world was very different from the way it is today. There were not enough solicitors to go around. Today there is a vast oversupply.

Following the split with the Major, one option for me was to keep our home in the Cotswolds, get a job in London and rent a flat during the week. I saw a few London firms and there was one in particular that I really liked the look of called Piesse and Sons. Piesse had been around for a long time and had an office on Cheapside in the City. The partner I met was an excellent man. They were looking for an assistant to work primarily with one of their biggest clients, Esso Petroleum. This would be a big, and very welcome, change from the sort of work to be had in Chipping Norton and Cheltenham. The partner, Michael Arsecott, and I got on very well. I was shortlisted down to two but Michael was rooting for me because we really got on together. I was very hopeful.

One evening came the 'Dear John' moment. Michael called me. The other candidate had prior City experience and was a little senior to me, so in the end they thought they would have to go with him. This was a blow.

Piesse and Sons soon after merged with Durrant to form Durrant Piesse and then that in turn later merged with Lovell White and King ('Lovely White and Clean' as it was known in 'the trade') to form Lovell Durrant. Today it is Hogan Lovells and about number eight in the world rankings.

It was back to the drawing board.

I got lots of letters, went to a few interviews and got a few offers but nothing that really caught my attention. I had put an advert in the Law Society's *Gazette* and that had produced plenty of letters of interest. I was starting to despair of finding something interesting when along came a letter from a firm in Manchester called John Gorna and Co. It was a relatively small firm with four partners, but a few checks revealed that it was very well thought of and had a very good client base.

I arranged an interview. John Gorna himself, who was then in his fifties, was a fascinating and very successful man. The practice had originally been set up many years before by one Louis Blomberg, a successful Jewish property lawyer. Louis regularly took his lunch at the French restaurant in the Midland Hotel, then Manchester's finest. The head waiter in the French restaurant was John Gorna's father and Mr Gorna senior apparently one day told Louis Blomberg that his son John would like to be a solicitor. He was taken into articles by Louis Blomberg, qualified, became a partner and then Louis died leaving the practice to John who fairly rapidly changed its name to John Gorna and Company. Not much doubt as to the boss here then!

John was a charming man, short, immaculately dressed with large owl-like spectacles who spoke with a not unattractive sort of drawl, Mancunian style. He specialised, and therefore so did the firm, in commercial property with a fantastic client base including the Co-operative Insurance Society, Central and District Properties, Manchester United and the Edwards family, of whom much more later – and some strange names, but excellent organisations, such as the Independent Order of Oddfellows, the Independent Order of Shepherds and many others.

Some had been inherited from Louis Blomberg but John himself had attracted much work and had himself become a developer of commercial office buildings mainly in and around Manchester, and in consequence had made himself a great deal of money. He bought a brand new Rolls-Royce every two years, held court in a massive mahogany-panelled office with a boardroom table that seated twenty people, and insisted that the offices were filled with masses of fresh flowers every working day. There were three other partners, Percy Harris (property and a little company law), Peter Reynolds (property and some litigation) and Roger Broadhurst (property and property lending).

It would be a wrench to leave the house in the Cotswolds but in reality I felt that I had retired at the age of 27 without the intervention of a career. I had to put aside bucolic country practice and set out to make a career for myself in the great big world of business and commerce rather than pandering to the whims of country folk and small-town enterprises. The world of John Gorna was a world of fascinating clients, with large and challenging issues and this was the world that I wanted to inhabit.

We sold our lovely little home in the Cotswolds almost as quickly as we put it on the market. I bade the 'Mad Major' a less than fond farewell and started down a new fork in the road.

CHAPTER 10

Back Up North

We returned to Cheshire in April 1972 and I took up the job as assistant solicitor at John Gorna and Co. I was mainly responsible for litigation but with something of a roving brief and I mainly worked with Peter Reynolds, a good man with a decent sense of humour. All in all this was a different world from the one I had inhabited for the last couple of years.

Quickly I was drawn into all manner of interesting cases. Louis C. Edwards and Sons, a public company in the meat supply business, was getting rid of an unloved chief executive, a Mr Peacock. Louis Edwards and his brother Douglas (Dougie) ran the business with an iron fist. The two brothers, who were not at all alike, shared a large office which overlooked the massive manufacturing area (canned meat products) with two big desks facing each other. Louis was every inch the master butcher, a very large man who was the driving force of the business and his brother Douglas, the elegant, moustachioed former Lord Mayor of Manchester, was suave and urbane. The two often spoke as one.

Outside the family business Louis' big interest was football. He had built up a substantial interest in the shares of Manchester United Football Club, then a private company but still one of the best known clubs in the world. Louis had two sons, Martin and Roger, and a daughter, Kathryn. Dougie had two sons, John and Peter. Martin and John both worked in the business with their fathers and both tried hard to make an impact against the odds, given their somewhat dominant fathers.

Getting rid of the chief executive, Peacock, was a big deal and therefore I bore a big responsibility to get it right. I worked closely with Louis and Dougie but increasingly got to know Martin and John as well, both of whom I liked a lot. They had a difficult time with their dads and I remember well Martin and John making great speeches about the need to keep shareholders informed and advised (it was a public company). I was present at one such meeting where Martin and John were very vocal as to what should best be done for the benefit of the public shareholders. Dougie responded by saying imperiously to Martin, 'Your father and I will decide what is good for the shareholders!'

I was also involved in planning enquiries in London, difficult litigation areas for local captains of industry and a great relationship with John Gorna and the partners. After an initial period of two or three months a routine developed where at about 6.00pm most evenings I would call by John's office ('JG' as he was universally known in the firm). JG would always have the same drink at 6.00pm, a Tio Pepe sherry with half from a room temperature bottle and the other half from a bottle kept in the fridge. We had some great conversations and I learned a lot about property finance, yields, reversions, all manner of things.

I then met several people who were to have a great influence on my career. First was a bright Manchester barrister called George Carman, a friend of JG and the firm and someone who was instructed in all sorts of cases for clients. I started to use George too and quickly we became quite close. Before very long I was to spend a great deal of time with him in a case that would rocket-propel his standing and career.

Also I met again Stafford Pemberton whom I had known slightly in my early twenties around Bramhall and Wilmslow. Stafford's family were in the business of children's book publishing and he was a director at World Distributors, a major publisher based in Manchester. Stafford had been the guy who always had lots of money when the rest of us had not a great deal. At age 21 he took delivery of a brand-new white drophead E-type Jaguar, just the sexiest thing on four wheels and very popular with the girls. We got to know each other again and soon I was doing the World Distributors work and seeing a lot of Stafford. He would have a great effect on my career in the fairly near future.

I also started doing some work for a public company called Northern Developments plc, a home builder set up by a former bricklayer called Derek Barnes which, through aggressive expansion, had become the second-biggest home builder in the UK after Wimpey. The in-house lawyer there was Peter Bretherton.

I started to do more and more work for the Edwards family and within a few short years Louis C. Edwards and Sons, by then a struggling public company in the meat packing business, was to be used by one James ('Jimmy') Gulliver to create an enormous food retail and liquor empire, the Argyll Group, which, in the process, was to make all the Edwards family extremely wealthy. Above all, though, one man stood out from the rest.

Tony Sherring was a partner at accountants Deloitte Haskins and Sells in Manchester. Tony was a friend of the firm who one day recommended me to a client of his who had built up a medium-sized supermarket chain called

Whelan's Discount Stores. The owner, an ex-professional footballer called Dave Whelan, needed advice with a tricky problem.

Dave walked into my office and to this day I can still remember his first words: 'Hello, I'm Dave Whelan. I hear you can find pearls in oysters!'

I was then 27 and Dave was about 34. We hit it off from the word go. Dave was from Wigan and very proud of it; he had joined Blackburn Rovers as a teenager and quickly got through to their first team. He remembered playing against footballing legends like Stanley Matthews and Nat Lofthouse and had a very promising, if not in those days well paid, career ahead of him until disaster struck. Blackburn fought their way through to the Cup Final at Wembley in 1961, but Dave ended up on the wrong end of a tackle, broke his leg and had to be stretchered off the pitch. He was so badly injured he was not to play for Blackburn again. He spent a little time with smaller clubs like Crewe Alexandra but in reality his career in football was over, at least as a player. Using his redundancy money he started a market stall in Wigan, which he parlayed into a shop, then a small supermarket, then a large, and pioneering, discount supermarket which he had built up to four or five outlets by the time we met.

The particular problem he had was that Cow & Gate Baby Foods were refusing to supply him with baby foods because they maintained he was discounting the retail price to such an extent that many of their other retailing customers were complaining. They said that Dave was using Cow & Gate products as a 'loss leader', that is, selling retail for less than cost price.

I very quickly mugged up on the Retail Price Maintenance Legislation, hired a London barrister in George Carman's chambers called Frederic ('Freddie') Reynolds and threatened Cow & Gate with an immediate court injunction unless they recommenced supply. They folded like a pack of cards within days. Dave thought I had found a pearl for him! It was the start of a beautiful, but never uneventful, friendship.

Things were going well at John Gorna and Co. for me. I liked the people in the firm, I was acting for some really interesting clients and I could see a future opening up for me. I was still doing litigation work but through Percy Harris I started one or two corporate deals. There was nothing mega, just buying and selling private companies and understanding how that worked. I had always been an avid reader of the business sections of *The Times* and the *Financial Times* and at law school had enjoyed the sessions on valuation of companies. I thought it would be a good thing if the firm started to set out its stall to be known for more than commercial property and started also promoting itself as a company and commercial firm. We had the connections to get the work, we just needed to focus and I wanted to be the initiator of the new specialism.

Percy Harris was a good lawyer and he soon taught me what he knew about the world of share purchase agreements, representations and warranties and deeds of indemnity. I was getting more confident with every passing week. Then JG intervened. I thought he would be totally approving of this innovation but in fact it was quite the opposite. He didn't want to have a corporate department. Any work of that type that came in Percy could do and he wanted me to stick to litigation. This was our first disagreement.

Something else happened to change virtually everything. On a sunny morning in May 1972 at Battersea Park in London the wooden rollercoaster Big Dipper was taking on its routine crowd of thrill seekers. The ride had been designed by John Collins, the famous fairground impresario, in 1951 and, apart from a fire in 1970, had operated at Battersea without incident. On that day in May 1972 the cars went up the first steep slope but, as the train neared the top of the incline, the drive motor faltered and the train began to slip backwards. The design allowed for this possible risk and there were flanges on the side of the cars that were designed to dig into wooden planking at the track side to arrest and stop the backward movement. On this occasion they did not achieve their purpose; the rollercoaster car at the rear detached itself and hurtled backwards down the slope crashing horribly at the foot. Five children were killed and thirteen injured in the tragic crash.

Peter Reynolds had had some previous dealings with John Collins and his family and through this we became involved to provide advice. I was put forward to take the lead role.

Dealing with and defending a criminal charge of manslaughter was really not what I had in mind to occupy me for the next several months. Peter Reynolds felt we should take it on and JG had formed a view that there was some sort of public duty or *pro bono* type obligation that fell on us. Rather strangely, it was to represent the accused rather than the families of the dead children and those injured in the crash.

It was made pretty clear to me that the firm *was* going to take this on and that *I* was going to be in charge of achieving the right result, an acquittal.

Immediately I reached out to my new friend George Carman QC, assisted by Freddie Reynolds as his junior. We were to represent not the Collins family as the owners of the ride, but the manager of the ride, a man by the name of Hogan.

The third defendant was the surveyor (mechanical engineer) who had certified the safety of the ride only weeks before the disaster. He was to be represented by the prominent criminal solicitor, Sir David Napley.

In summary, our defence was that, given his lack of training and technical knowledge, our client Hogan was doing his 'incompetent best' in difficult circumstances and that there was insufficient evidence to show that he had shown 'reckless disregard' for the safety of the passengers.

The committal proceedings were held in Wandsworth in south London over a week-long hearing and during that time I got to know Sir David Napley fairly well. He was a former president of the Law Society (hence his knighthood), silky smooth and certainly the leading criminal solicitor of his generation. He had a particular interest in miscarriages of justice. I often grabbed a lift down to the courts with Sir David in his Rolls-Royce.

The case was committed for trial to the Old Bailey and I spent more and more time with George Carman preparing for the trial. It was a very high-profile case and one which might make or break George's career.

As the case progressed things moved on at the law firm. I and two other associates were to be put forward for 'equity' partnership at the firm. The other two candidates were both property lawyers and, although both decent sorts of guys, I'm afraid that rather arrogantly I didn't see them as being my equal. In short I thought I was better, more motivated to succeed and much more likely to generate significant revenues for the firm than either of them.

We finally got our written offer of partnership. JG had 55 per cent of the profits and the three others had 15 per cent each. We were each offered a 2.5 per cent interest for a total of 7.5 per cent, some coming from the three junior partners, thus ensuring that even after dilution JG still had just over 51 per cent of the action.

This didn't seem that enticing to me. The other two seemed to be up for accepting the offer, so I arranged a face to face meeting with JG in his office. Having carefully prepared his usual Tio Pepe for him I thanked him for the offer and asked him the extent to which it was negotiable.

His answer was clear and unequivocal: 'It's not!'

No maybes, no ifs, no sliding, no manoeuvring; just a simple NO! To be honest this really wasn't how I imagined it would be. I was happy at the firm which I thought was a good law firm that I could help make into a great law firm but ... it was take it or leave it.

Never knowingly undersold I reluctantly decided to leave it. JG said he was sorry, or maybe he said I would be sorry, but asked that I saw out the Big Dipper case before I went. I said that of course I would do that and in the end we agreed to disagree.

It was another fork in the road.

CHAPTER 11

The Big Dipper

Now it was the late summer of 1973 and I was again looking for alternative employment. I was 27, married with a two-year-old daughter and an expectant wife due to deliver our second child in November. I thought again about going to London but then, out of the blue, I heard that another prominent Manchester lawyer was starting a new firm and he was on the lookout for founder partners – his name was David Blank.

David was Jewish and had his unusual surname because when his father arrived in England to escape the Nazis, the immigration official couldn't spell his last name so just wrote down BLANK.

David had been the founding partner of a very successful Manchester law firm called David Blank, Alexander and Co. (with 'Tinnie' Alexander) and the firm had built a very good practice. Some ten years earlier, in 1963, David had decided to give up the practice of law and concentrate on his outside business interests which included a small publicly quoted conglomerate called the Cranleigh Group plus, together with his friend and client Frank Ford, another public company called Duple Motor Bodies which made luxury coaches. He had also set up an insurance guarantee and bonding company called General Surety and Guarantee Company in which he had then later sold a controlling interest to Swiss Life, at a considerable profit.

What JG was to commercial property, David Blank ('DB') was to corporate law. He was to be another great tutor. There was already another young partner who had accepted an offer, Ian Simpson, a good corporate lawyer, as well as a more junior solicitor, John Alcock. While JG had a Rolls-Royce, DB had a dark blue Bentley, and a chauffeur.

To start off, DB would have 50 per cent of the equity and Ian and I would have 25 per cent each with a guaranteed minimum profit share, guaranteed by DB, for the first two years. DB would provide the clients and the working capital and we would focus on corporate and commercial work. It was a great offer. I was in!

Before that I had the Battersea Big Dipper case to get through which started at the Old Bailey in the early autumn. The prosecution case was presented by Treasury Counsel, Henry Pownall QC, who was a first class act. George was going to have his work cut out to secure an acquittal for our man.

Our client Hogan was a decent 'salt of the earth' sort who honestly didn't deserve to go to prison on multiple counts of manslaughter. George Carman had Hogan summed up, as if trying to pigeonhole him by way of explanation to me, as 'the sort of man who doesn't necessarily change his socks every day'!

George Carman had a troubled home life, not helped by the fact that George Best the footballer, a client of George's, had taken a shine to George's then wife and had taken to leaving his red E-type Jaguar outside George's home when he was away!

Night after night I spent with George going through all

the angles, how we might tackle this piece of evidence, how he would get the jury on his side.

The day of his closing speech grew closer and George became more and more nervous. The night before, we promised ourselves an early supper and a good night's sleep. As it turned out I virtually pushed him through his apartment door after quite a few whiskies, making him promise that he would be at his best by 10.00am for the biggest day of his life.

As things turned out he was. George had the most amazing powers of recovery, often after almost no sleep. We settled into our seats in the show court of the Old Bailey and I sat next to David Napley in the solicitors' row. George rose to his feet and proceeded to deliver one of the greatest closing speeches of all time.

The jury hung on to his every word. David Napley nudged me and whispered, 'Where did you find this chap? He's magnificent!'

The jury went out and returned after only a short time to deliver a verdict of 'not guilty' on Hogan. Within months David Napley was hired by Jeremy Thorpe, the leader of the Liberal party, when he was accused of attempted murder. David in turn hired George Carman QC and George was off down the route of fame and fortune.

Nevertheless, these were not easy times. In retrospect, the 1970s was a very difficult decade, not only for Britain but for what was then known as the Western world, i.e. the industrialised nations, generally.

The rate of inflation had started to accelerate in the 1960s as successive governments set about achieving full employment. Determined to avoid a return to the high unemployment levels of the 1930s, successive governments (both Labour and Conservative) implemented Keynesian policies to keep demand high, using public money to prime the economic pump. The result, in a Britain with some archaic industrial management and workforce practices, was the creation of greater demand than supply – the classic cause of inflation.

However, this was just a foretaste of what was to come in the 1970s. Anthony Barber, the chancellor of the exchequer in Edward Heath's government, pumped money into the economy as never before in 1971 and 1972 following the news that unemployment had broken through the 1 million barrier, a shocking total following 30 years of full employment. Unfortunately, Britain's expansion coincided with a world boom, sparked by the decision in the United States to print money rather than raise taxes, in order to pay for the country's increasingly expensive involvement in Vietnam. In 1971 the US turned from being an exporter of oil into a net importer; and on 6 October 1973, Yom Kippur (the Day of Atonement) in the Jewish calendar, Egypt and Syria attacked Israel. Within 24 hours major Arab oil-exporting nations had announced plans to reduce oil production. Ten days later they announced an oil embargo against the USA in response to its support of Israel, and increased the price of petroleum by no less than 70 per cent!

The Yom Kippur War ended with an Egypt/Israel cease-fire on 25 October, but Arab frustration at Western nations' support for Israel continued and on 23 December the oil-producing nations agreed on a further increase in the price of oil. The price had doubled since the beginning of 1973. This was a great shock to the developed nations of the world which had enjoyed decades of cheap oil.

As panic buying and speculation took hold, the price rocketed. Tens of billions of pounds, dollars, deutschmarks, francs and lire were taken out of the world economy and put in the Arabian desert. Until they could be recycled into the system, the world was going to suffer.

In an attempt to choke inflation, Heath's government tackled the symptoms – rising prices, dividends and earnings – without tackling the cause: too much money. In the autumn of 1973, just before the oil crisis, the government introduced stage one of an incomes policy which would allow index-linked rises if inflation rose above 7 per cent. Because of the oil-price hike, inflation rose quickly above that level and the automatic pay rises produced a ratchet effect, pushing it higher and higher.

The National Union of Mineworkers submitted a large claim and imposed an overtime ban on 8 November 1973. Heath panicked and declared a state of emergency on 13 November. A month later he declared a three-day week to preserve fuel, and though negotiations with both Arabs and the miners continued, the only results were the continuation of high oil prices and the actuality of a miners' strike rather than just the threat. In the end, and for some people three weeks too late, Heath called an election with the implied platform of: 'Who governs the country, the government or the unions?' The electorate decided it wasn't sure who should govern the country. The Tories had finally shown some signs of standing up to the unions, but Labour might get the miners back to work. Neither party gained an overall majority, but Labour came away with more seats. Heath tried unsuccessfully to negotiate a coalition with the Liberal Democrats, so Harold Wilson formed his third administration.

It was against this political and economic backdrop that I embarked on the next stage of my career.

CHAPTER 12

New Firm

On 1 October 1973 I entered into partnership with David Blank and Ian Simpson at 76 Cross Street, Manchester, just 150 yards from my previous office in John Gorna's firm.

It felt good to be a part-owner of the firm and quite quickly I found that when I told my contacts and clients of my move, many wanted to come over with me. Almost immediately, Dave Whelan was about to expand again with the acquisition of a very big new site not far from central Manchester.

Stafford Pemberton brought World Distributors over (I was handling most of their work by then anyway) and, crucially as it turned out, Peter Bretherton, the in-house lawyer at Northern Developments, wanted to keep in touch and fed me some small matters to deal with.

Then on 10 November 1973 our second child Jonathan was born and everything seemed to be moving in the right direction. Everything, that is, apart from the economic situation, which, as we have just seen, was about to take a very ugly turn for the worse.

In the general economy, things had not been that wonderful in the run-up to 1974.

Harold Wilson and the Labour party were back in power.

Property prices in the early 1970s had taken quite a jump, credit was fairly cheap and lots of banks had money to lend (sounds familiar doesn't it?). But the storm clouds were gathering. Whenever you overhear that property (real estate) is a sure-fire bet and will continue on an ever upward spiral, say nothing, leave the room and quietly start to sell. It's taken me a long time to learn that lesson and not many people had learnt it in 1974.

I think it started with a 'secondary banking crisis', that is to say those who had borrowed short and lent long suddenly realised that they couldn't get their money back easily and started to default. The Bank of England stepped in with its 'Lifeboat Fund' to bail them out. By then it had hit the stock market, oil prices were racing away, confidence was sapped daily and it got worse and worse.

All this was obviously having an effect on business levels at our new office. We increasingly found that we had time on our hands, which is the last thing you want as a lawyer when your whole existence depends on selling that time to someone else who has money to pay for it!

Lunches at the St James Club in Manchester, which I had joined in my John Gorna days, were useful for getting to know everyone in Manchester but time lay heavy and the low point or, depending on your view point, the high point was when I won the club snooker championship in 1974. A great snooker player makes a poor lawyer. We were not making enough profit to pay ourselves in full and David Blank was having to tip more money in to keep up the payments.

I decided that enough was enough and it was time to roll up my sleeves to find some profitable work as quickly as possible. One man's misfortune is another man's fortune and so it was with Northern Developments plc. You will remember that Derek Barnes had set up the business originally in

Blackburn, Lancashire. He was a bricklayer who managed somehow to get his hands on a couple of building plots and begged, stole or borrowed enough to build a couple of homes which he quickly sold at a good profit. Those were the years of plenty for homebuilding in the 1960s. The business took off and by the early 1970s Northern Developments was a public company with a market capitalisation of about £35 million (about £700 million in today's money).

Derek still owned 50 per cent of the shares. He was likeable, straight-talking and a total maverick. In 1973 an American homebuilder had heard of Northern Developments and decided that they were going to buy it. They sent a message to Derek that they were coming over mob-handed to buy Derek out and bid for the rest of the company.

A week or so later they arrived at Elizabethan House in Blackburn, the HQ of Northern Developments, to be told that Derek was not around. They sent a message to Derek to say that they would pay him about £25 million for his shares alone.

This was in the days before mobile phones, so it took two or three hours to track Derek down to a building site where he was up to his knees in mud in the foundations of a house. He was given the message about the Americans and the £25 million. Without missing a beat he said, 'Well, you can tell them to piss off back to America – I'm not interested!'

Two or three years later, when one evening I was riding the train back from London to Manchester after a particularly bad meeting, I reminded Derek of this story and asked him why he had done what he did. You will see later what he replied.

Northern Developments in early 1974 owed a lot of banks a great deal of money. Derek had fuelled the amazing growth of the business on a mountain of debt, aided and abetted by banks who were falling over themselves to lend him the money to do it. ND owned land all over the country and just so long as demand for residential housing stock exceeded supply everything worked out fine.

That had ceased to be the case. Sales were drying up, interest rates were rising, and banks were getting very, very nervous. I talked to David Blank about ND and he said that we should get hold of Derek as soon as possible and get him to instruct us to make the first move with the banks by going to them, before they made a move, to explain the situation and to negotiate a moratorium on the entire banking syndicate.

There were about 25 separate banks who were owed varying amounts of money. The bank that was owed most money was Williams & Glyn's, later part of Royal Bank of Scotland, which was owed about £4.5 million and, to put that in context, it was the largest loan that the bank had out at that time. How's that for inflation? (It is £90 million in today's money).

What was obvious was that if one or more of the banks foreclosed on their security and then put the property on the market for the best price it could get, an avalanche would start and it would spread quickly through the residential housing sector. Values would plummet. Banks would lose vast amounts of other people's money and the average home-owner would see the value of their own property take a nosedive, causing a further loss of confidence. Retail spending would dry up and, not to put too fine a point on it, the whole country would face Armageddon.

This was serious stuff and definitely something that I was up for getting stuck into.

Through Peter Bretherton, and through an accountant we knew called Brian Tomlinson who was also close to

Derek, we got Derek to come into the office and we laid out a plan.

We would take overall charge of negotiations with all the banks to secure a 100 per cent moratorium. Given that ND was a public company we needed a merchant bank on board and the one we knew best was Slater Walker Securities, which had been the 'go-to' merchant bank for the previous few years. Slater Walker had been founded in 1964 by James Slater, a manager at British Motor Holdings, and Peter Walker, a Conservative MP and later a Cabinet minister. It was a very powerful operator in the City of London in the late 1960s and early 1970s, making many successful raids on public companies. Their activities led to the use of the term 'asset-stripping'. [During] the financial crisis of the mid-1970s, largely caused by an explosion in the price of oil following the Arab-Israeli war, Slater Walker got into financial difficulties and had to be rescued by the Bank of England.

We would be paid monthly and we would get the bank to release our fees so long as the negotiations continued on track. If we were successful in getting a 100 per cent moratorium signed up within twelve months we would also get a large success fee. We would have saved the company, and perhaps even the country!

Derek agreed and I was duly appointed as the leading man on the job which was quite a responsibility at the age of 29. It was only when we started our discussions with the banks that I realised the magnitude of the task that lay ahead.

Today, having learnt lessons, I know that it would be very unwise to have a syndicate of banks which required 100 per cent approval to make decisions or changes. One or more smaller banks will always exploit that situation to try to get the bigger banks to pay them off. That was exactly the problem we had at ND. There was no formal syndicate. More and more banks had wanted a piece of the ND pie so had crawled over each other to get in on the lending.

After a month or two we got the whole lot of them into the biggest boardroom Slater Walker had at St Paul's Churchyard opposite St Paul's Cathedral. We explained the financial position and particularly the huge risk that would be faced if any bank decided to jump the gun and break ranks. We had the Bank of England's tacit support, of course, and every bank would be treated in the same way irrespective of the amount of their outstanding loans.

Apart from the British banks we had American banks, French banks, secondary banks, Japanese banks, in other words, banks of every hue and colour. It was a tough meeting but I loved it!

I outlined the basic principles of the moratorium agreement and said we would get them a first draft within days. The meeting broke up with not too much rancour, but that was to be just the start of a hair-raising negotiation over months involving every trick and turn of human avarice, fear, ruthlessness and just about everything else you can imagine.

We were just about to embark on the year of our Lord 1975 and what a year that would be for me. The New Year kicked off with my first drafts of the moratorium agreement for ND circulating the banks and their lawyers. I was completely swamped, mainly spending the time in London at Slater Walker's offices in seemingly constant negotiation with the banks and their lawyers, ND and Derek Barnes, who did *not* want his hands tied by the banks.

Although I was totally consumed with this job I was very satisfied with the way my career was now going. Still only 29, I was dealing with the biggest rescue bid almost of all time, we were being paid well and there was all to play for.

Then two more things happened. As I was spending more time in London I thought it would be a good idea to get a rented flat for the firm rather than spending money constantly at the Grosvenor House Hotel on Park Lane which was David Blank's favourite. One day I was looking round some flats in Dolphin Court along the Embankment, a favourite haunt of Members of Parliament who needed crash pads in London during the week. While waiting for an agent to show me around I looked at some small adverts in the lobby of the building and one in particular caught my eye for a motor car.

> '1965 Bentley S3 midnight blue
> Titled Owner – £2,500 ono.'

I was fascinated. My old pal Rodney Hylton-Potts had an S3 Bentley and suddenly, impulsively and obviously stupidly, I decided that I should have one as well.

I rang the telephone number given and the phone was answered with a languorous drawl, 'Yeees …?'

The owner had an apartment in Dolphin Court. He would be down in an hour and would meet me in the lobby and take me for a test drive. An hour later this slightly foppish, well-dressed young man appeared and introduced himself as John Jermyn ('Jermyn' as in the street in St James's, he explained, in a sense giving a slight impression that he may own it).

We set off and the Bentley S3 made its stately progress around Chelsea and Belgravia and back to Dolphin Court. John and I sat down for a coffee and he started to tell me about himself. His title was the Earl Jermyn; his father was the Marquess of Bristol.

The family seat was a stately home called Ickworth just

outside Bury St Edmunds and although the house and park were owned by the National Trust the family had a lease on the East Wing, with fourteen bedrooms, and still owned 4,500 acres around the house, 3,000 more acres of prime land in Sleaford, Lincolnshire, a 1,000-acre estate in Essex and 'some rather good pictures and furniture'.

John was approaching his 21st birthday and clearly he and his father did not see eye to eye.

I told him all about myself, what I did and what I was working on. He asked me if I would look through all his trusts for him to advise him on what actions he needed to take.

Basically we got on like a house on fire. I thought he was interesting and had a great self-deprecating sense of humour, and he clearly needed help and advice. I drove back up to Cheshire in the Bentley S3 as its new proud owner with a boot full of trust documents that I had to read.

At about the same time Stafford Pemberton had decided to leave World Distributors and set up his own children's book publishing company called (intriguingly!) Stafford Pemberton Publishing Company Limited. It would concentrate on producing and distributing children's 'annuals', a book bought normally at Christmas for and by children and teenagers. This sector of publishing had started off with 'annuals' of comics like the *Beano* and the *Dandy* but moved on to other things like popular TV shows, rock bands and so on.

A very early signing Stafford made was for a band from Scotland called the Bay City Rollers. The band took off in a major way and SP Publishing sold hundreds of thousands of Bay City Roller annuals at a great profit margin. This was soon followed by another band, Abba, which exploded and the Abba annual was another massive seller. SP Publishing was on the verge of something very big in 1975.

On the domestic front we decided to move to Alderley Edge in Cheshire and found a Victorian house which had been built in 1861 for a prosperous Manchester solicitor, in the middle of the Edge with an acre of gardens and right next door to Louis Edwards of Louis C. Edwards and Manchester United fame.

The home had been split into two flats by the widow who had lived there for many years but it was no great job to turn it back into a single house. Incredibly as I look back now, the price we agreed was £43,500 (about £600,000 in today's money) for a five/six bedroom house in the heart of the very best location south of Manchester. So we had a new home in June 1975.

My partners at David Blank and Co. were less than impressed by the new 'asset' on the partnership books, the Bentley S3. They were even less impressed when, after only a week or so, the gearbox failed and was about to cost another £1,500 to fix.

I called John Jermyn and told him of the problem. I thought there was no point in beating about the bush: 'John. If I'm going to be your new lawyer on a signed retainer then I will have a conflict of interest in suing you for the failed gearbox.'

Lord Jermyn signed the retainer. I was about to become an expert in the world of landed estates, trusts and their taxation.

One evening in early October 1975 I was watching television with Pamela – there was a pilot for a new American TV detective show called *Starsky and Hutch*. It was very good. About ten minutes after it finished the phone rang. It was Stafford Pemberton – had I seen the show and did I like it?

'Yes and Yes.'

'Right, pack your bags; we're off to California to find the producer.'

CHAPTER 13

California Here I Come

I was 30 years old and not only had I never been to California, I didn't know anyone who *had* been to California. I hadn't even been to America. Compare that with today when I can hardly think of anyone who *hasn't* been to California! We had to prepare in haste and the first thing was to get a B2 visa from the American embassy – no visa waiver programme then. This was duly granted on 29 October 1975 and shortly after that Stafford and I took off on a non-stop flight to Los Angeles.

Fourteen hours later we were driving through the streets of Beverly Hills where it was early evening. To us then it was truly a magic place. Compared with 1970s Manchester it was a paradise. Everywhere looked so affluent, the people in the street were so good-looking and everyone seemed so upbeat and welcoming.

We decided to spoil ourselves by staying at the famous Beverly Wilshire Hotel in the centre of Beverly Hills. We had a suite at the end of a corridor and the reception room looked out over Wilshire Boulevard to Rodeo Drive and the famous Brown Derby restaurant. We got some sleep that night, ready for the day ahead when we would do our best to fix a meeting with the producers of *Starsky and Hutch*.

We knew the production house was Spelling Goldberg Productions, co-owned by Aaron Spelling and Lenny Goldberg. It wasn't too hard to get through to them on the telephone the following morning to secure an appointment with their head of business affairs, Marvin Katz.

Just being British with an English accent was such a leg up at that time. Most people we found were quite happy to fix a meeting so they could listen to our accents and ask us about 'Olde England' and the Queen.

We hit it off with Martin Katz from the word go. The show was the first big series that Spelling Goldberg had produced and I think they were surprised it had been such an instant hit, particularly outside the USA.

Aaron Spelling didn't travel outside of the United States because he absolutely refused to fly anywhere. I think he had once had a bad experience, so if he travelled internally in the States it was by train. As his shows took off and his wealth rocketed he was able to hire his own personal railroad carriage which he had tacked on to the back of a regular service.

Marvin had done his background checks on Stafford and he was certainly up for a deal. We agreed a reasonable advance against a realistic royalty and in virtually no time at all we had a deal. I got on so well with Marvin that I asked him whether Spelling Goldberg had lawyers in the United Kingdom. Of course they didn't because this was the first show to explode onto the international scene for them. Never known for being backward, I asked Marvin if I could represent Spelling Goldberg in the United Kingdom. He set up a meeting with Aaron Spelling and we hit it off so, in no time at all, I was now retained to represent Spelling Goldberg, and later Aaron Spelling Productions, in the UK.

What a trip. We had secured a successful signing of a deal

for Stafford Pemberton Publishing and a new client, and a very exciting one at that, for me.

Stafford and I were back in our suite at the Beverly Wilshire celebrating over a bottle of wine when an almighty din started up in the corridor outside. It sounded like a bunch of kids playing football and our door was the goal! After ten minutes or so of this racket we'd had enough, so I threw open the door to see two black children with a football. I was about to 'remonstrate' with them in a fairly direct way when the door to the adjoining suite opened and a huge black man with a striking physique and handsome face came out into the corridor, looked at me and said, 'Is everything all right?'

I suddenly realised who it was; Muhammad Ali, the heavyweight boxing champion of the world and one of my heroes!

I melted into a pool of supplication. 'Oh yes champ – I was just about to say what beautiful children they are and ask if I could join in!'

We shook hands and had a good chat, mainly about 'Smokin' Joe Frazier if I remember correctly. This capped the trip and we returned to England on a massive high.

Meanwhile back in the office we were finally getting to the endgame with the saga of Derek Barnes and Northern Developments. The moratorium agreement with all the banks was finally in an agreed form despite all the usual last-minute jockeying, particularly from banks with a smaller exposure trying to blackmail the bigger banks into buying them out. I got them all into the main massive boardroom at Slater Walker in St Paul's Square Churchyard and finally one by one they all signed up.

The major terms were to make sure there was an orderly disposal and realisation of the massive land bank as well as hundreds of completed houses. The main restriction on Derek and the company was that he didn't try to buy any *more* land.

After a year of blood, sweat and tears which had dominated my life, the sense of relief at pulling off this huge deal was immense. Our success fee was paid. I felt I had earned it. Unfortunately the celebrations were short-lived. About two to three weeks after the signing one of the main bankers called me in a state of high dudgeon. 'Your client is in breach of the agreement so the moratorium is dead and we are appointing a receiver.'

I calmed him down and got the story out of him. It appeared that Derek had been to a land auction and had successfully bid for, and had knocked down to him, some building land for about £1 million. This was £1 million that neither Derek nor the company had. That was that. The banks had had enough and so, one by one, they all pulled the rug and appointed receivers. The game was up.

A day or so later we had a post mortem meeting in London when the receivers explained how they wanted to run things. Afterwards I rode back on the train north with Derek. He was philosophical but in no way contrite. I reminded him that less than two years earlier he had turned down an offer of over £20 million in cash for the shares. I asked him why he had done that. He said that he had worked out that if he took the cash he would be, in terms of hard cash in the bank, the second richest person in the country. He thought if he held out for a year or two longer he would get a cash offer that would make him the richest *cash* millionaire.

I reminded him of what Nathan Rothschild once said when asked how he became so rich. He had replied, 'I always sold too soon!'

The year of 1975 rounded off with confirmed instructions to act for Spelling Goldberg to represent all their interests and protection of all their copyrights in the UK. At the same time I had now read all the papers and trust deeds for Lord Jermyn and we were ready to move forward on that front. All in all 1975 had been quite a year.

Looking back now, I remember 1976 mainly as the start of 'the Hollywood Years'! *Starsky and Hutch* became an enormous worldwide hit show and in the UK magazines, toy manufacturers and indeed anyone who thought they could make a buck out of 'ripping off' the *Starsky and Hutch* copyright was at it, and we waded in with gusto.

I have to admit that film copyright and merchandising law had not figured large in my experience up to that time but I was a very fast learner. Within a couple of months I had a fairly good grasp of the basic principles and I was learning more and more every day. I fired off dozens of 'letters before action' to infringers and very quickly started negotiating settlements.

Invariably the settlement involved a cash sum representing past royalties and more often than not the grant of a merchandising agreement so that the infringer could become legitimate or pay a royalty on all sales to Spelling. They also normally paid my costs. Some of the biggest infringers were up for a fight and hired lawyers. I arranged for Marvin Katz to come over to London for a week and take a suite at the Grosvenor House Hotel on Park Lane. I arranged for almost back-to-back meetings with infringers and their lawyers in the suite and Marvin and I had a well-practised routine.

I had already billed Marvin as 'Mr Hollywood' to the infringers so most of them were very keen to meet this important man from 6,000 miles away. I would answer the door to the large suite and usher the guests into the very large reception room overlooking Hyde Park.

Marv took a strategic position at the far side of the room and would always be looking out over the park as I brought in the guest infringers (or 'prey'!). I would then solemnly announce their arrival and Marvin would turn around very slowly to greet the guest with an air of imposing grandeur. We called this the 'slow turn from the window' routine and we still laugh about it today, some 35 years later.

Routine or not, it worked and we settled off and licensed most of the remaining infringers, collecting a large amount of damages in the process. News of our success soon got back to Aaron Spelling so an early return visit to Los Angeles was quickly organised.

Marvin knew most of his counterparties as head of business affairs at nearly all of the other studios – Universal, Paramount, 20th Century Fox et al – so soon, meetings were arranged for me to meet all the right people to see if I could represent them in the UK. To be honest it wasn't too hard. Most had rarely seen an English solicitor over there and once the point of reference, Aaron Spelling, was overcome I proceeded to pick up most of them as clients.

My visits to Los Angeles became almost a monthly event as the work built up and up. *Starsky and Hutch* was soon followed by *Charlie's Angels*, another huge hit for Spelling. 'Hutch', the actor David Soul, turned out to be a great singer and was soon a huge hit as a pop star on both sides of the Atlantic. As we knew each other from the set of *Starsky and Hutch* it was only natural that I should become his personal lawyer in the UK as well.

We were instructed on smash hit films, *Star Wars, Superman* and *Saturday Night Fever,* and started to get more and more work from US licensees of products who wanted to extend their distribution to the UK and Europe. I had settled into a routine of staying at the Beverly Hilton or the Beverly Hills Hotel, renting exotic cars from Budget Rent-a-Car on the corner of Wilshire and Santa Monica and spending the days driving from studio to studio meeting more and more people and getting more and more work. It was all very hedonistic!

One day during that summer of 1976, Marvin took me along to a drinks party at the home of an agent friend of his on the beach near Santa Monica. It was a very pleasant and relaxing day until along came a new guest and his wife who obviously had had a few drinks on the way but he was great fun and I fell into a long conversation, aka drinking session, with him.

He was an actor and I remembered seeing him in a film called *Stardust* with David Essex where he played the Hollywood agent for a mega rock star from England (Essex). He had a great line that he delivered from his penthouse office overlooking the whole of Los Angeles on a lovely sunny day, where he waved his arm expressively over the view and said to David Essex, 'Just another shitty day in Paradise!'

We were getting on famously and I asked him what he was working on. He said he had just got back from Texas where he had shot a 'pilot' for a new TV 'pot boiler' that he felt had no future and would go nowhere. He was very wrong, and I had just spent the day with 'JR', the soon to be world famous Larry Hagman!

Back in the UK as the year progressed things just kept getting busier and busier. I had now got to grips with all the paperwork surrounding Lord Jermyn and his trusts. John had just had his 21st birthday and regrettably was pretty much at loggerheads with his father and his trustees.

When a lawyer writes a book such as this there is a very

difficult line to be studiously observed. A lawyer must never break that bond of confidentiality that he owes to his client and as during the course of this book I refer to clients, famous or otherwise, by name, I will never reveal anything that I believe that they themselves would regard as confidential. I hope that I stick to this discipline rigorously and that the reader's enjoyment is not adversely affected in the result.

With that caveat spelt out, I can say that Lord Jermyn's trust affairs were extremely complicated but the net result was that I had to master in short order the archaic world of the Settled Land Act, entailed interests and accumulation and maintenance settlements, as well as trust taxation both in the UK and overseas. I rapidly became an expert (I had to be!) and the net result after several battles was that the vast bulk of the assets which had been in trust for John were distributed to him to be held in his own name.

It also became clear in fairly short order that if John was to save a huge amount of tax that would cripple the estates he would have to leave the UK and establish himself abroad for a period of time. We selected Monte Carlo, which suited John in many ways and I fairly quickly secured a *carte de séjour* for him to live in Monaco. As I look back over John's life, of which you the reader may learn a good deal, it is clear to me that the world at large took the view that John was a vacuous aristocrat of the worst kind who squandered his vast inheritance. This popular view is largely unfair and, during his life, John tried hard to be a good businessman and to accept his responsibilities. He was also effortlessly a charming and very amusing companion.

Having got access to his funds and assets and knowing that he must spend much time in Monaco, I suppose it seemed natural to him that he should acquire what is normally the ultimate folly, a yacht; not just any old yacht but a very large one. He told me he had located the ideal vessel and that it was currently moored up in Gibraltar where the current owners were living on it.

It was about 135 feet long, built in Southampton in about 1936 and was a classically designed motor yacht full of wood panelling and polished brass called *Braemar*. He had set his heart on it. It would be kept in Monaco and I was to go with him to buy it. We arrived there, according to my passport, on 26 August 1976, and checked into the Rock Hotel which was very *fin de siècle*!

A delightful couple owned and lived on the boat (or ship!), which indeed was magnificent, at least at the dockside, and it had not been on any sort of voyage for quite some time. I'm sure we must have had a report from a marine surveyor but whatever, John was determined that this was to be his and so a deal was agreed.

The old saying is that there are only two good days when you own a (large) yacht – the day you buy it and the day you sell it! I well remember the day of purchase and remember even more vividly the day it was sold, many expensive years later, in the port of Villefranche in the south of France. It was nevertheless a fun trip and it would certainly give John a major challenge and open many doors of amusing experience to both of us over the following few years.

CHAPTER 14

Not Again!

Back in the office my practice seemed to be going from strength to strength but I was starting to get very frustrated with my partners.

David Blank was a wonderful and very astute corporate lawyer who taught me a great deal but the reality was dawning on him that he did not possess the same powers of attracting work that he had in his earlier years. My two other partners, Ian and John, seemed content to float along with pretty much a 'nine to five' existence that I found frustrating and annoying. It probably wasn't true but it seemed to me that I was doing at least 50 per cent of the work but only getting 25 per cent of the profit.

I had met socially another solicitor called Tony Hill who had a practice called Hills which he had set up, focused mainly around property clients. I got it into my head that there would be mileage in putting together the two practices, using our strengths in corporate, and now entertainment and trust law, and his in property. I also felt that Tony would be much more of a kindred spirit to me and that we would spark off each other to build a bigger and better firm. We had some exploratory meetings but it soon became clear that Tony thought my partners were pretty stick-in-the-mud and they thought he was too racy, for which read entrepreneurial.

The rather desultory negotiations soon ground to a halt. In time this provoked a confrontation with my three partners who wanted to know what I wanted. I told them the truth which was that I felt I was working harder than any of them and if I was to stay I wanted a bigger share of profits. They came back to me with a proposal. I could increase my share of profits to 35 from 25 per cent BUT only on the basis that I entered into a restrictive covenant that if ever I left the firm I would not act for any of the clients for at least two years. In other words it was a completely unacceptable proposal!

By now we were well into 1977 and I started to think about other alternatives. In reality I didn't particularly want to leave. It would be disruptive for me as well as my family and my clients and I was quite proud of what we had built up over the last three years or so. I had rather vague talks with other law firms but increasingly I had a feeling that the only way I would be truly fulfilled would be to start my own business.

I thought of moving to London, always the 'Mecca' for lawyers given the vast volume and variety of work. I had a meeting with a lawyer called Stanley Lee who had his own practice in Lincoln's Inn Fields. He was definitely my sort of guy, a very savvy corporate lawyer who enjoyed doing his own thing. He made me a generous offer – he would admit me immediately and share the profits equally.

I was tempted but our children were just starting school in Cheshire, we had taken on a 'project' Victorian mansion on the edge of Alderley Edge and apart from my entertainment clients, and growing general American client base, most of my contacts and clients were all around the north-west of England.

So Stanley and I decided to go into business together under the title Lee Lane-Smith, with offices in London and Manchester. I think we were the only solicitor firm, at that time, to have offices in both the North and London. We had Stanley's office at 52 Lincoln's Inn Fields and I found a small suite of four rooms on the first floor of a Victorian street in central Manchester, 20 Kennedy Street.

My David Blank partners did not take the news well. Everything seemed to slide quickly from a civilised 'stand-off' to all-out war. The 'war' became worse by the day as they started to work out how many clients and files would be walking out of the door with me. They were wondering how what was left was going to keep the three of them in anything approaching luxury.

Rather woundingly David Blank accused me of being fundamentally a sole practitioner, unsuited to practising law with other partners. This was pretty wide of the mark as later events were to demonstrate. As we got closer and closer to the leaving date, 30 September 1977, the more unpleasant everything became. Every file was argued over with the firm demanding money for every scrap of work in progress.

I was very grateful to National Westminster Bank who extended the new business an overdraft of £10,000 (£150,000 in today's money). A lot of that was used up paying off David Blank and my old partners.

The last day in the office came, and typically for autumn in Manchester it was pouring with rain. The last remaining thing I needed was my desk chair (with back support for my bad back) which probably was worth 10p. I asked if I could take it with me.

I gave them the money and took the chair down in the lift to the ground floor. My new office was perhaps 300 yards away so I stepped into the street and held the chair on top of my head as I walked through the pouring rain to my new life.

Ten minutes later I sat behind the desk in my new little office and let out a huge gasp of relief.

At last!

I was my own master, in charge of my own destiny. I was probably ever so slightly queasy but still ready for my new life. So what exactly was it that I wanted to achieve over the next 25 years or so? I was just short of 32 years of age.

Over the previous two years I had spent a good deal of time in the offices of American law firms and I had learnt that the very best way to grow a law firm was to produce a totally committed service where the interest of the client *always* came first. I would adopt that credo, totally committed to clients, totally committed to quality and, to give myself a target, I would dedicate my professional life to attempting to create, not the biggest and best law firm in Manchester, nor the biggest and best in the United Kingdom, but the biggest and the best law firm in the world.

The real journey was about to begin in earnest and I stood again at another fork in the road.

I had chosen the route to follow; there was no looking back so now it was onwards and upwards!

CHAPTER 15

Lee Lane-Smith

The first day I was open for business was Monday 3 October 1977. The deal I had cut with Stanley Lee was that he would be entitled to 5 per cent of the profit of the Manchester office and I would get 5 per cent of the profit of the London office. I had two full-time employees; my secretary Ann who had been with me at David Blank's and Gillian, the David Blank receptionist, who decided she preferred to be with me. To keep the books we had Doreen, on loan from my accountants for a day a week. The office space was about 750 square feet but it had a great feel and atmosphere from the beginning.

On 16 August 1977, just six weeks earlier, Elvis Presley had died in Memphis at the age of 42. Suddenly the world was going mad with Elvis merchandise and I could see that his estate was going to get exploited big style unless someone got a grip on what was happening.

Elvis Presley was almost certainly the most celebrated musician of the twentieth century. He was commercially successful in many genres including pop, blues and gospel. With estimated sales of over 600 million units he is the best-selling solo artist in the history of recorded music. He was nominated for fourteen Grammy awards and won three, including the

Grammy Lifetime Achievement Award at the age of 36. When he died tragically at only 42 years old, 80,000 people lined the processional route from his home, Graceland, to the Forest Hill Cemetery and President Carter said, 'Elvis Presley has permanently changed the face of American popular culture.'

Through Stafford Pemberton I found out that the secretary of the Elvis Presley fan club in the UK was called Todd Slaughter and I tracked him down. I told him of my experience protecting famous names and copyrights and saying that Elvis's estate was going to get mercilessly ripped off unless something was done quickly.

He told me that Colonel Tom Parker, Elvis's manager, had signed a worldwide deal with an American merchandising company called Factors Etc., Inc. and that the owner of Factors was due to arrive in London in a day or so. He told me where they would be staying and said he would tell them about me. Three days later, following one of my rather brazen 'I'm a lawyer and you need me' discussions on the telephone, I was sitting down with the owner of the rights to Elvis worldwide.

I was instructed to protect the estate throughout the UK and to supervise other lawyers in Europe and, within days, letters before action were hitting the desk of a multitude of infringers, written on the notepaper of Lee Lane-Smith.

The letters started out 'We represent the estate of the late Elvis Presley …'

You couldn't make it up!

Being instructed by the estate of the 'King' came quickly on the heels, or should I say 'hooves'? of another major and unusual instruction that autumn. Red Rum had won the Grand National steeplechase in 1973 and 1974. In 1975 he came second to L'Escargot and in 1976 was beaten into second place by Rag Trade.

In 1977 his trainer, Ginger McCain, entered him again at the age of twelve (the horse not Ginger!). Red Rum not only won the race for an historic third time but he won it by 25 lengths. 'Rummy' was a national hero and was getting very many merchandising opportunities. McCain and the owners came to me to handle the work and I was delighted that if I was to act for any horse it should be Red Rum, one of the greatest of all time.

So with Elvis Presley, Red Rum, a good chunk of Hollywood and the start of a specialisation in landed estates, 1977 came to an exciting and fairly spectacular close with a major cocktail party held at our home in Alderley Edge. About 150 people turned up for what proved to be an annual event for the next few years.

Just as the party was getting under way, Dave Whelan rang to say he couldn't make the party – too far from Wigan! – but he had received an approach to sell Whelan's Discount Stores which he had decided to accept and he wanted to get me on board in the New Year to handle the transaction. He also wanted me to meet another friend of his, Arthur Snipe, the founder of a very successful public company called Mining Supplies, who was looking for a new corporate lawyer.

1978 promised to open with a bang, and it didn't disappoint as we shall see shortly!

By January 1978 I was starting to settle into my new little office and the routine that I would keep up for most of the next 25 years or so. I would get up at about 5.00am, subject to weather go for a short run, have breakfast and jump in the car by 6.30am at the latest, to beat the traffic, and be in the office by 7.00am. I would get the percolator going for fresh coffee, start work, light a cigar (small Swiss) and crack on. My secretary Ann and receptionist Gill arrived by 9.00am and we got stuck in.

From the beginning I told Ann and Gill that we were all on first-name terms and that would continue no matter how large or grand the firm became. This rebounded on me many years later when based in my grand penthouse office at the top of our own eleven-storey building in the middle of the City of London. One morning I was walking across the lobby to the lifts with a fairly important new client when a young man, who I assumed was about seventeen and had just started in the photocopying room, came out of the lift, looked me up and down, must have recognised me from a photograph during his induction session and then said, 'Whatcha Roger – everything alright mate?' in a broad cockney accent. I couldn't blame him. He had obviously been told the tradition as part of his induction.

In January 1978 work was starting to flow well. Clients were very supportive and I suppose that I was just so immersed in the business and their issues that I was giving a good client service. The problem was that I was doing every type of legal work; some company law, real estate transactions, disputes, commercial agreements, landed estates. The list went on and on, including all the copyright infringement and licensing work that was continuing to build almost by the day.

I can't quite remember how but one day I received an approach, probably an unsolicited letter, from one Kathryn Lloyd-Jones. She told me she had just finished her degree and was looking for a two-year training contract. She came in and seemed very keen, pleasant and willing to get stuck in and best of all didn't cost a lot! So I took her on as my first employee. She became an immediate 'gofer'/personal assistant and learnt quickly. Her then boyfriend was a barrister, just admitted, and he used to call in from time to time.

I really needed more help than Kathryn and then got

another approach from one Jeremy Fieldhouse. I had met Jeremy during my days at John Gorna. We played chess together most lunch times. After I left he had also departed to Birmingham to join a very good firm called Pinsent and Co., where he specialised in commercial property work. After a couple of years there he was keen to come back to Manchester.

Jeremy's father Roy had been a close confidante of John Gorna in commercial property work and his brother Paul had taken over the family agency business Isaac Nield and Co. Jeremy was keen to give it a go and we seemed to have enough real estate work to get him going, so he joined as a salaried partner (no share of the profits in the firm) but with the title of partner.

The notepaper was starting to fill out, given the London end where we had Stanley Lee and John Hamilton, and one or two more juniors. Altogether, by 1978, Lee Lane-Smith had six partners on the notepaper with offices in London and Manchester. I don't recall any other Manchester firm with a London office so it was quite a good public relations angle.

The attitude of the other Manchester firms was interesting and typical of the legal profession at that time. The 'old-line' firms then were Addleshaw Sons and Latham, March Pearson Skelton, Slater Heelis, Vaudrey Osborne and Mellor. Their attitude to me was, I think, that I was a jumped-up curiosity that wouldn't last the pace and in any event they were so deeply ingrained in the community that it really wasn't necessary for them to react in any way to me to shake themselves up. In other words they were largely totally complacent. That was perfect – just where I wanted them to be. By 2013 every single one of those once famous Manchester firms, apart from Addleshaws, had disappeared into oblivion.

Dave Whelan came through with his corporate deal. Over my long career in the law and the world of business I met endless successful businessmen, some of whom went up like a rocket and down again like a lead balloon. In truth I can count on one hand the men that I regarded as having just natural flair, instinct and a general nose for business and I put Dave Whelan right up there. Nobody taught Dave the fundamentals of business. His dad was a singer/entertainer on the working men's club circuit in the North going under the stage name of Tony Rigaletto (the Italian tenor – from Wigan!).

After Dave broke his leg at Wembley in the Cup Final his playing days at the top of the game were effectively over. He had used his limited redundancy money to start a market stall in Wigan market which he built up, with a lot of help from his lovely wife Patricia, into a shop, then a discount mini-supermarket.

In the 1970s supermarkets were just starting to take off but Dave's concept was much more along the Tesco line of 'pile it high and sell it cheap'. That is, fantastic value. From Wigan, Whelan's Discount Stores had spread across the northern part of Greater Manchester and by early 1978 had about seven outlets.

Ken Morrison from Yorkshire had taken over his family shop and had been pursuing a similar strategy to Dave, but across Yorkshire, through his Morrison's Supermarkets. Ken was ready to do his first acquisition and Whelan's Discount Stores was the target.

In his own book Dave reveals that the price he agreed with Ken Morrison was £1.3 million. It is a testament to the ravages of inflation that 35 or so years later that seems like such a comparatively small amount of money for a corporate transaction. (It is about £12 million in today's money.)

It certainly seemed a lot of money back then, enough for Dave to consider whether he might retire, in his early forties, on the proceeds.

Ken Morrison was not a Yorkshireman for nothing. He and Dave battled hard over virtually every penny but always in a good-natured way. Ken's lawyers were a hard but fair Bradford firm and I picked Stanley Lee's corporate law brains to make sure Dave was protected from possible pitfalls. The deal involved a final stocktaking which Ken insisted he was going to do himself. Memorably, on the day in question, Ken managed to reject about four Mars Bars on the grounds that they were just past their sell-by date, thus saving about £1. In Yorkshire every penny counts, and so it should!

After completion I went off with Dave down to Majorca where he had, and still has, a place not far outside Palma. We went to negotiate a move there for four to five years so that the 30 per cent gain on the sale price might be mitigated by Dave being non-resident. It seemed that in Spain one could negotiate a figure for tax payments that was mutually acceptable, but, after only 24 hours, Dave was bored and decided there and then to return to the UK, pay the tax and get on with the rest of his life.

Part of the deal with Morrison's had involved extracting from the business a small retail sports and fishing goods shop that Dave had picked up along the way called J.J. Bradburns. We carved this out of the assets sold and this small single shop then became the foundation store for what was to become over the next 25 years or so one of the largest retailers in the UK, JJB Sports. Around JJB there lies many a tale in the years to come.

Around this time Dave introduced me to one of his great friends of that time called Arthur Snipe. Arthur was another very sharp, and fairly abrasive, businessman from South

Yorkshire. He had spent some of his early years around the coal mining equipment industry and had designed, and patented, some revolutionary gadgets that vastly improved the performance of the automated conveyors that took freshly mined coal from the coal face and away to its transportation from the mine.

He had started his own business, Mining Supplies Ltd, in 1960 and it had been so successful that by 1965 it was a public company and Arthur had already made a considerable sum of money from the issue of shares to the public. He had bought a beautiful house and estate near Newark. Dave gave me a good write-up to Arthur who was looking out for a new law firm for the company. The mighty Slaughter and May had acted on the IPO but that had been thirteen or so years earlier and the ties were not close. One day Arthur started to tell me that he wanted to make a bid for another public company called Lawrence Scott and Electromotors based in Norwich and Manchester.

Mining Supplies had developed a new coal cutter to pair up with their armoured coal face conveyors and Lawrence Scott and Electromotors were the power train. If the new product took off (it did) they would be placing orders for a lot of motors so Arthur's logic was to buy the company that made the motors to secure the line of supply. He hoped to negotiate an agreed deal, but if not he was quite prepared to launch a 'hostile' takeover bid for Lawrence Scott.

Arthur's son-in-law Michael Bell was in effect the managing director of Mining Supplies. I say 'in effect' because Arthur was not the sort of man who was about to concede that anyone, apart from him, had any power of decision making. Michael was apprehensive about such a large step but was not about to question Arthur's judgement.

Our merchant bankers, Singer and Friedlander, sounded

out the board of Lawrence Scott and received a short and sharp rebuff. They were not up for an agreed deal. It then emerged that Slaughter and May also represented Lawrence Scott so could not represent Mining Supplies who had to nominate its own corporate lawyers for the fight.

I, of course, immediately put my hand up and said, 'I can do that!'

In truth I had done little public company work at that time and certainly had never handled a hostile takeover bid. Arthur gave me the job and we immediately got stuck in. Stanley in London helped me again and battle commenced. I learnt an awful lot in a short space of time and loved the cut and thrust of a public battle, particularly pitting myself against a firm like Slaughter and May.

The Lawrence Scott board had, we quickly found, lost the confidence of their major shareholders. The price we offered was fair, probably too generous, and their defences quickly crumbled. We had won hands down. We soon found out that the company was in a far worse state than we thought and was going to need a lot of work to turn it round. Mining Supplies were short on manpower so I was drafted in as a sort of 'hitman', spending two days a week at the headquarters in Norwich, getting to understand the business and the people and generally trying to figure out what to do with our new possession.

We also quickly found that their bankers, Barclays, were very unhappy with Lawrence Scott and wanted their money back. In the meantime they expected Mining Supplies to guarantee the debt.

In a tense meeting at the Barclays head office in London we explained that there was no way we were going to give a guarantee and that it was in their interest to leave us alone to get on with the task of sorting it out. Barclays agreed.

The chief executive of Lawrence Scott was a typically bombastic man who seemed to blame everyone but himself for the problems. I terminated him. We sold off two or three peripheral subsidiaries that had nothing to do with the main business to generate some cash to give back to the bank. There was a large manufacturing plant in Manchester. Everything needed to be transferred to Norwich to save cash and improve efficiencies. The Manchester workers and their union wouldn't entertain it and took over the factory, ejected the local management and declared that they weren't going anywhere. There were finished motors in the factory that we could not get out because we couldn't get in!

This attracted a lot of newspaper and general media attention, not least because it was about to tie in with what became the 'Winter of Discontent' when the unions rebelled against Jim Callaghan's Labour government. In typical Arthur style he determined direct action was called for. He organised for two helicopters to go in armed with security guards one weekend. The helicopters landed on a Saturday, ejected the few workers who were present sitting in, changed all the security locks and airlifted out the motors that were needed.

Game, set and match to Arthur. But now the workforce laid siege to the site itself! After weeks of stand-off we finally did a deal to organise redundancy funds for most of the workforce with some skilled men moving down to Norwich. The profile of the hostile bid won and the subsequent legal issues that flowed from the deal did the fledging law firm of Lee Lane-Smith no harm at all in the marketplace.

The entertainment practice was also flourishing with more work flowing in all the time. David Soul ('Hutch') was enjoying a meteoric take-off as a recording star and was hugely popular around the world including the UK in particular. David's image was being 'ripped off' mercilessly and unless something was done it would get out of hand and he would lose out financially. So David came to see me to figure out what might be done.

The problem then, as we had found out with trying to protect Elvis Presley, was that, while it was understood that a fictional TV show like *Starsky and Hutch* would enjoy copyright, and sometimes trademark, protection, English law did not recognise that any individual had a 'right of privacy'. So if, for example, a bag manufacturer brought out a 'David Soul' bag with a picture of David on the side then as long as the picture did not breach copyright (it wouldn't if it was acquired from the photographer who took it) then there was nothing that David could do.

This was because, in the eyes of the English courts, David's business was that of TV/movie/record star *not* that of licensing the rights to his own image. So, the way I saw it, if David *did* have a business which commercialised his image rights then that business could prevent pirates from cashing in on that business without a proper licence. David was in reality a test case and he knew it. He understood the argument and wanted to stop the commercial abuse but likewise didn't want to appear to be money-grabbing by setting up a company simply to profit himself further by licensing his image rights.

My solution to this was to set up a new charity, The David Soul Foundation, which would own the company and David would assign his image rights to that company and any profits would go to David's own charity. David loved that idea and so it went ahead. David was a very, very nice guy and he and I got on well. He was quickly rising to 'superstar' status. Through *Starsky and Hutch* his face was recognised around the world and his music, written by a

great English composer called Tony Macaulay, was top-
ping the charts on both sides of the Atlantic and around
the world. His first record 'Don't Give Up On Us Baby'
topped the charts.

Over dinner one night in London, the night 'Silver Lady'
went to number one in the USA and UK simultaneously
in October 1977, I told David that I thought the biggest
risk he ran was that one day he might start to believe his
own publicity. For a guy who pretty much always seemed to
have his feet on the ground he thought it couldn't happen.
Unfortunately, really through the fault of those around him
rather than David himself, it did.

We got the new licensing company up and running,
granted some commercial licences and then waited for the
first commercial exploiter who was prepared to take us on.
They weren't long in coming along. We issued proceedings
and got ready for the battle in court.

The English legal system is undoubtedly the finest in the
world and one of our greatest exports. However on a very
limited number of occasions it can let itself down. I said
'itself' but more often than not it is the very rare 'rogue'
judge who will let the side down.

The framework that we had set up to justify David Soul's
case to prevent infringement was based on well-established
English law principles of 'passing off' someone else's 'good-
will' as your own. As well as sound relevant case law from
around the Commonwealth, mainly Australia, there were
certain established American law principles that should also
be persuasive.

I forget now the name of the judge we had that day but
I knew from the get-go (as they say in America) that he was
going to be a problem. As our QC rose to his feet to open
the case the judge volunteered:

Oh yes – I can see this is going to be one of those cases where you are going to tell me about the law in Australia and America and all sorts of other places around the world apart from what the law is here in England!

It pretty much went downhill from there. The judge obviously took the view that David was lucky to be as famous, and rich, as he was around the world and really shouldn't bellyache about his picture appearing on products of which he might not approve. The judge's view seemed to be: 'That's showbusiness!'

It was a disgrace. We lost, which also established the (wrong) precedent in English law, and David understandably lost faith in English law and decided he didn't want to take the case to the Court of Appeal. This was a great pity because around the same time we had had a case for Aaron Spelling on *Starsky and Hutch* where the magazine publishing our material claimed that although a film is protected by copyright a single frame from a film, which had come from the cutting room floor, was a 'transparency' and was not therefore 'part of a film'. This was a quite nonsensical argument since the single frame clearly started its life as part of a film (series of moving pictures).

We had sued the magazine for breach of copyright and Martin Katz had come over from London for the hearing at the Royal Courts of Justice in the Strand. The normal judge was ill so we ended up with a deputy, who was about as crass as the judge in the David Soul case. After three days he found in favour of the magazine, accepting their argument that the single frame wasn't part of 'a film'. Marvin was horrified and so was I. Happily Marvin, and Aaron, weren't about to leave things that way and agreed to take it to the Court of Appeal.

A few months later Marvin was back and saw the majesty of English law in action as three judges in the Court of Appeal took less than an hour to state that the deputy judge in the court below didn't know what he was talking about and of course our interpretation was the correct one; and furthermore that the hapless magazine, advised by a very conceited City law firm partner who had got up my nose from the beginning, would also pay all the costs of both sides as well as a very substantial amount of damages to Aaron Spelling.

The sweet smell of success!

1978 rolled on into 1979 and things at the law firm continued to go from good to great. Our pioneering work for the film industry was bringing in more and more similar work. Having sorted out Lord Jermyn's complicated family trusts we were consulted by other great families to help with their trust and tax issues. Through a friend of John Jermyn's I was introduced to the Earl of Rocksavage.

David Rocksavage was the heir to the Marquess of Cholmondeley with two marvellous estates in Cheshire and Norfolk. David and his father Hugh enjoyed a wonderful relationship but there were many complex tax issues that needed to be addressed and that were to take up a great deal of my time in the years to come.

Through another friend of John's I was recommended to Henry Bath. The Marquess of Bath lived at Longleat, a wonderful house and estate in Wiltshire. Lord Bath was a first-class man who unfortunately did not see eye to eye with his very eccentric son and heir, Alexander, who lived a bizarre lifestyle with 'wifelets' and exotic art adorning parts of Longleat House.

At the same time the real estate business seemed to be doing well under Jeremy but I was flooded out.

Kathryn Lloyd-Jones dumped her barrister boyfriend and now turned up quite often with her new man who was about to qualify as a solicitor called Nigel Kissack. His family originated from the Isle of Man where he had been at school. He seemed to turn up most evenings to meet Kathryn and then hang around to see what we were up to. Nigel could see that the work was everywhere and offered to help out. In the end I simply told him that he seemed to me to be spending more time with us than at the law firm where he was supposed to be working so he might as well come and join us full time. So Nigel joined.

Mining Supplies was keeping me busier and busier. Quite apart from sorting out Lawrence Scott, Arthur had decided that now he wanted to expand to service the coal mining industry in America. He saw that I was spending a good deal of time in the USA, mainly on my entertainment work, so decided that Michael Bell and I could head up the thrust into America. Arthur wanted to build a new factory there to manufacture the same components that he manufactured in the UK but wanted to be near to the US coal mining industry.

Michael focused on the southern part of Virginia and I managed to find out that there was a fantastic financing package available for approved projects there which was called an Industrial Revenue Bond. In short, provided the money was to be used to invest in something that would create jobs (ours would in spades) then long-term finance was available from insurance companies at a very attractive 'low' rate of interest. The rate was 'low' because it was tax free in the hands of the lender.

We needed US$3 million to build our new factory and Michael chose a site, approved by Arthur, near to Abingdon in south Virginia. I hired lawyers in New York and 'bond counsel' in Richmond, Virginia.

Because this was a great project politically in Virginia, Michael and I normally got the use of the Governor's private plane as we were flying around. We also used Concorde to ferry back and forth to Washington and New York. What a great treat that was.

On the day of the final closing I left London Heathrow on Concorde first thing in the morning, I arrived in New York an hour and a half *before* I had set off from London and was met at JFK by the Governor's plane to transfer me to Richmond, Virginia where I arrived at 9.00am local time – the same time (local time) as I had left Heathrow five hours earlier.

Concorde was some plane – I just hope supersonic travel comes back again.

CHAPTER 16

First Deal

T he business was growing well but I hadn't made a lot of progress towards becoming the biggest and best in the world. By 1979 we were eight partners and starting to outgrow the office at 20 Kennedy Street, despite taking over more and more space in the building. At the same time we had found that there was another firm of solicitors next door to us at 21 Kennedy Street. It was called Brett Ackerley and Cooke and was one of the oldest and longest-established solicitor firms in Manchester.

However, it was very small with Robert Cooke on the verge of retirement and his son Michael running the private client practice. Michael was a delightful man about my age with a wicked sense of humour and a particular line in self-deprecation. The only other partner was called Keith Reeves who was acceptable, up to a point, but really not my sort of person. I'm not really sure what 'my sort of person' is or was except that I found Keith to be rather boring and anal. Michael was quiet but very pleasant and was clearly fascinated by what we were up to as his father had run their business with an iron 'Victorian' fist for years.

It really wasn't very profitable, because it was badly run, but it had some excellent clients having acted for

Barclays Bank for many years, mainly in the area of property work for the bank and estate administration. Haydock Park Racecourse was another client where there seemed to be some good work to be developed. Michael Cooke told me much later that he was hypnotised by our arrival in Kennedy Street and the fact that a solicitor would drive a white Porsche 911 Targa!

We had to start looking for a new office. Jeremy was the one who pushed this hard. I enjoyed the fact that our overheads were low, our cash flow was great, we had no bank debt and therefore no stress. Jeremy found a new development at 11 St James's Square in the centre of the city. There was plenty of space, too much in fact, but I started to learn that it was important to look ahead and plan for expansion.

It struck me that if I acquired Brett Ackerley and Cooke I could get Michael, who would run the private client practice, some good new clients to develop and it would help fill up the space. Keith Reeves was not going to be part of the deal so we had to pay him off. This was my first ever 'acquisition' and to be honest it didn't really seem too difficult. Their business was also run very conservatively. They had no bank debt, in fact they had cash in the bank and, of course, all the client account deposits reconciled to a penny. In fact having paid off Reeves there was still cash left over, so I was ahead of the game from the outset!

We still had to fit out the new premises but again good fortune struck. Lord Jermyn wanted to sell his tenanted estate in Lincolnshire, about 2,500 acres of prime fenland. His agent Bill Marriott told me the price he wanted to achieve and through Jeremy's brother Paul Fieldhouse, we contacted Barclays Bank Pension Fund who quickly agreed to pay the top of the price range that Bill had demanded. A very grateful Lord Jermyn paid us a very generous fee for dealing with the whole issue quickly and very profitably and that fee basically paid for the fit-out of the new office.

It really looked wonderful, very bright and modern and very much along the lines of what I had seen so often in America. We even imported an entire rosewood tree from Scandinavia to make three giant desks, a boardroom table and full panelling for the boardroom.

As we moved in Michael Cooke joined us to set up the private client department and I had made my first, if small, step along the road to the Great Vision.

Not so much a fork in the road but a great sprint along it.

Lord Jermyn also had an input on our American expansion. The yacht *Braemar*, he had decided, was going to be dispatched over the Atlantic to be chartered out in the Caribbean in the winter months. John had hired a bear of a man called Mike Jeske as his captain. Mike (I think he was Scandinavian) was simply fearless. This was just as well since being totally fearless turned out to be an essential prerequisite for captaining this particular vessel. Mike had sailed the *Braemar* over the Atlantic with only one or two crew with him. Two engines packed up so he limped the second half of the voyage, finally pulling into English Harbour in Antigua.

John and I were over in the States on a business trip looking at farmland and he decided that we would round off the trip by visiting the *Braemar* in Antigua to see what needed to be done to sort out the (latest) problem. We had the greatest trouble trying to book a flight down from New York to Antigua as there was some sort of strike on. The best we could manage was a flight down to Miami then a connecting flight to San Juan, Puerto Rico and from there it seemed there were local flights over to Antigua. As we landed at San Juan I noticed that there seemed to be about half a dozen propeller planes of the local airline lined up on the tarmac which I thought looked promising.

On arrival we went over to the desk of the airline, Prinair, to book on the flight to Antigua for the following day. There seemed to be quite a queue at the Prinair desk. I soon found out why. Eastern Airlines were on strike so it was only the local airline, Prinair, that was operating and their flights to Antigua, one each day at 9.00am, were full up for days.

The man on the desk seemed not only unperturbed by the huge inconvenience that this caused to would-be passengers, but also blind to the opportunities that this presented. I pointed out that there seemed to be a good many Prinair aircraft available on the tarmac, so why not put an extra flight on to satisfy demand?

The man thought that his boss wouldn't go for that. John voiced his opinion that therefore the man's boss must be a 'fucking idiot' which the man thought hilarious and he collapsed into fits of laughter. John asked if there was a price for the airline itself; if the man's boss was indeed such a 'fucking idiot' he didn't deserve to own the airline which would be much better under the more entrepreneurial ownership of Lord Jermyn. The man thought this was even more hilarious! We weren't getting very far.

To cut a long story short, over the next two to three hours I managed to charter a ten-seater plane for the following morning, and contacted Prinair who promised to round up eight passengers from the waiting list for me to take to Antigua at a fare per head that covered the whole charter price and meant that John and I not only got away to Antigua but also went for free! With all that organised I felt pretty pleased with myself, and John and I happily went out to dinner in San Juan believing we had pulled off a dream solution.

The following morning we were down at the airport at 8.00am and found our ten-seater charter plane all fuelled up and ready to go. I set off for the Prinair desk to collect my eight passengers. As I strode towards the desk, with the same Prinair man behind it, my heart began to sink. There was no one else around! The man behind the desk greeted me like his long-lost cousin. He was so pleased to see me again. With a heavy heart I asked him where my eight passengers for Antigua were.

He perked up further and informed me brightly:

My boss started thinking about everything you said last night and decided you were right. So he put on another flight which took all the passengers on the waiting list. It's a pity you weren't here because there were two free seats!

He was very fortunate that both John and I had a dark sense of humour since without it I have little doubt that we might well have responded by sticking a palm tree right where the sun don't shine! Thirty minutes later John and I sat in splendid isolation in our chartered ten-seater plane down to Antigua. We did at least have the pleasure of spending three nights on board the *Braemar* in English Harbour with all crew including a chef on board.

Braemar was actually very comfortable, provided one never left the harbour! From our talk to Mike Jeske it was obvious that the *Braemar* needed a lot of work to make it fully seaworthy. The best thing was to sail her (slowly) up to Fort Lauderdale in Florida where there were shipyards competent to sort out the problems. There seemed little choice.

Three nights after our arrival we boarded a British Airways flight at midnight out of Antigua to London, the flight having originated in Barbados. It was crowded and very dark as we moved along the cabin looking for our reserved seats. As we found them there was a man sprawled out and fast asleep over our two seats. John was not about to tolerate anyone getting between him and a seat, so after a verbal alert had failed to raise the somnolent figure John pulled back his leg and delivered a great kick up the backside.

This did the trick and the man rose blearily up, turned round and stared up at Lord Jermyn. 'Oh. What? Who? How are you John?'

It was the Queen's cousin Lord 'Patrick' Lichfield who on balance didn't seem in the least bit vengeful that his backside had been kicked by a fellow Earl!

As a postscript, two months later we were back in Fort Lauderdale at the shipyard to fix a schedule of works, a price and a contract. It was eye-wateringly expensive.

We spent a few days there and Pamela flew out to join me as well as a few of John's friends. We loved Fort Lauderdale. It was clean, on the ocean plus the Intracoastal Waterway, with great restaurants, weather, clubs and golf.

I was by now spending so much time in America that I thought it would be good to have a base there so we, or rather the firm, bought an apartment in a block overlooking the beach and the ocean which we owned for seven or eight years and where we enjoyed some great times.

The *Braemar* eventually got fixed, at great expense, but never got a single charter in the Caribbean and so it returned to the Mediterranean for the 1980/81 season. By now even John had accepted that even with his family's prodigious wealth he really couldn't justify keeping the *Braemar*. It had in fact managed to secure a charter when back in the Med out of Monaco. Nigel Burgess sent Lord Bristol a letter reporting on the charter to an American party. He reported that

Braemar had left Monaco bound for Portofino with a party of eight on board in fine weather.

One day into the cruise disaster struck, summed up splendidly in one sentence in the letter of report. 'Basically – everything went very well until the fire!' The engine room caught fire and most of the guests jumped overboard! That was the final straw.

It got moored up at Villefranche not far from Monte Carlo and went on the market. Amazingly (and I suppose this just proves the 'greater fool' theory) we heard through the agent that there was a potential buyer. His name was Mike Batt. He had originally been in the Manfred Mann Band in the 1960s but had focused, very successfully, on song writing including all the songs by the Wombles! Don't knock it if it makes money!

Mike was sick of the tax rates then in the UK – up to 98 per cent – so had decided not only to go non-resident, as of course was John in Monaco, but also to take his family on a two-year voyage around the world. *Braemar* was to be his dreamboat to fulfil this ambition. He had it put into dry dock in Villefranche and sent the marine surveyors in. Of course the boat (or ship!) had just had a fortune spent on it in Fort Lauderdale.

John called me up to bring down the ship's papers to complete the deal. John and I set off from Monaco to meet Mike Batt at the harbour in Villefranche. John had a beautiful red Ferrari and it was a most perfect day. We bowled up to the quayside and met up with Mike Batt. He was full of his plans for his world trip and clearly was totally intoxicated by the *Braemar*. The marine surveyor had (amazingly) given the all clear and *Braemar* was in the process of reversing out of the dry dock into the harbour as I handed over the signed bill of sale and collected the banker's draft for the agreed amount. With some ceremony Mike and family boarded the vessel and the *Braemar* reversed majestically into the centre of the harbour and then moved slowly forward to set forth on its world voyage. Mike was waving from the boat to us on the quayside and the captain pushed forward the throttle to drive the engines to exit the harbour. As the *Braemar* picked up speed there was suddenly a sickening crack and the prop shaft severed. For the time being, the voyage was at an end having never got out of the harbour.

John and I were off in the Ferrari to bank the money in Monaco faster than you can say 'lawsuit'! We later found out that Mike had it repaired and finally set off on his world voyage, taking two and a half years and taking in a return trip to English Harbour in Antigua and to the island of Montserrat where Paul McCartney joined him on board. After that I imagine that *Braemar* had exhausted Mike's financial resources and so was sold.

Mike Batt tells the story that a few years later a former deck hand on *Braemar* rang him to say that *Braemar* – now renamed as something else – was for sale in the Greek islands. 'Why don't *we* buy it?' he suggested.

Mike's response says it all. He said, 'You buy it – I'll be *your* deck hand!'

CHAPTER 17

Down Under

B y 1981 we had settled into the new offices and things
were continuing to prosper. Having successfully established a factory in America, Mining Supplies was now
interested in conquering Australia where there was an equally
active coal mining industry. Arthur and Michael called me
to join them on the exploratory trip and we set off in April
1981, the first visit any of us had made to Australia. We
enjoyed a very comfortable flight in first class on Singapore
Airlines to Singapore for an overnight stop and then on to
Sydney.

We arrived in Sydney at about 6.30am on what I knew to
be a public holiday – Anzac Day. Because it had been raining so hard when I left home in Cheshire two days earlier,
I carried a raincoat over my shoulder, pretty unnecessary in
the 90° heat of Singapore, and I had it over my arm as we
made our way to the taxi rank at Sydney airport. Our taxi
driver looked me up and down and said, 'See you got your
raincoat with you mate. That'll be useful. It hasn't rained
for six months!'

Our taxi driver was a true wag. As we drove in I explained
that it was our first trip to Australia and that we knew it was
a public holiday. What did he recommend that we did for

our first day? He responded, 'Basically you have two choices. Either you can get pissed or you can watch everyone else getting pissed!'

It seemed that Australia was likely to be my sort of country, which it was. I loved it.

We had a productive few days in and around Sydney and established the Australian Longwall Mining Corporation to complement the American Longwall Mining Corporation we had set up a couple of years before. We returned to the UK via Mauritius and Johannesburg where Mining Supplies was supplying the coal mining equipment to SASOL (the South African government-owned entity that was converting coal to oil).

I didn't take to Johannesburg in 1981. Apartheid made the whole city feel surreal and cruel.

I was to return to Australia much sooner than I expected following a call one weekend in late summer 1981 from Lord Jermyn.

Looking back now, it is hard to understand the intense paranoia felt in the UK back then about the Soviet Bloc behind the Iron Curtain. There was still a strong feeling of threat that the eastern borders of western Europe might be overrun by communists who would grab all the assets of the West. This unfounded concern led to many landowners in the UK seeking to diversify their assets into overseas territories perceived to be at a safe distance from the communists like the USA and Australia.

Lord Jermyn had already bought one or two small farms in Georgia (USA) and called me to say he had decided that he wanted to acquire 'a big chunk of land' in Australia. Please would I arrange this? This was presumably based on my wide experience of Australia following a four-day visit to Sydney four months earlier!

Of course I set to it, locating a great agricultural consultant, one John Bingle, through my trade consultancy contacts built on the Mining Supplies mission earlier that year. The Bristol Estates land agent Bill Marriott was to join us on the trip and we set off again via Singapore to Sydney, arriving on 26 September 1981. John Bingle had arranged for us to see some farms within two to three hours' striking distance from Sydney. However, the prospect that created maximum interest from Lord Jermyn was a huge 55,000-acre property in the middle of Queensland called Burenda Stud, a well-known sheep farm and stud station.

To get around more quickly John had chartered a private plane and so it was that in late September 1981 I found myself landing at a strip near Charleville in Queensland with John, Bill Marriott and John Bingle.

The tour of Burenda Stud was memorable – as most experiences involving John Jermyn always were. It's fair to say that at first John's reaction to Australia was somewhat mixed. John was used to a relatively cultured life that revolved around London, Paris, Monaco, his yacht and his stately home in Suffolk. Australia was down to earth, generally unimpressed by English aristocracy, and 'no frills'.

John had arrived at Burenda in fairly severe heat in the outback dressed as if for a cocktail party at St James's Palace. Styled jacket, collar and tie, plus a gigantic tie pin studded with diamantes in the shape of the family crest. He regarded the farm manager who was to show us around with an air of amused indifference.

We piled into some sort of SUV and set off for a tour of the estate. To give the reader some idea, 55,000 acres is a lot of land. I think it was about twenty miles from end to end and, for some reason, to visualise the size of it we worked out that it was roughly ten times the land mass of Bermuda.

This became a statistic that John thereafter employed frequently when describing it to friends and acquaintances back in Europe. When asked how big Burenda was he would feign an air of aristocratic indifference and say, 'Not sure really – although it's ten times bigger than Bermuda!'

At one stop we pulled up by a sheep watering stand where we met a gnarled old Queenslander. He must have had some limited pre-briefing from the farm manager as to the antecedents of this exotic creature with Gucci loafers and a diamante tie pin arriving in the noon heat of a wild Burenda. He was introduced and asked John cheerfully, 'How are you enjoying Australia so far, my Lord?'

John took his time in replying, implying that he was giving the question some serious thought. Finally he said, 'Well – I find that visiting Australia is a bit like being invited to join a rugby team – frankly I'd rather play croquet!'

A couple of hours later John focused on the farm manager, asking him first to point out the boundaries of the property from a vantage point. We could see some large hills, or small mountains, in the far distance.

'Well, if you can see it you own it,' ventured the farm manager. It started to dawn on John that this inspection could take some time. 'How long will it take to view the entire property?' enquired John.

'Well, my Lord, I've been here two and a half years and I still haven't seen it all!'

'That's it,' said John. 'We're going to fly around it!'

Which we duly did. The sheer size of the estate and the possibility of much better land use under the supervision of John Bingle persuaded John that he had to buy it. Which he did.

Life acting for John was never dull!

Meetings with John were normally held in the wonderful

surroundings of the East Wing at Ickworth close to Bury St Edmunds.

John's ancestor, the (in)famous Bishop of Derry, built this magnificent extravagance starting in about 1795, but in 1956 the principal house and the park of around 200 acres in which the house sat were gifted to the National Trust in settlement of death duties although the East Wing (which was in reality the only part of the vast house that the family had ever actually lived in) was leased back to the incumbent holder of the Marquisate of Bristol.

Outside the park were around 4,500 acres still owned by the family, or more specifically John.

Invariably I would get ready for a 10.30am start together with John's accountant Michael Chappell and sometimes the agent for the estates. We never expected John to be there by 10.30am and he rarely surprised us.

We would talk through most of the business whilst we awaited the moment when John would grace us with his presence. In reality most of the business was conducted before John ever showed up.

Normally he breezed in at around 1.30pm dressed immaculately with Coronet tie pin in place, double-breasted suit and a pretence that he was ready to discuss affairs of state.

The meetings followed a set pattern. We would roll off the things that we had been talking about while we waited for him and the provisional decisions that we had come to and to which we sought his endorsement.

Each provisional decision was normally met with an 'Absolutely' or 'Yes of course' or occasionally 'Serves the bloody man right!'

We then normally moved on to the budget – which involved a wonderful graph that Michael always prepared and updated which showed the existing amount of total assets, liquid and illiquid (mainly the latter), and a quite alarming demonstration that, in the absence of some fairly severe constraints on spending, the money would run out at a prescribed and predicted time in the (increasingly near) future.

John always met this forecast with bright spirits, normally explaining recent mega spending splurges as 'an aberration' or 'totally unforeseen but not to be repeated'. In this way we would convince ourselves (or he would convince himself) that everything would work out fine in the end.

John's thoughts would then move to lunch at around 2.30pm and we would retire at the butler's quiet summons – 'Luncheon is served My Lord' – to the dining room.

Despite our customary promise never to drink at lunchtime the good claret would come out and John would start to get into his stride for the day.

On one particular day in summer after a long lunch John disappeared from the room to return after a few minutes with a beautifully crafted wooden box which he opened lovingly to reveal a pair of pearl-handled Colt 45 handguns.

'Ever fired a Colt 45?' said John airily, as if assuming that we normally fired off all sorts of small arms regularly but not perhaps with guns by that particular manufacturer.

'I've never fired a handgun John,' (in fact I was pretty certain mere possession of them must be illegal).

'Oh. We'll soon fix that! Let's go down to the East Dereham Gun Club – they have a jolly good range there.'

I enquired as to how we might travel there.

'Well, we'll go in the helicopter of course. Grab your glasses – let's go!'

With that the four of us trooped out to the helicopter (John with a large glass of port in hand) and we all (very nervously) got in with John at the controls.

The rotor blades whirring, we rose into the sky above

Ickworth at which point John threw an AA road map at me in the co-pilot's seat.

'Don't you have a navigation system?' I asked.

'Never bother with all that malarkey,' replied John cheerily, 'I think we follow the "A" road towards Ipswich – you'll find it alright.'

We swooped on several unsuspecting villages, each one met with a curse from John along the lines of 'Bugger! I'm sure it was here last time.'

Eventually John tired of this and said, 'That's it – we're going down to ask the way.'

With that he dropped the helicopter straight into the garden of a private house, causing mayhem with the flowerbeds.

'Get out and ask,' he said.

In my pinstripe suit I descended from the craft (it might just as well have been a spaceship to the rather elderly but delightful lady who greeted me at her back door).

'What a surprise to have you drop in,' she said to me as the helicopter blades gradually laid her garden to waste.

She invited me in for a cup of tea and I thought the least I could do was accede. Not surprisingly, this 80-odd-year-old lady had no idea where the rifle range was located. We said our goodbyes and I returned to my 'spaceship' which by now had virtually obliterated her garden (and her neighbour's).

'Any luck?' enquired John as I re-entered.

'No, afraid not,' as we ascended into the skies.

'Oh bugger this – we're going home,' said John as we swerved round on a new course.

'Soon be back,' observed John as we raced through the skies. 'Ickworth is just up ahead.' I looked hard at the horizon and certainly there was a large structure there, but it didn't look much like a stately home to me.

'Are you sure that's Ickworth?' I observed.

'Don't you think I recognise my own bloody house!' said a rather indignant John. Five minutes later it was clear even to John that we were hurtling towards the sugar beet factory in Bury St Edmunds.

'Where the bloody hell is Ickworth then?' said our trusty pilot.

'Over on the left,' I said as fortunately the park and mansion hove into view.

'Damn confusing,' said the pilot. Five minutes later we landed back safely on the helipad.

'Sorry we couldn't get any shooting in,' said our genial host. 'Still, not long until dinner!'

CHAPTER 18

More Hollywood

B ack in the UK the practice was still going from strength to strength. It was starting to feel like a proper law firm now with a corporate and tax department headed by me, property under Jeremy, litigation under Nigel Kissack and private client under Michael Cooke. The entertainment practice was still going strong with Nigel now doing most of the copyright infringement and licensing work.

We had lost one client – David Soul. This came about because for some reason I had been trying to put together a film deal, obviously intoxicated by Hollywood. I wanted to acquire the rights to a story called 'Sparky's Magic Piano' to make a film musical out of it. The rights to it were held by its creator, one Alan Livingston who lived in LA. Alan was president of Capitol Records and as such was the man who had brought the Beatles to the USA – big dollar sign! When I met him to discuss the Sparky project he was president of 20th Century Records which was doing very well under his stewardship. Alan and I got on like a house on fire. He was a very kind, down to earth guy.

David Soul was by then a very big recording star. But I was very worried about David's record company which was a pretty small label and I knew that, despite selling millions of records, David was not getting his royalties in anything like a timely manner. Alan Livingston told me that he believed David's record company was in danger of going bankrupt and David was at risk of losing a lot of money. Alan wanted to sign David to 20th Century Records.

I attended a meeting with David at the offices of his lawyers Gang Tyre Brown in Hollywood. Apart from David and his lawyer, others present were David's agent, Jules Shar, and his business manager.

I told them of my great concerns about David's record company. It was quickly obvious that between them they had all set David up with this deal and didn't take kindly to my intervention. In short I was asked to step outside and then was told they would 'be in touch'. The following day David called me. He was very uncomfortable saying that the other advisors wanted me out (very Hollywood). He was upset because he and I got on so well but what could he do? I told him not to worry and that I just hoped everything worked out for him.

Within six months David's record label did go bust, owing him a fortune in unpaid royalties.

Having lost one 'star' I was fortunate to have that star very quickly replaced by another, and one which was to shine very brightly for a considerable number of years afterwards. Early in 1981 Aaron Spelling had come out with a new TV show called *Dynasty* which was in essence his answer to the success of *Dallas*. The first series had gone pretty well on the ABC network but Aaron was looking to spice it up.

I was in his office one day with Marvin when Aaron said, 'Hey Roger, you're English, you must know this actress called Joan Collins.'

I explained to Aaron that although I had a very wide circle of friends and acquaintances back home there were about

50 million people in the UK and I didn't know them all! Of course I had heard of Joan, she had recently had something of a surge of popularity after two films called *The Stud* and *The Bitch*. Both based on books written by her sister Jackie.

Aaron told me that he was going to hire Joan as the wicked former wife to spice up the show. Aaron said he thought Joan's lawyers were not good enough for her so he was going to tell her to instruct me in the future! So it was that a few weeks later Marvin and I went onto the *Dynasty* sound stage with Aaron to meet Joan. She was shooting a scene where she sweeps imperiously down the huge spiral staircase of the family mansion in a stunning ball gown.

We waited at the foot of the stairs, and as she swept down the shot ended – 'Cut'.

Aaron stepped up: 'Hey Joan, how are you doing? This here is Roger. He's your new lawyer!'

It was quite an introduction! I think Joan said something like, 'Well, at least you can buy me dinner.'

And so the following night I went out with her and her then husband Ron Kass. Happily we all got on exceptionally well and that was the start of a very happy relationship that lasted through many years and a number of husbands. We will return to more stories of Joan as the years roll by, but she soon turned *Dynasty* into a worldwide hit and into the bargain turned herself into one of the most recognised women on the planet – not far behind HM the Queen!

1. My parents, 1944.

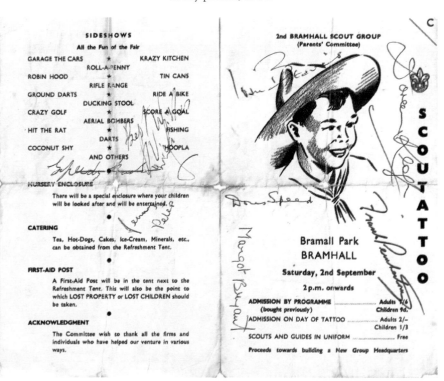

2. Trailblazers – September 1961.

3. The Beatles.

4. First date with Pamela – my father's Masonic Lodge, circa 1966.

5. Our engagement
day, 1968.

6. Our wedding,
20 September 1969.

7. A young advocate, 1970.

8. Sixty Four Society dinner, circa 1970;
'Curls' (far right seated, medal and glasses) tragically died shortly after this.

9. Windrush Vale, Naunton 1971.

10. Bentley S3 – a suitable car for an aspiring young solicitor!

11. With David
Soul (Hutch) and
his 'minder' Don
Murphitt, circa 1978.

12. The Marquess
of Bristol – in
reflective mood.

13. The Lee Lane-Smith 'look': Nigel Kissack (second from left) and Kathryn Lloyd-Jones (third from right seated) with some team members in the early 1980s Manchester office.

14. 'Young buck' lawyer – Manchester, 1983.

15. Gerald Ronson.

16. Sir Gordon White
with Joan Collins.

17. The Manchester receptionists – 'American style', 1985.

18. Will Holt – game changer, circa 1990.

19. The family at home, 1990.

20. Home in Cheshire.

Alsop Wilkinson's managing partner has a clear image of his firm in the year 2000

Practising for a global future

Lane-Smith: high partner involvement

In the news

Roger Lane-Smith

Fourteen years ago Roger Lane-Smith, now the managing partner of Alsop Wilkinson, had an office and two secretaries in Manchester.

In nine years' time he expects to be on the management committee of a global, multi-national partnership of lawyers.

That's fairly ambitious: the sort of thing you can only say when you are 14, or when you are very close to achieving it. Lane-Smith is close to achieving it.

At the start of this month his firm announced an association with the Kuwaiti firm Al-Ayoub & Al-Majid, with offices in Kuwait, a partner in Cairo and associations in Jordan and the Persian Gulf. Last week it announced that it was opening a Moscow office.

Alsop Wilkinson has the third-largest law firm in Hong Kong, and an alliance with US law firm Donovan Leisure Newton & Irvine.

Donovans senior partner Rod Hills says: "In 35 years of visiting London professionally I felt he, better than anyone else, shared my view of how lawyers should practise."

Lane-Smith explained: "We share a philosophy of high partner involvement. We don't want the leverage of a high assistant to partner ratio. We just want to confine ourselves to the high-class problems."

There is no secret to Lane-Smith's success. No family connections, ("My grandfather's cousin was FE Smith," he says, but there were no nearer legal contacts). He was in no magic circle.

His success has come because "he's a superb lawyer and a consummate businessman", says his friend Ian Burton, senior partner of Manchester's Burton Copeland.

Lane-Smith is identified with Alsop Wilkinson, and Alsop Wilkinson with Lane-Smith. But what if

he were to fall under a bus? One new appointment said: "If I go back to the office and find he's gone, I'll walk straight out again."

Lane-Smith says: "I'd like to think I've created a team spirit. I don't think that would go away. I'm an ideas man, but if I'm not here it's not going to fail." There is evidence that is right. Women in the firm speak of him with affectionate disrespect, usually a good sign.

Lane-Smith does have a life outside the office. He is married with a teenage son and daughter, he likes golf and deep-sea fishing. He chain-smokes small cigars.

The Kuwait deal is one of the landmarks in Alsop Wilkinson's progress. It is going for international public work on the scale of the blue-chip City firms: Lane-Smith wants a hand in the reparations work in Kuwait.

There is already a City-Kuwait

Group, with Alsops as an associate member, but believes Lane-Smith: "The idea that it can be handled on a contract basis in the City is just politically unacceptable. Washington wouldn't have it, Kuwait wouldn't accept it. It needs to be tripartite."

Lane-Smith is keenly aware of the political input in overseas jurisdictions. Donovan Leisure's Hills was formerly chairman of the US Securities and Exchange Commission (and his wife Carla is currently Secretary of State for Commerce); Abdullah al-Ayoub was formerly the government's official in charge of prosecutions in Kuwait.

The firm he envisages in the year 2000 would have Far Eastern offices in Hong Kong, Malaysia and Singapore and US offices in Los Angeles, New York, Washington (where Donovans has existing offices), Atlanta and Houston. Houston is going to revive, he says: oil is picking up.

It would have European offices in Frankfurt, probably Geneva and Vienna ("a mini-financial centre serving Prague and Budapest"), offices somewhere in Italy and Spain as well as the new Moscow office and the existing offices in Paris and Brussels.

Note 'existing offices'. At the moment Alsop Wilkinson shares a Brussels office with Donovans, and has facilities at the US firm's Paris office. What would the year 2000 firm be called? "Alsop Donovan." A full partnership? "Yes."

But in Britain Lane-Smith sees no new offices; Liverpool, London and Manchester are enough.

Alsop Wilkinson is a member of the Legal Resources Group, and there is a feeling some of the partners wanted a merger. That's unlikely, says Lane-Smith, "but it may be forced on us".

Nick Gillies

ALSOP WILKINSON

11 St. James's Square
Manchester M2 6DR

Telephone: 0161-834 7760
Telex: 677369 DX: 14329
Fax: 0161-831 7515

Our ref:

Your ref:

Other Offices in: London ● Liverpool ● Brussels ● Hong Kong ● New York

22. The Alsop Wilkinson
notepaper in 1996 – the 175th
anniversary of that firm – just
before the DLB and AW merger.

23. Winning 'something' from Princess Margaret (Sebastian de Ferranti in foreground).

24. With Pamela at the Dealmakers' dinner.

25. In a golf Pro–Am with Dave Whelan – the 'Pro' is Brian Huggett.

26. Roger and 'The Rockettes'

27. *Back, left to right:*
Barry Dunn,
Dave Whelan,
Brian Ashcroft, me;
front, left to right:
John Fairhurst,
Martin Wilde,
Tony Jacklin
(Birkdale, 2005).

NEWS RELEASE

12 February 2010

DLA PIPER RECEIVES OUTSTANDING ACHIEVEMENT AWARD

Legal Business Awards 2010 recognise DLA Piper's transformational rise in the global legal market

DLA Piper received the "Outstanding Achievement Award" at the 2010 *Legal Business Awards*, held in London on 11 February. The special award, which marks the magazine's 200th edition at the end of 2009, was introduced in order to recognise the firm that has made an unrivalled impact on the business of law over the past two decades.

DLA Piper was selected ahead of other nominees including Clifford Chance, Freshfield Bruckhaus Deringer and Linklaters for this coveted award in recognition of its phenomenal rise within the global legal market over the past 20 years. The award was presented to Sir Nigel Knowles, joint Chief Executive Officer, whose unwavering commitment to the strategic vision to combine geographic reach with a broad range of legal services has transformed DLA Piper's legacy firms into one of the world's largest legal practices through a series of UK and international mergers.

"The past two decades have been truly remarkable. The global legal market has undergone tremendous change, which in turn has been a catalyst for development and opportunity within the sector, said Sir Nigel Knowles. joint Chief Executive Officer at DLA Piper."

Sir Nigel continued: "I am delighted to accept this Outstanding Achievement Award which I feel is recognition of our fantastic journey over the past 20 years. A journey that would not have been possible without the tremendous teamwork, or the support of our clients."

Legal Business Awards recognise the work and accomplishments of the legal profession and its lawyers in the UK and internationally.

ENDS

Regards.

Nigel

Sir Nigel Knowles
Managing Partner

DLA Piper UK LLP

28. Message from
Sir Nigel –
'Finally made it!'

Finally made it !

29. With Marvin 'Mr Hollywood' Katz at our home in Provence, 2011.

30. With John Timpson in Mustique, February 2013.

31. Sir Nigel Knowles.

32. Roger Lane-Smith
portrait by John Swannell.

CHAPTER 19

Game Changer

As the early years of the 1980s progressed life was fun, business was good, the family was progressing well and I was about to pull off a life-changing deal. The venture capital, now called private equity, industry in the UK was in its infancy mainly because, prior to the Companies Act 1981, in attempting to raise finance to buy a target company, it was illegal to use the assets of the company one was attempting to buy to secure the debt for the deal. This made it almost impossible to raise any substantial debt to do such a deal. The 1981 Act changed all that and made this possible for the first time.

It was not all wine and roses. Yet another recession hit British industry in 1980. A dramatic change had arrived on the political scene in May 1979 when the electorate, tired of a decade of the collective approach, voted in Margaret Thatcher, a woman who promised a new start. It had been a miserable decade for a once-proud nation. After further sharp slippage down the world's economic league, the country had reached a stage by early 1979 when the prospect was not of decline *relative* to our main competitors, but of *absolute* decline. The country had had enough, and the Labour prime minister James Callaghan, so recently berated by the *Sun* newspaper for saying 'Crisis, what crisis?' when he arrived back from a conference of world leaders in the Caribbean in the middle of yet another winter of industrial disputes (in fact, Callaghan never said those words, but that was the *Sun's* headline and everybody believed it), realised that the country wanted a change. He said to his aide, Dr Bernard (later Lord) Donoghue:

> There are times, perhaps once every 30 years, when there is a sea-change in politics. It then does not matter what you say or do. There is a shift in what the public wants and what it approves of. I suspect there is now such a sea-change – and it is for Mrs Thatcher.

While the unions had been on the rampage in the mid-1970s, the middle classes had felt that they were in an alien land, and agreed with Patrick Hutber, the city editor of the *Sunday Telegraph*, when he wrote in his book, *The Decline and Fall of the Middle Class*:

> That this is a time of crisis for the nation is common-place, but it is equally a time of crisis for the middle class who are subject to unprecedented pressures, and, at the same time, to unprecedented denigration.

Hutber went on to say that he felt it was wrong for everyone to be reliant on the state for everything. Finally he pointed out that high taxation discouraged the payment of high salaries. This might be thought of as a social advantage, but in an increasingly international economy it meant that British companies would not attract the best people, and even if they did, it would not give them much incentive to work hard.

While Hutber was attacking socialism, and the dreadful damage wrought by inflation, the Tory party ousted its leader, Edward Heath, who had put in place many of the doctrines of his opponents, the Labour party – restrictions on wages, prices and dividends. In his place the party elected a woman who, under the tutelage of Sir Keith Joseph, had grasped certain essentials of the remedy required to restore economic sanity to the country.

Joseph had ruled himself out as a possible leader by a speech in Birmingham in early 1975 which stated that people at the bottom of the social scale were having too many children and were ill-equipped to bring them up (!). Whether it was true or not, it smacked of racialism and elitism, and when he withdrew his challenge to Heath's leadership Margaret Thatcher was able to take it up.

From February 1975 until she came into power in May 1979, Thatcher and her supporters prepared the ground for a revolution in Britain's economic attitudes. Hugh Young, in his biography, *One of Us*, summed up her position when she assumed power:

> She brought to that post no great technical expertise, but a handful of unshakeable principles.

They were not particularly original purposes. But they were commitments made with the fire of the zealot who could not imagine she would ever become a bore. Tax cutting was one of them. In four years as opposition leader, she had hardly made a single economic speech without alluding to the punitive rates of tax. Usually this was in reference to upper rates. 'A country's top tax rate is a symbol,' she said in February 1978, 'very little revenue is collected from people in this country who pay tax at the highest rates. A top rate of 83 per cent is not much of a revenue raiser. It is a symbol of British socialism – the symbol of envy.' Restoring the morale of management, she said around the same time, was the prime requirement. 'No group is more important, and yet none has been so put through the mangle and flattened between the rollers of progressively penal taxation and discriminatory incomes policy.' So tax cuts were the first objective. They were the traditional Tory nostrum, to which the leader brought her special proselytising zeal. The second was good housekeeping.

The third fundamental therefore defined itself; the control of public spending. And again a kind of pietistic morality went hand in hand with a supposed economic law.

This was music to the ears of businessmen, but to a certain extent – even if not spelt out with quite the same rigour – they had heard it before. It will be remembered that Heath had come to power in 1970 making not dissimilar noises, only to buckle under to corporatist solutions as soon as the going became rough. Would this woman be different?

We know now, not least from the memoirs that have been published by several of her colleagues, that Margaret Thatcher did not have the full-blooded backing of the whole of the Cabinet, or indeed of many leading businessmen, for some of her stronger measures.

The general financial climate from 1980 to 1982 had been the worst since the war, certainly in terms of corporate failures and rising unemployment. The result of tight monetary policies allied to another sharp hike in the price of oil following the overthrow of the Shah in Iran, which in turn brought a sharp rise in the value of the pound (viewed by this time as a petro-currency thanks to Britain's near self-sufficiency in oil from the North Sea), was to create the most difficult trading conditions that British companies had experienced since the 1930s. ICI, generally viewed as the bellwether of British manufacturing industry, cut its dividend and Sir Terence Beckett, the director-general for the CBI, promised the government a 'bare knuckle fight', saying at the CBI conference: 'We have got to have a lower pound – we've got to have lower interest rates.'

The prime minister remained firm, and declared on the day that unemployment passed the 2 million mark (Heath had lost his nerve when it passed 1 million): 'I've been trying to say to people for a long time: if you pay yourself more for producing less, you'll be in trouble.'

Heavy wage inflation, allied to the near-doubling of VAT in the first budget of the new administration (introduced within weeks of their winning power), meant that inflation soared again to an average 13.3 per cent in 1979, 18.1 per cent in 1980 and 11.9 per cent in 1981.

The result of all this, allied to a very tough attitude towards unions and strikes (epitomised by the government's approach to a national strike in the steel industry, a strike they were determined to win whatever the cost), meant that the government's and Thatcher's popularity fell to new depths by the end of 1981. But Thatcher pressed on regardless, and although she had invited people from the whole spectrum of the party into her Cabinet, she took little notice of what many of them said. Indeed, she made it quite clear that:

> If you're going to do the things you want to do – and I'm only in politics to do things – you've got to have a togetherness and a unity in your cabinet. There are two ways of making a cabinet. One way is to have in it people who represent all the different viewpoints within the party, within the broad philosophy. The other way is to have in it only people who want to go in the direction

in which every instinct tells me we have to go. Clearly, steadily, firmly, with resolution. We've got to go in an agreed and clear direction.

She wasn't going to 'waste time having any internal arguments'.

Thus, at the depths of the recession and with unemployment still climbing sharply, she strongly supported Sir Geoffrey Howe's budget in the spring of 1981 which further intensified the squeeze on both companies and the consumer. Initially Howe had been against any such budget, and even the Treasury felt that some relaxation of monetary policy was possible. However, Thatcher had now taken on two extra-parliamentary advisors, Sir John Hoskyns, a former army officer who had built up his own very successful computer software business, and Alan Walters, a former professor at Birmingham University and the London School of Economics, who had established his monetarist principles long before the phrase was heard in political circles. (Indeed, he had predicted the inflation of 1974 as early as 1972, analysing the explosion of credit in that year of the Barber Boom.)

Hoskyns and Walters stiffened Thatcher's resolve in the early months of 1981. To them it was a matter of credibility. The government had to show everyone once and for all that it was not going to move forward 'with enormous and insupportable borrowings'. It had to convince the financial markets that it would get inflation down. And it worked. The markets saw that there was a prime minister who stuck to her guns, and they applauded her toughness and resolution. As many predicted the U-turn that tough-talking governments of both parties had indulged in since the war, Thatcher went to the party conference and told them: 'You turn if you want to; the lady's not for turning.'

Not that Thatcher and her Conservative government worked instant miracles. Indeed, the country was immediately plunged into another inflationary crisis as more trouble in the Middle East, including the deposing of the Shah of Iran, led to another sharp rise in the price of oil. This was exacerbated by Thatcher agreeing to implement in full the awards recommended by the Clegg Commission, set up in the so-called 'Winter of Discontent' to grant a whole new raft of inflationary wage settlements. The belief of the new administration in increasing indirect tax (raising VAT from 8 to 15 percent) and reducing direct taxation did not help in the short term either.

In 1982 I met three people who were to co-join to help create a groundbreaking deal in 1984.

First, and as usual, Lord Jermyn played a part. John Jermyn was spending more and more time in America and had bought a beautiful town house in Sutton Place on the East Side on Riverview Terrace overlooking the East River and the 59th Street Bridge. John had spent a fortune buying the house and converting it into a splendid mansion where at the front the view was over the East River and at the rear was a 'trompe l'oeil' of Ickworth House in Suffolk. John had a grand opening cocktail party at the house to which a large number of the 'beau monde' of New York society came along.

I had spent a few minutes talking to Fred Hughes, a lawyer who was with his client Andy Warhol. Fred was great, while Andy was totally weird. I moved a few feet along to where a tall, rather elegant figure stood by the stairway and we fell into conversation. He was English and told me his name was Gordon White.

I had heard of him. He and his good friend James Hanson had built quite a conglomerate in the UK called Hanson

Trust. Gordon had recently become Sir Gordon and had arrived in New York some time before to seek to grow the Hanson business in the United States. He succeeded in this and was often referred to as Britain's most successful buccaneer in the USA.

We just hit it off. We talked for hours and Gordon was particularly impressed by all my entertainment clients on the West Coast, where he spent a week each month holed up in a massive suite at the Beverly Hilton. He knew Joan, and I was fascinated by his approach to business and his lightning grasp of the corporate world. We started to hang out together in New York and Los Angeles.

At some point Gordon told me the story of his first deal in the United States. He had come over to New York with a fund of £50,000 (not £500,000 or £5 million or £50 million) advanced by Hanson Trust.

For a year or two Gordon kept his head down, seeing how everything worked and how business was done differently from the UK. He was particularly concerned that his first deal may be the defining one and he wanted to make sure it was right.

Eventually he lighted upon a suitable target and over a period of time agreed a deal with the very tough American owner. He lined up bank loans secured on the assets of the target and was putting in the minimum of cash that he could get away with.

The day of the closing came and the deal was consummated. Within the hour Gordon knew something was wrong. There should have been a substantial cash balance in the target's bank account – US$3 million – but it had disappeared. The vendor had withdrawn it and disappeared off to his house in Miami.

Gordon knew that he could not call James Hanson and

tell him the first deal had gone badly wrong within hours. He told me that he realised that he would have to think and act 'American'.

He called the seller in Miami and said, 'You just stole US$3 million of my money.'

The response was along the lines of, 'Go screw yourself!'

Gordon jumped on the next available flight to Miami, went round to the seller's house and knocked on his front door.

'What the fuck do you want?' said the seller, hardly in a pleasant tone.

Gordon replied slowly and menacingly, 'You stole US$3 million of my money. Unless I go back to New York tonight with a cashier's cheque for US$3 million then I'm just going to have you blown away!'

Gordon got the money and never had to tell James Hanson what happened!

At about the same time many of my landowning and commercial clients in the UK were having to move their interests and trusts offshore, given the swingeing tax regime left behind by the outgoing Labour government in 1979. I had developed a very strong relationship with Lazards in Jersey where many of my clients now operated their offshore trusts and interests.

Through Lazards in London I was invited to a lunch at their offices one day in 1983 when sitting next to me was Roger Brooke. Roger, then just over 50, had joined Pearson's, the public holding company that then owned Lazards, and also had briefly been managing director at EMI, the musical and electronics group, until it was taken over by Thorn. Roger was then looking for something else to do. His friend Michael Stoddard of Electra Investment Trust had got him to go to New York to meet Henry Kravis of KKR, the emerging king of venture capital in the USA. Roger had decided to go in with Electra and two or three other institutions including Investors in Industry (3i) to form a new company called Candover Investments. He had just started business and we had a fascinating chat. I kept his card.

Finally, our daughter Zoë was at a preparatory school in Wilmslow and had got to know Victoria Timpson, a year older than her, and then Pamela met Alex Timpson, her mother, and so, as these things happen, we ended up at a dinner party together and I was sitting next to Alex. She told me about her husband, John. He was in the long-established family business, Timpson Shoes, that had 200 or so retail shoe shops plus a separate shoe repair business. Timpson had some years before been taken over by a public company, United Drapery Stores (UDS).

John was now running Timpson, but of course as an employee not an owner. He was frustrated by that. Alex organised a meeting with John for me. He told me the whole story and how UDS were starting to look like a sitting duck as a takeover target and how, if that happened, he had no idea what would happen to him and the Timpson company under new owners.

At some point I popped up with the remark, 'Well, why don't you buy it back then?'

John said he had not thought that it was possible for him to buy back his family company but I suggested we at least see what might be fundable. I had just finished reading a biography of the financier Charles Clore and through that I saw that Clore had bought many companies by selling, or selling and leasing back, their freehold real estate assets. In going through the portfolios of Timpson shop assets it was clear that over the years many high street freeholds had been purchased.

The trading entity was being charged a notional rent for occupying the freeholds but if we got control of the freeholds then *we* could sell them off for cash to institutions and lease them back. We soon realised that there was perhaps as much as £50 million tied up in real estate (about £450 million in today's money).

We called in Paul Orchard-Lisle of Healy and Baker. His father Aubrey had been a close advisor of Charles Clore. Quickly he established that we were right. Cash could definitely be raised on a number of the valuable freeholds. I also introduced John to Roger Brooke of Candover who in turn brought in the man who had just joined him as chief executive, Stephen Curran. Immediately, they saw the potential as well. This could be a very fundable deal as well as a very large one.

This would be by far the largest private management buyout (MBO) ever attempted in the UK at a price of more than £40 million. What we needed now was a willing seller and more than a touch of luck.

UDS did not want to sell. They thought they had an independent future, so their CEO Stuart Lyons told John in the autumn of 1983. We had done a great deal of work so far to no benefit and so we were justifiably somewhat deflated.

Then our luck changed.

As I mentioned, since about 1978 I had been working frequently with Lazards Trust company in Jersey on various offshore tax structuring issues for clients. The managing director there, Simon Scrimgeour, of the old stockbroking family Scrimgeour Kemp-Gee, had become a close business colleague and friend.

Lazards were setting up another trust company in the Cayman Islands and as a result I had visited there on business and fallen in love with the islands, so started to take the family there on holiday. That Christmas and New Year of 1983/84 we had rented an apartment on Seven Mile Beach as usual.

On 1 January 1984 I had chartered a boat for a deep-sea fishing trip with John Edwards (my client from Louis C. Edwards days) who was now a tax resident of the Cayman Islands. We set off at 9.00am to head out to 'the Drop' where the reef dropped away sharply and we could hope to find marlin, tuna and other sporting fish.

Our luck was in. Within an hour, we had a huge blue marlin on the line and I was in the chair fighting the fish. An hour and a half later my muscles were straining and turning to jelly. I could barely fight on as the huge fish displayed all the characteristics of a submarine going in the opposite direction. Finally I reeled it in and we got it aboard. It was 150lbs of fighting fish but would also be delicious to eat. I collapsed in a heap of blubbering muscle and pulled on a beer. A sense of enormous relief that the ordeal was over flowed through my veins. Then the boat's marine ship-to-shore phone rang.

It was a call for me from John Timpson, very unusual in those days before the mobile phone. John came through on a crackling line. The message was that Gerald Ronson of Ronson Corporation had just launched a hostile takeover bid for United Drapery Stores. Game on!

Gerald Ronson was a well-known property entrepreneur who made his first fortune in filling stations and he clearly had seen the same potential in the real estate of UDS as we had. He had substantial firepower and was a serious player, but I didn't know him. Twenty years later I did meet and get to know Gerald and we had lunch together twice but back in 1984 I had no lines in.

Come what may, UDS was now 'in play'.

Now the pundits combed through all the facts and figures surrounding UDS and quickly reached the conclusion that at the price of the Ronson bid it was cheap. He would have to pay more. Then the second piece of luck dropped in. It was announced soon that Hanson Trust were poised to make a counterbid for UDS, which they duly did. Now there were two bidders but at least I knew Sir Gordon White of Hanson.

Ronson upped the ante and bid again at a higher number than Hanson. There were two competing bidders, a joy for UDS shareholders. At this point I thought I needed to intervene so I picked up the phone to Gordon White in New York. I told him that I was working on putting together an offer for Timpson of at least £40 million. I wanted him to know that in case it helped him finance a higher Hanson offer.

The Hanson share price was riding high so if they could buy good assets for shares and then sell the assets it was a great way of raising cash for the Hanson machine. Gordon thanked me and said he thought they would put in a final knockout blow for UDS. They soon did. And Gerald Ronson ruled himself out of a final competing offer. Hanson had won the day.

Now I knew we had a real chance of pulling this massive deal off. With John's blessing I approached NatWest, the banker to Timpson, to see how much they would lend on the deal. They were enthusiastic and yes, they were on too. So now we had sale and leaseback through Healy-Baker, equity finance through Candover and bank finance through NatWest. We were looking good.

Understandably, Gordon wanted to complete the deal and get his feet under the table before talking turkey with us. His right-hand man on the deal was Tony Alexander, a northerner based in the Hanson Trust Knightsbridge office.

An anxious few weeks were to pass by before my next conversation with Sir Gordon White. In the meantime, the law firm seemed to be going from strength to strength. All the hard work was paying off. I had a pretty good idea what other lawyers were making in Manchester per partner and we were making more than twice as much. We were by far the most profitable law firm in Manchester and the firm that able young lawyers wanted to join.

However, although we were very profitable, I hadn't made much more progress on my grand plan to be the biggest and best in the world.

Then one day came a phone call from Alan Greenough. I didn't know Alan at all. He was a partner in a firm called Alsop Stevens Batesons, based in Liverpool, who also had a City of London office. Alsops was a quality act.

Formed originally in Liverpool in 1821 by one Thomas Harvey, of the Harvey Bristol Cream sherry family, it had built up a very strong practice around banking (Barclays Bank in particular), shipping and insurance, institutional pensions, real estate, private clients and litigation. They had opened in the City of London in the 1950s and had a small, five-partner practice there but again with a quality client base.

Alan asked if he could come to see me and of course out of curiosity I agreed. When he arrived a few days later for the meeting I liked him immediately. He was a kindred spirit. He told me that Rayna Dean of Price Waterhouse in Manchester had described Lee Lane-Smith as the most progressive law firm in Manchester. This was very flattering – and true!

He was keen to capitalise on Alsop's client base and reputation and wanted to move into Manchester so as to make Alsop the legal powerhouse of the north-west. They could open on their own but preferred to join with an existing Manchester firm which knew the market.

For me it had come at a perfect time. We were getting lots of good work from all over the place but I could see there was certainly a 'glass ceiling', whereby big corporations and merchant bankers were reluctant to use us just because we were fairly new and young and did not possess that patina of establishment 'clout' which undoubtedly was possessed by Alsops as well as by firms such as Addleshaw Sons and Latham in Manchester. Going in with Alsops would help me break through that ceiling and I could see we could quickly grab the mantle as the top commercial firm in the north-west.

I met some of the Liverpool partners. They were very nice old-school establishment figures. Their financials were not so impressive. The firm was not in my view being run as a business, more as a gentleman's club, but I could see a huge potential in turning this juggernaut round. We had some rather half-baked discussions which we had to shelve as suddenly the Timpson MBO reared its head.

Hanson had completed the purchase of UDS. Healy-Baker could deliver at least £30 million in sale and leaseback cash, NatWest were up for £5 million and so were Candover, so we had around £40 million in the locker.

I called Gordon again at about 5.00pm one evening. He told me he was in the back of a car in Surrey on a poor line. He asked me to remind him how much we would offer for Timpson.

'At least £40 million.'

'OK, you're on for a meeting. See you in a couple of days.'

Two days or so later John Timpson and I turned up at Hanson Trust at 190 Knightsbridge to meet Tony Alexander and Sir Gordon White. It was a typical Gordon meeting, friendly but businesslike. Did we have the money? How quickly could we move? Who was behind us?

We said that we needed a week or so to finalise our offer but we needed to cease any intercompany movements of cash so we could know how much working capital we had. We agreed to freeze all intergroup cash movements immediately.

That night John called me in a state of great excitement. Peter Cookson, the Timpson finance director, had calculated that by a stroke of pure luck our 'freezing' of cash movements could not have come at a better time. We were sitting on at least £4 million of surplus cash. Candover, NatWest and Healy-Baker all put their hands to the pumps and two weeks later we were back in front of Gordon and Tony, this time joined by Stephen Curran of Candover.

What was our best offer?

£43 million.

'Not enough,' said Gordon.

'We don't have any more cash,' say I.

'We need £45 million to deal,' said Gordon.

'We'll give you £44.5 million so long as you lend us the extra £1.5 million for two years on a loan note,' say I.

'I'll speak to James Hanson,' said Gordon.

Five minutes later Gordon and Tony returned hands out-stretched: 'You have a deal!'

Well, that was just the start of it. It was an incredibly complicated deal with lots of moving parts, any one of which if it fell by the wayside, could cause the whole thing to crater. Hanson was fair but firm and definitely wanted to keep the momentum going. Gradually more and more members of the law firm were drawn into parts of the transaction to a point where after a couple of months virtually every lawyer in the firm was working on the deal and we were on a 'contingency fee', that is, no deal – no fee.

I had agreed with John that we would get a fee of £250,000 (£1.5 million in today's money) if the deal completed and that figure was included in all the financing but only if the deal completed. The progress of the deal almost merits a book in itself. Many people did not believe we could pull it off – too big, too difficult – but I now had the bit between my teeth. This deal *was* going to happen.

There were lawyers and financiers everywhere and I felt like a military commander as I tried to steer this vast army. We finally got to the contract signing meeting. It was a huge room somewhere in the West End, I can't remember where – I was punch drunk!

There must have been more than a hundred people in the room around a huge boardroom table, with me at the head directing operations. There were hundreds of documents to be signed. At one point Tony Alexander of Hanson called out: 'Has anyone lost a lawyer because I seem to have one too many?'

Finally everything was signed and the announcement went out on the Stock Exchange. The following morning the business papers were full of it. 'Biggest ever MBO in history', etc.

I was elated but in fact completely drained.

We completed the deal and billed the fee, which was promptly paid, thank God! Had it failed it probably would have been the end of the firm; huge stakes indeed.

CHAPTER 20

Alsops

The Alsops merger had had to go on hold because of the Timpson deal but now we were back at the table, probably in a much better negotiating position with the deal completed, and already we were becoming known as the law firm to use to handle a difficult and complex MBO transaction. Already I had been retained by another UDS subsidiary, Farmers Shoes, to negotiate their MBO from Hanson.

Venture capitalists, banks and merchant banks all wanted to meet to see how we could all benefit from the new gravy train. Alsops would undoubtedly catapult us forward in my grand ambition. This deal needed to be done. Alan Greenough and I started to spend a lot of time together. Alan was a first-class corporate lawyer and he could see how the Timpson 'stardust' could propel the merged firm forward.

However, I was not about to give up my control on how things were going to be run. Also my profit share meant that I would be taking at least twice as much as any other partner in the merged firm, but then I was generating a huge amount of fee income. The Alsop partners were generally nice, but naturally suspicious of me. They probably saw me as some sort of shooting star who might burn out quickly. It was a gamble for them.

We agreed that the firm would be called Alsop Stevens Bateson Lane-Smith. What a mouthful! To all intents and purposes I would be the managing partner and Derek Morris, a delightful man and much respected pensions and funds partner, would be the senior partner.

Finally the merger was announced in the autumn of 1984. Alsops was immediately the largest firm in the north-west with offices in Manchester and Liverpool, offices in the City of London and also one associated office at 30 Rockefeller Plaza in New York together with my old friend Roger Boyle who had recently left his old firm of Millbank Tweed Hadley McCloy to form his own firm, Boyle, Vogeler and Haimes.

Now I was managing partner of a serious law firm with great clients, a good reputation and the first firm that had gone national in the United Kingdom, with a toe in the water in America. We were on the way and I was still just short of my 39th birthday.

I haven't mentioned Stanley Lee (the Lee in Lee Lane-Smith) for some time. Stanley and I had always got on like a house on fire but in reality we had completely different aspirations. Stanley was happy with the relatively small office we had in Lincoln's Inn Fields and although he was offered a place in the Alsops merger it definitely wasn't for him. He wanted to keep his independence as well as the name Lee Lane Smith. We dropped the hyphen!

The next three to four years seemed to pass in a blur of activity. Alan Greenough and I made a great corporate team and many lawyers wanted to join us. In terms of corporate transactions we were more and more the firm to go with for the big deals. Alan landed the £50 million buyout of the Norwest Holst Construction Group and through Gordon White again I put together the MBO of the Farmer Shoe retail business backed by Clarks Shoes.

I had joined the board of Timpson after the deal as had Stephen Curran of Candover. On the back of the Timpson deal Candover was starting to put together even bigger deals and was quickly establishing a reputation as a market leader in the private equity industry.

My private client practice continued to grow with more and more work from Bristol Estates, the Cholmondeley family, the Marquess of Bath at Longleat and many others who were drawn by our reputation as very experienced tax and trust lawyers on difficult matters particularly around landed estates and the aristocracy. One of the London partners, Peter Rainey, was a magnificent if slightly eccentric brain in this area of activity and I knew I could always rely on him and Donald Mason in Liverpool to cope with the most complex of such problems.

In 1983 Arthur Snipe at Mining Supplies got into a little problem with the taxman which caused me a great deal of work to deal with the issue in a sensitive manner, but Arthur had to step down from the board and I joined as a non-executive director, with Michael Bell promoted to chief executive.

Dave Whelan was steadily building JJB Sports into a major private sports chain and I was spending much time with Dave and his accountant, David Fairhurst. David was and is the most genial and able of men. He went out of his way to introduce me to others of his clients who needed corporate help and we built a firm trust and friendship that continues to this very day. As the business grew we hired more and more new partners and lawyers and the business continued to grow and grow.

The 'showbusiness' side of the practice was still burgeoning with most of the work being handled by Nigel Kissack. Joan Collins had become a world superstar through her role as Alexis Carrington in *Dynasty* but still she continued to call me several times a week. When she had made her two films with Brent Walker Productions, *The Stud* and *The Bitch*, after a slow start the films, based on books written by her sister Jackie, had taken off and proved worldwide hits. However, Joan and Jackie didn't seem to have received very much in the way of royalties and they both suspected that George Walker of Brent Walker was under-reporting royalties to them.

They asked me to investigate. I read their contracts carefully and noticed that they had the right to send in a firm of auditors to check the books and records. Through a friend at Ernst & Young I got hold of an expert partner on film accounting. Then with only a few hours' notice I sent them in to Brent Walker to check the books and records. They found a complete mess, including the predictable excuse that a fire had destroyed many books and records. They found more than enough evidence of a very substantial under-reporting of royalties to Jackie and Joan.

I then reached out to my old friend George Carman QC. This was right up George's street – high-profile, Hollywood, super-attractive women, possibly 'bent' film financier. George took it on with relish, although I held back from telling the solicitor on the other side that I had brought in the most feared cross-examiner in the legal profession.

George was desperate to have a face-to-face conference with Jackie and Joan but the trial date was now only two weeks away and it was time to strike. George had been rehearsing with me his opening speech to the judge as he proceeded to lambast George Walker, showing that he or his organisation had concealed very large amounts of income.

I made the call to George Walker's solicitor. I told him that the Ernst & Young audit had shown under-reporting that seemed to verge on fraud and as a result I had decided to retain George Carman QC who was very much looking forward to getting his client George Walker in the witness box.

Within hours Walker's counsel had been on the phone to George, and he to me. It was as if we had hit all the buttons on a cash register at the same moment. Their offers went higher and higher by the hour as George and I held out for more and more. Eventually we felt that in all conscience we could extract no more and we settled. Joan and Jackie were delighted and the newspapers were full of the story of George Walker's capitulation!

It was during this period that I had come to have a meeting with the famous, later notorious, publisher-cum-press baron Robert Maxwell. Maxwell, a Jew born in Czechoslovakia, had escaped Nazi occupation and fought in the British army. After the war he worked in publishing and built up Pergamon Press, as well as serving as an MP. He then went on to buy British Printing and Publishing Corporation, Mirror Group Newspapers and Macmillan Inc. as well as other publishers. He lived lavishly in Headington Hall in Oxford and sailed his luxury yacht, *Lady Ghislaine*.

My old client, Stafford Pemberton Publishing, which had kick-started an awful lot of my copyright and merchandising practice, had fallen on hard times. The company had made a great deal of money out of publishing children's annuals and those profits had gone in part on luxury cars, Ferraris and Rolls-Royces, as well as expansion into areas that they did not fully understand like the children's toy business. The company still had some valuable assets and a talented team but was running short of money.

One evening Stafford called me at home to say that he had just had a long telephone conversation with Robert Maxwell who had recently bought the British Printing and

Publishing Corporation (BPPC). This was the same BPPC that three or four years earlier I had successfully sued in the Court of Appeal for breaking Aaron Spelling's copyright in the *Starsky and Hutch* TV series.

Maxwell had offered to buy Stafford's company for around £2.5 million, much less than it had been worth two to three years earlier but not a bad price in the circumstances. Maxwell wanted to agree the whole deal the following day at his new BPPC offices in London. Stafford needed me to be there with him.

I dropped everything and by 10.00am the following morning we were at BPPC offices for our appointment with Maxwell. The appointed time for our meeting passed first by one hour then two until finally, two and a half hours late, we were finally ushered into the presence of the 'great' man.

Maxwell was a very large man and indeed a very fat one. As we sat in his office he constantly took phone calls and clearly was trying to impress us by showing that he was involved in many deals and that he was ruthless. He told us that BPPC had been in a financial meltdown but he was now saving it. Every single cheque issued was now to be signed personally by him.

After some considerable time spent listening to him brag I asked if we could please talk about the subject of Stafford's company; after all, that was the reason we were there. He asked how much he had offered for the company. We answered: '£2.5 million.'

He told us that, now he had read through the financials, the company wasn't worth £2.5 million.

He then said, 'It seems to me that you, Stafford, are just waiting for something to turn up, and when that is the case in my experience the only thing that does turn up is trouble!'

He wouldn't pay £2 million, nor £1 million, nor

£500,000; in fact he wanted us to put the company into liquidation. He wanted us to sink all the creditors and he would then buy all the assets on the cheap. He would cut Stafford in for 10 per cent!

I was appalled and so I let him have it. 'Mr Maxwell, you dragged us down to London at short notice, you kept us waiting for nearly three hours, you constantly take calls during our meeting and then you insult us by making a derisory offer for my client's company. You have totally wasted our time and now we are leaving.'

We stood up to go. Maxwell got up too.

'You seem like a bright sort of lawyer,' he said. 'I have a lot of business interests in Manchester and I need a good lawyer up there. Can I have your card?

'No!' I replied as I walked out with Stafford. Thank God I did! Maxwell was found dead in the Atlantic Ocean in 1991, having fallen off his yacht, and his death triggered the collapse of his publishing empire. It was discovered that he had stolen hundreds of millions of pounds from his companies' pension funds.

Overall things had worked well with the Alsops deal. The firm was doing better and better and in the North there was now no real doubt that we had overtaken our main competitor, Addleshaws.

Although no-one formally had titles, I was to all intents and purposes the managing partner and still on a profit share of twice the next most senior level. I was earning this because I did bring in a lot of work.

New partners continued to join. Tony Neary, the England 'golden boy' rugby union captain and former colleague of mine from John Gorna and Co., came over, bringing with him an excellent new partner, Paul Webster, who later was to be very influential in building up our banking practice and who would become a close ally. Another partner joining was Will Holt, the in-house lawyer at a large public company, British Vita. Rothschilds, for whom we now did good work, had recommended Will and he brought British Vita with him as a client and was to be a key figure in later mergers.

I had developed a great relationship with Alan Greenough who had moved to Manchester following the merger and was now a very productive corporate partner who brought in a lot of work and also had a good sense of humour. In some quarters I know the firm was being called 'The Roger and Alan Show'!

We had between us capitalised well on the MBO scene and we were one of the leading corporate firms in the sector, attracting some top talent as new partners such as Michael Prince, one of the senior in-house lawyers at 3i.

London had to be our next target. The Alsop London practice was quite good with some interesting work. The Alsop firm had for years acted for the Bowring Insurance family and London partners like Michael Clarke, Stephen Blair and others had a very good name in the insurance and international reinsurance markets. Peter Rainey was a great brain, if rather idiosyncratic, and a well-respected lawyer. We had a decent shipping/maritime practice in London and Liverpool with good partners and clients including Ocean Group and a pretty decent restructuring practice headed by Paul Gordon-Saker.

But in London terms we were a flea bite on an elephant. We would get nowhere near my global dominance aspirations unless we cracked London – and big-style. I started to look around for prospective candidates to merge with us in London. My business colleague Stephen Curran was now going great guns at Candover Investments with more and more big deals. I called on Stephen to ask who he used in London law firms and who he might recommend.

Their main corporate law firm was Ashurst Morris Crisp, one of the longest established firms in the City from where two partners, named Slaughter and May, had left some decades earlier to found that eponymous law firm. I knew Geoffrey Green there pretty well and there was no chance that they were likely to be a merger candidate. Stephen told me he had recommended lawyers to represent management teams and he particularly mentioned Michael Collins and Peter Wayte of Wilkinson Kimbers and Staddon based in Lincoln's Inn. Maybe they would be interested in talking?

I had just gone through a second major back operation and was laid up in hospital. I started making some calls, got hold of Peter Wayte and arranged to meet him. At about the same time, through a headhunter, I had arranged to meet Barry Driver, a lawyer from Hong Kong, in the American Bar at the Savoy. Barry was a New Zealander who had set up in practice in Hong Kong a few years before.

I had never been to Hong Kong, although the reader may recall that at a fork in the road some seventeen years earlier I was within a whisker of joining Johnson Stokes and Master there, until the unfortunate incident with the unlocked cloakroom door!

Barry was looking for an English law firm to joint venture with him in Hong Kong. Alsops had a good reason to think about this. We had a good shipping practice with a lot of international work that could be developed particularly in Hong Kong and Singapore. Although a good number of London firms had offices in Hong Kong, no regional law firm did and it seemed to me that a good number of our existing clients could well use us in Hong Kong and it would be a good hook to pull others in on the back of this.

I decided to go over to take a look in November 1987 with the rather cynical and reluctant approval of my executive committee.

Some years earlier Ocean Group, through their subsidiary Straits Steamship in Singapore, had asked David Mawdsley, one of the shipping partners, if Alsops would open an office in Singapore to support them but no one could spare the time to bother to go to Singapore so the opportunity was lost.

I arrived in Hong Kong on 7 November 1987, landing at Kai Tak airport in downtown Hong Kong after a sharp right-hand turn into the runway over Kowloon, always a hair-raising experience! As I came out into the early evening of Hong Kong after a long flight I remembered an old story.

Someone arrives for the first time in Hong Kong and is met at the airport. Hong Kong had, and arguably still has now, a certain smell and the new arrival asked his host what the smell was. 'Money,' said the host.

For me it was love at first sight. The noise, the wonderful people, the buildings, the sight of Hong Kong Harbour, the Star Ferry crossing from Kowloon to Central, the confluence of British colonial order with English law mixed with Chinese entrepreneurship. It was a truly heady cocktail.

Apart from Barry and his partners I had some people to look up. Tony Neary's brother Steve had been my assistant at Gorna's in the early seventies and had gone off to Hong Kong to make his fortune, and had done so. Rothschilds gave me an introduction to their office, and our friends at Coopers Lybrand had opened the door to their office. Through Nigel Kissack I had an introduction to an old friend of his from his school days in the Isle of Man, Camille Jojo, whose family was of Lebanese extraction but now lived in Manchester. So I had some compass points.

Barry's office was on Canton Road in Kowloon and

quickly I realised that the legal and business centre was on the other side of Hong Kong Harbour on the Island and the business district was called simply 'Central'. I quickly learnt other things. 'The Bank' was always taken to refer to the Hongkong and Shanghai Banking Corporation at its futuristic office in Central – HSBC to us today.

'Land' was Hong Kong Land which together with Swire owned much of Central. Jardine Matheson and the Swire Family had been the founding colonials of the territory. The concept of 'Feng Shui' or good luck spirits was everywhere. An office building had 'good' or 'bad' Feng Shui and on this turned every decision. The HSBC building had been specifically designed with Feng Shui in mind.

I just fell for the whole ambience hook, line and sinker.

Hong Kong Island was owned by the United Kingdom in perpetuity but much of the mainland side, Kowloon and the New Territories, was held on a lease from mainland China and was due to revert to China in 1997, ten years hence from my first visit. The problem was that the water for Hong Kong Island came from the New Territory. No water – no future.

The British government under Margaret Thatcher had negotiated a deal whereby the entire territory, including the British freeholds, would be handed to China in 1997 in exchange for a guarantee that for at least 50 years thereafter Hong Kong would remain broadly untouched. One country – two systems.

Back in 1987 this was a real cause for concern but the more I talked to influential people around Hong Kong the more I began to realise that the reversion back to China in 1997 was more likely to be an opportunity than a threat. Generally the people I talked to were upbeat about the future and also upbeat about an Alsops presence if we believed that it was what our clients truly wanted and needed. If we didn't provide the facilities then it was all too easy for clients to go to another UK firm in Hong Kong and from that it was a short step to those clients moving over in the UK as well.

It was also clear to me that Barry's firm wouldn't cut it. The office was in Kowloon instead of Central. The quality of the partners was not up to our standards in the UK and their way of practice was generally orientated towards private clients rather than business and corporates. However it was also fairly clear that for Alsops now to set up a totally stand-alone practice in Hong Kong would be very expensive.

I knew Alan Paul, a partner at Allen & Overy whom I had worked with in London at the time of the Farmers Shoes acquisition from Hanson Trust. Alan was shortly to open a new office in Hong Kong for Allen & Overy. His budget was well over £1 million.

So on the evening that I arranged to have dinner with Camille Jojo I had conflicting emotions. I was convinced that Alsops should open up in Hong Kong but I knew we were in the wrong location and the people were not right.

To say that Camille and I hit it off would be an under-statement of monumental proportions. From the minute I first met him Camille and I were like brothers, and we remain that way today nearly 25 years later. Camille still lives and works in Hong Kong but he is also my next-door neigh-bour, owning the next-door farm to me in Cheshire, where he intends to retire at some undetermined time in the future.

We had arranged to meet in the restaurant at the old Hilton Hotel in Central (demolished years later to form the Cheung Kong Centre). Camille had qualified in the UK and then worked in-house for Grand Metropolitan, a major real estate and liquor distributor. In 1981 he had moved to Hong Kong where he had joined Johnson Stokes and

Master. After a few years there he joined McKenna & Co. in Hong Kong to handle construction litigation as well as restructuring (insolvency) work. McKenna's was a fairly old-time London-based practice that had made its name acting for building contractors and was generally a quality firm. Camille was fairly happy there but the more we talked the more he liked the idea of joining Alsops as a partner (he was still a senior associate at McKenna).

In my view, Camille was the man for us who could lead our charge in Hong Kong. My resolve was to return to the UK with a recommendation that we have a joint venture with Drivers but also that we bring Camille in as a partner to Alsops (UK and Hong Kong), get new offices in Central, allow Camille to recruit and go from there.

When I got back, however, I found there were bigger fish to fry in the immediate term.

CHAPTER 21

Wilkinson Kimbers

O ur initial meetings with Wilkinson Kimbers had gone reasonably well. Their senior partner, David Cooke, was head of commercial real estate and a truly nice man. Michael Collins was the corporate partner Candover had first gone to and Mike was also a super guy that I felt I could really relate to and I immediately saw him as the head of a merged London office. Peter Wayte I found to be a good lawyer if somewhat self-opinionated. George Godar was a very impressive intellectual property lawyer. These four were the main players out of about sixteen partners in total.

WK was an old-time London firm which could trace its history in the City of London back to the 1820s. It had a range of work in London that frankly we lacked, particularly in corporate, real estate and intellectual property, and it was not too big a bite. We fairly quickly knocked out some preliminary terms but then came news that Peter Wayte in particular had gone cool on the deal. It went quiet for two to three months and I was starting to cast around for replacements when David Cooke rang me one day to ask if we could resume talks.

Of course I agreed. It then became clear that they didn't

want to agree to the merged firm having any say over how they divided up their 'share' of the merged profits.

They, or rather Peter Wayte, reckoned that they would generate about 40 per cent of the net profit and wanted that enshrined in the partnership articles including also a provision that they alone as a group could decide how their 40 per cent would be divided up between them. Michael Collins in principle would head up the merged London operation.

We should have walked away. To agree to the proposed profit split in that way was almost suicidal and had 'disaster' written on its forehead. But we didn't walk. We ploughed on because to pull off this deal would make the merged firm the first true North/South, quasi-national law firm and would give us the base from which to continue with the 'grand plan' of UK then global prominence. So we agreed those terms, although even then, at the last minute, Peter Wayte absented himself from the final negotiation meeting (he sent another partner, Gordon Day, in his place). I think that Peter wanted to be able to say that he was not really in favour of the deal if it didn't work out too well.

Part of the deal was that WK would vote two of their partners onto the board. We assumed that one of those would be Michael Collins who then would become managing partner of the merged London office. They had their vote, and voted in David Cooke and Peter Wayte.

Michael was furious. And so was I. All the WK partners knew that Mike was set to become managing partner and not to vote him onto the board was just perverse. It looked like the merger was going to get off to a bad start!

Quite soon after these events I was sitting with Alan Greenough in his office in Manchester. The office in Manchester was still booming and was very profitable and I really had no wish to move. However, we simply could not have the London office descend into turmoil because of lack of leadership.

Suddenly I said to Alan, 'Maybe I should go to London to run it.'

Alan took his opportunity immediately. 'If you do that I promise I will run Manchester the way it is now and promise to stay for at least five years so there will be no need for you to concern yourself.'

That was it. I decided to go to London to take over as London managing partner, but not before I had got Hong Kong on the move.

The new Alsop Wilkinson executive committee included certain members who I thought of as allies – like Alan – with a number of pretty conservative guys who needed a lot of convincing about everything.

David Cooke and Peter Wayte of WK now joined the committee. David was always a sensible and pragmatic man. Peter, on the other hand, seemed more than overly cautious and resistant to ideas of innovation. I found this particularly irritating since all the time I had been running Alsops, for the last four to five years, we had financially been very stable indeed and generally a pretty happy ship.

This issue of a Hong Kong office had been agreed as part of the merger but with a very limited budget which if I recall correctly was less than £50,000. It would be hard to open a very small sweet shop in Hong Kong with that money today.

To its credit the partnership had agreed to a joint venture with Driver (Alsop Wilkinson Driver in Hong Kong), to admit Camille Jojo as a partner in AW with Camille and I being the two partners with primary responsibility for the new office and in principle to take new additional offices in Central. These we found on the 40th floor of Jardine House right in the middle of Central, situated very close to the Star Ferry terminal, which was convenient for a quick hop over to the Kowloon office on Canton Road which Barry also wanted to keep on.

Pamela and I then spent the next four months in a rental apartment on Caine Road in the Mid-Levels as I worked with Camille and Barry to get the office moving. Those few months were just so invigorating. It was like starting again but this time in a completely new environment 6,000 miles from the UK. I just totally loved Hong Kong – the thrill of business life and the fun and novelty of a new social life. We were very happy although Pamela was ready to get home to England after the four-month stint.

Back in the UK we found a small apartment just off Sloane Square and, because we wanted to keep our home in Cheshire (it was a good thing we did), the firm agreed to put up a loan to help us buy the apartment.

Nothing quite consolidates a merger and nothing makes lawyers happier than a big influx of new work that can then be used as evidence that without a merger such work would not have come in. I got fairly lucky fairly quickly. First an old friend and client who I had met back in the Slater Walker days, Richard Lee, contacted me to say that he and two colleagues, David Suddens and Andrew Johnson, were in talks to acquire from Coloroll plc some 50 to 60 companies which became known as the Crowther Cloth and Clothing Division in an MBO to be led by David Suddens, a corporate high-flyer who previously had been at Courtaulds.

The deal was to be financed by Charterhouse Development Capital, part of Charterhouse Banking Group, now headed up by my old friend Victor Blank (David Blank's nephew). Blank had been made a partner in the legal firm Clifford-Turner, now Clifford Chance, in 1969 at the very young age of 26. There he specialised in corporate law and co-authored a book on mergers called *Weinberg & Blank on Takeovers and Mergers*. He left Clifford-Turner in 1981 to become head of corporate finance at Charterhouse where he masterminded the buyout of Woolworths.

An American bank would provide the 'senior debt'. The price was likely to be over £90 million and the deal intensely complicated. Because we were to act for the management our fee was contingent on success! Nevertheless this deal started to produce a very large slew of work for the merged London office and gave me a big chunk of work to get my teeth into in my first month as managing partner of the London office.

At around the same time I got a telephone call at home in Cheshire one Sunday morning from an accountant friend who was married to a former girlfriend of mine. Peter was now the finance director of a public company called James Ferguson Holdings plc. Peter asked me if I had ever heard of an investment entity called 'Barlow Clowes Gilt Fund'. I said that I vaguely remembered some advertising in the financial press but that was about all.

Barlow Clowes' offices were based in Poynton, an outly-ing suburb of Manchester, about eight miles from my home. Peter told me that he thought my advice was needed rather urgently. Could I come over to their offices immediately? Being of a naturally curious disposition, and sniffing the scent of a 'big deal', I was there within the hour!

I learnt that James Ferguson had two particular subsidi-aries called Barlow Clowes Gilt Managers and also Barlow Clowes International, which was notionally run out of Gibraltar. These two funds, which were licensed by the Department of Trade and Industry (DTI), basically attracted funds from the public by offering a high return (2–3 per cent over the government bonds) but with all the security of a gilt-edged stock.

They had taken in a lot of money – about £85 million into the UK fund and about £120 million into the international fund (about £250 million and £360 million in today's money).

I was introduced on arrival to Peter Clowes, the chairman and chief executive. They told me that they were starting to get calls from the DTI and the Bank of England who were concerned to know if all investor funds were safe and secure. Peter explained the nature of the funds. These mainly were populated by Independent Financial Advisors (IFAs) who were introducing their clients to the funds and got a generous introductory commission for so doing. The funds appeared to yield a cash return well above bank deposit rates but stated that the money was 'principally' invested in government securities (gilts), although the small print made it clear that they were free to invest in other stocks and bonds and in fact virtually anything else. They paid out the interest monthly and if an investor wanted his cash back it was paid promptly with accrued interest.

All this was fine provided it actually was what it appeared to be.

I asked first about the UK gilt fund and said I assumed that it was all represented by gilts certificates or cash. Peter said that largely that was true. They had certificates for around £50 million of the £85 million and substantial cash balances – they were working on a reconciliation at that very moment.

'OK. So what about Barlow Clowes International Fund? Where is the £120 million?' say I.

In a classic moment there was a pregnant pause and Peter then said, 'Well, that's a slightly longer story!'

It certainly was.

What then started was a marathon session that went on almost day and night for the next few days. I said that I wanted all the assets, of whatever nature, wherever located and in whatever form, brought in to the boardroom where they could be logged and scheduled and gradually accounted for to establish whether or not there was a shortfall. I advised Peter and the other directors to cooperate to the full with the Bank of England and the DTI.

A well known insolvency practitioner, Michael Jordan of Cork Gully, was being lined up by the authorities assisted by a solicitor, David Freeman of DJ Freeman & Co., a medium-sized but well-known London firm. I quickly made contact with Michael and David and told them what we were doing. Over the next hours and days seemingly endless vanloads of documents arrived in the office.

Share certificates for gilts, quoted shares and bonds, unquoted shares in private companies, large and small, title deeds to properties at home and abroad, houses, many farms, two to three 'jet aircraft', three or four large private yachts, bank deposits – they came in thick and fast.

Within two days Michael Jordan and David Freeman had arrived on site. By now the newspapers had the story and 18,000 or so investors were all scared out of their wits. Daily at 5.30pm David Freeman would report to the Bank of England to say how much progress we had made that day. And still the paperwork piled in. Shares in retail shop chains, private breweries, more farms and houses and it was all logged. It soon was becoming clear that there was certainly a shortfall and probably a very big one.

After about four days and nights of this we were all pretty exhausted. We got to about 8.30pm on the fourth night and we were all sitting around the gigantic boardroom table surrounded by paperwork and logs of assets. Peter Clowes was completely drained. I said, 'Is that it? Is there anything else you should tell us? Any more assets you recall should be itemised?'

'No,' said Peter, 'I'm pretty sure that's the lot. Would anyone like a drink?'

After four days and nights of non-stop work and stress we were all up for a drink. Peter came back into the room a few moments later carrying three bottles of red wine. 'Sorry, no spirits,' he said, 'only red wine.'

We really didn't care. Anything would do. He poured a glass for each of us and we raised it to our lips and drank it. 'That is really quite good,' I said, looking at the label. Chateau something – a French wine.

'I wonder who owns it?' said someone else.

Suddenly a look of dawning realisation passed over the face of Peter Clowes. 'Oh my God – I believe we do! I just totally forgot!' he said.

The Barlow Clowes affair gave the firm a good deal of work and a worthwhile profile as a national firm involved in attempting to trace and recover assets from one of the then largest financial scandals to hit the UK. No fewer than 18,000 investors lost their investment in Barlow Clowes which was wound up by the High Court in May 1988, owing £190 million (nearly £600 million in today's money). Many of the victims were retired people who had lost the entirety of their life savings. Peter Clowes was eventually convicted of fraud and theft and given a ten-year prison sentence.

It also meant that one of my London partners, a very good man and insolvency and recovery expert, Paul Gordon-Saker, was able to help me on the case and without doubt the profile it gave the firm landed another huge job, Polly Peck International, the conglomerate built up by Asil Nadir. Like many other things, this turned out not to be quite what it seemed!

Barlow Clowes also gave me the opportunity to get to know again a great friend from Guildford Law School, Ian Burton. Ian was with a smaller, mainly criminal practice in Manchester which he had set up a few years earlier. He had made a major impression on the Manchester scene but defending Peter Clowes on the imminent criminal charges of fraud on a grand scale would demand a London presence. I persuaded Ian to open a small London office to handle the Barlow Clowes affair and some others that we were able to put his way. Ian never looked back and today all these years later is still one of my very closest friends, as well as being the senior partner of just about the best known fraud and international affairs law firm in London, with a huge reputation as the 'man to see' if a prominent businessman, oligarch or member of the aristocracy finds himself in a tight corner!

Back on the corporate front the MBO of Crowthers also generated a vast amount of work.

It also gave me the experience of working with one of the great corporate lawyers of my generation, the Hon. Nigel Boardman of Slaughter and May, who was acting for Charterhouse.

Nigel, the son of Lord Boardman, formerly chairman of NatWest Bank, was and is a smooth operator. Nigel always assumed in any meeting that whenever he spoke everyone would hang on his every word, and whatever his view was on almost any topic was empirically the right one.

Despite that, he and I got on well. Perhaps we had similar personal characteristics! And finally, after much stress and many long nights, the deal was completed to great fanfare, although, within two short years, it was washed away by the tsunami of the 1990 recession which was about to claim many casualties.

Nevertheless, Alsop Wilkinson was up and running and I now had to take up the challenge of running the London office where, during my short absence in Hong Kong, factions had been forming and financial discipline slipping, as partners, as so often happens, fought for their place at the table.

The real hard work was about to begin!

CHAPTER 22

Reality Dawns

W hen I finally got to the enlarged London office to take over as managing partner I found a very difficult situation. In the absence of any sort of leadership an 'ad hoc' form of governance had quickly evolved with the formation of a large number of 'committees'. There were buildings, staff (HR!), marketing, library, IT and God knows whatever else committees. Also, everyone seemed to be spending an inordinate amount of time jockeying for position and of course that was having a pretty negative impact on profitability.

I had been used to running Manchester, always the busiest and most profitable office, but now I was pitched into a new situation where there also seemed to be pockets of resentment that simply did not want to take management directions from anybody, including me. Pretty soon executive committee meetings started to become increasingly difficult, with me in the spotlight from all sides on the new issue which was 'London office profitability'.

Alan Greenough, who I thought had been my close ally over the last five years, now began to complain about London's profitability. At the same time he had gone on a hiring spree in Manchester very quickly after I handed over the management reins to him. We were still very busy in

Manchester but I started to get concerned. Any downturn and quickly we would be overstaffed.

Peter Wayte continued in the somewhat cautious and negative way he had started, although I have no doubt that he firmly believed that his own opinions were the more valid. I put up with this for two to three months while I took stock of everything that was going on and then made my play.

I called a meeting of all the London partners one evening and very simply laid it on the line. I had been appointed to manage the office in London and so manage I would. I said that with immediate effect all existing committees were disbanded and that I was taking direct charge and responsibility for the operation. I wanted the partners to focus outward on client engagement and service and leave the rest to me. I made it clear that either I was going to do the job on my terms or I would leave them to it and return to Manchester.

That was the turning point. I now had the freedom to set decent financial targets, start a selective recruitment campaign to grow the business and run the office on tightly organised lines. Almost immediately the financial performance improved as we set realistic but stretching budgets and set to making it work.

In Hong Kong, Camille had joined and we had found new space in Jardine House. In a few short months we made a major strategic partner hire. Stewart Crowther had trained in London with Coward Chance and then had moved out to Hong Kong where he had joined World Wide Shipping, the major merchant shipping fleet established by the legendary Y.K. Pao, which went on to become one of the biggest, if not the biggest, fleet in the world. Stewart was interested in joining AW because it was a new operation in Hong Kong but had shipping connections in London and Liverpool which went back over many years, and he could see the chance to build a major new force in shipping law in Hong Kong and the Far East generally. He brought World Wide Shipping with him as a client and I had the great pleasure of meeting up with Stephen Pan, the CEO of World Wide, who I thought was quite simply one of the most intelligent men I had ever met. Even today almost 25 years later we still keep in regular contact and I see Stephen whenever I can out in Hong Kong.

So Hong Kong was starting to gather momentum with quality work brought in by Stewart and Camille. I sent out to Hong Kong a bright young couple who had recently married, Charles and Jane Reynard, corporate and litigation respectively, and they quickly fitted into the local scene.

In London we now started to recruit good new partner candidates who were looking to join a firm that had ambition and a plan. New partners joined in most disciplines including shipping, reinsurance, corporate and real estate and also we were very fortunate in acquiring through John Grimwade, a headhunter that I used a lot, the entire private client department of global giant Clifford Chance. This brought in bright new partners like Andrew Young and Glenn Hurstfield, and a whole slew of top new clients from around the world.

I was starting to get into my stride.

However, the general economic background at the end of the 1980s and, for the first few years of the 1990s, was not easy. By the time of the general election in April 1992, Britain had suffered a recession which, if not as severe as that of the early 1980s, nevertheless caused a great deal of pain in the manufacturing industry and elsewhere in the economy. The stock market crash of 1987 had been telling the world something, but for a time it was not clear what. Investors were feeling very pleased with themselves by the summer of 1987, and by October the City was wallowing in an orgy of self-love. The Tories were in for another five years (Margaret Thatcher had been comfortably re-elected in June 1987), money – serious money – was there for the taking, the markets were going up after the usual summer hiccup, then BANG! It all stopped. First New York, then Tokyo and Hong Kong, then London, then New York again, then Hong Kong, Tokyo and Sydney, then London, Paris and Frankfurt all turned into screaming, yelling pits of hysteria as the markets lost a year's gain in 24 hours. To exacerbate the situation, the hurricane in Britain three days before prevented many dealers from reaching their screens.

It was only twelve years or 3,000 trading days since the FT 30 index had stood at 147. Now it lost 183.7 in a single day. If anyone thought that was difficult to cope with, the Dow Jones fell by over 500 points, and it was only five years or 1,250 trading days since that index had been around 600. But that of course was part of the reason. The indexes had risen a long way, and once punters wanted to cash in some of their profits there could only be one result. Black Monday, 19 October 1987 (my 42nd birthday!), was so called after Black Monday in October 1929 – which had itself been named after Black Friday 1869, when a group of punters tried to corner the gold market, causing panic that led to a crash and a depression.

So many records were broken on this Black Monday – biggest one-day fall, biggest volume, more deals on the New York Stock Exchange that day than in the whole of 1950, etc. – that everyone ran out of superlatives, except that no one thought it was particularly superlative. As this was the nuclear age, John Phelan, chairman of the New York Stock Exchange, described it as 'the closest to meltdown I'd ever want to get'. In the same way that almost everyone over the age of 55 can remember exactly what they were doing when they heard that President Kennedy had been shot, every investor will remember what they were doing on 19 October 1987. It was serious. By the middle of Tuesday, as the Dow was plunging again – by then it had lost 800 points in less than five days' trading – the New York Stock Exchange was in touch with the White House and considering the suspension of trading. At that moment the market rallied and, although it might only be a dead cat bounce, it was at least a bounce and it removed the pressure for a moment. If New York had suspended trading, the effect on prices in London would have been catastrophic, as that would have been the only escape hatch. The Hong Kong Exchange did suspend trading, and that exerted extra pressure elsewhere, especially in Sydney. Why were the falls so massive? Prices could not keep going up forever. 'Why not?' asked Sid, who had been persuaded to buy British Gas and other privatised stocks. Good question. No one knew the answer, but they never had before. This did not explain the precipitous plunge. Programme trading by computer and portfolio insurance went a long way to explaining it.

Portfolio insurance had grown dramatically in popularity in the twelve months before the crash – the pension fund assets in the USA that were managed in this way had grown from \$8.5 billion to \$60 billion. In simple terms, it meant that by trading in the futures market on the indexes, a portfolio could be insured against a fall. Thus you could buy with impunity, which helped to drive the market up, and if it turned you were covered in the futures market, which would just as certainly drive the market down. In theory this is great, but the concept has, in retrospect, a rather obvious flaw: if the market is falling, not everyone can be a winner or emerge unscathed. Someone has to buy what everyone else wants to sell. In the week before Black Monday, the portfolio insurers had not been able to sell the stock they wanted to, so by the Monday the pressure was immense. On Black Monday itself, as the insurers sold the futures below the prices in the market, no one would buy the actual stocks when the futures showed they could fall much further, and no one wanted the futures while the portfolio insurers were the obvious sellers. The result – a free fall.

There were moments of wry humour. In the US, Alan Greenspan, chairman of the Federal Reserve Board, was flying to Dallas to make a speech. The markets were falling as he boarded the plane, so he was greatly relieved when he arrived at Dallas to be told that the Dow Jones was down 'Five Oh Eight' – until he realised that the 'Oh' was not a decimal point.

On Tuesday in New York, in spite of another huge fall in London in response to Wall Street's 500-point drop the previous night, we witnessed the classic dead cat bounce, and the Dow gained 200 points in the first hour. Then the insurers moved in again on the futures and down went the market again, 225 points in two hours. There was real panic now – any further falls (and the futures market was signalling another 300 points) would send many dealers to the wall. The futures market in Chicago stopped trading, apparently believing that the decision to close New York had already been taken. As everyone waited, the first sign of a turn came for the little-used Major Market Index in Chicago, where there was a rally. New York 'touched it out'; some corporations helped by announcing that they were buying their own stock; and the day finished with a 100-point gain – the largest ever. The immediate crisis was over. The post-mortem began.

The consumer boom that had built up around the world

in the 1980s did not lose its momentum overnight, and most of 1988 was another good year, especially in Britain. Chancellor of the Exchequer Nigel (now Lord) Lawson had read his economic history books and knew that what turned the Wall Street crash of 1929 into the world depression of the 1930s was the tightening of credit everywhere and the mistaken attempt to balance budgets. He, and others, were determined that that should not happen this time, and lowered interest rates to maintain liquidity in the financial system.

Unfortunately, he overdid it. Most British consumers are not directly affected by the stock market (though many of them are through their pension funds) and, though the crash made dramatic headlines and hurt a few large private investors, the mass of people went on spending, confident that their main asset – the house they lived in – was still worth far more than they had paid for it.

The house price spiral was given a final upward twist when Lawson announced the end of double tax relief on mortgages for unmarried couples living together.

However, the new law would not apply until August, and the early summer of 1988 witnessed the final frenzy of house purchase at what, in retrospect, came to be seen as silly prices. What those who were buying failed to notice was that the interest rate cycle had turned. After reducing interest rates at the end of 1987 and the early part of 1988, Lawson realised that the British economy was overheating badly. The mature, some would say sclerotic, British economy could grow only at about 3 per cent before it hit capacity restraints and ran into inflation and balance of payments problems. Lawson took a long time to realise that the economy was growing much faster than this. (One of the Thatcher government's public expenditure economies had been to cut down on the

Whitehall department supplying statistics on the economy, and these were taking a long time to become available. It proved to be a very expensive cost saving.) However, by early summer 1988 the overheating was obvious as the inflation rate turned upwards and the balance of payments deficit ballooned alarmingly. Lawson should probably have raised taxes in his 1988 budget instead of reducing them, but the real problem was the amount of liquidity in the economy. He tackled this by raising interest rates.

The only problem was that a national economy is a big ship, and big ships take a long time to stop and turn round. People did not realise the implications – and nor, in all fairness, did most businessmen, financial commentators or politicians. The balance of payments got worse, and interest rates went up again until they eventually reached 15 per cent. This meant that most people were paying 18–20 per cent on their overdrafts, loans and mortgages. It may have taken some time to stop the ship, but stop it certainly did, and with some very nasty related and self-feeding consequences.

Not only had house prices risen very sharply in the 1980s, but the financing of them had become very easy – 90, 95 and even 100 per cent loans had become available. On a £100,000 mortgage, 10 per cent was £833 a month – quite a lot of money, but manageable if both partners were earning £1,500 a month. The sums looked differently by the end of 1989, when repayments had moved up to £1,600 a month and one of the jobs looked a little shaky. If the worst happened and one of the partners lost his or her job (and high interest rates also bring recessions), the couple would have to sell the house and move to something cheaper. And it was only then that the real calamity of the house price spiral hit home. The house that had been bought for £110,000 with a £100,000 mortgage could not be sold, certainly not at £110,000, nor at £100,000, nor even at £90,000 or £80,000. It could perhaps be 'given away' at £70,000. The couple faced disaster. They could not keep up the mortgage payments, but if they sold the house they owed the mortgage company £30,000. John Major, who took over from Nigel Lawson as chancellor when Thatcher determined that he should take the blame for this fiasco, said: 'If it isn't hurting, it isn't working.'

On Black Monday I was in our then City office at 29 Mincing Lane in EC3. I was completing the purchase of an engineering company for MSI and we were paying the purchase price by a 'Vendor Placing'. Essentially this was issuing MSI shares to the Vendor and immediately placing them for cash in the Stock Market.

The Vendor's lawyer had been difficult throughout and was still arguing every minor point.

I got a message to call MSI's brokers. The market was collapsing – we had twenty minutes to do a deal.

I walked back in to the meeting room and said, 'The market's in freefall. Sign now or we walk.'

They signed and got the money!

CHAPTER 23

Manchester United

I was still back in Cheshire most weekends and kept up all my clients and contacts in and around Manchester.

The Edwards family who I had met in the old days of John Gorna back in the early 1970s were still friends and clients. Their original public company, Louis C. Edwards and Sons plc, had been transformed by retail and supermarket entrepreneur James (Jimmy) Gulliver who had bought into the Louis Edwards business, then closed the meat processing operation and turned it into Argyll Foods which had become a major 'go-go' stock of the late 1970s and 1980s, which had also had the effect of making most members of the Edwards family fairly wealthy in the process. Louis Edwards had always been interested in Manchester United Football Club and had steadily over a number of years bought up more and more shares.

Louis' son Martin, who had become a good friend, had himself carried on this tradition and had got to a point where he owned 51 per cent of the voting shares and was the chairman and CEO after his father's death. My other friend Dave Whelan had had extensive talks with Martin about buying a part of his shareholding. Martin had kept on buying shares as they became available and as a result had borrowed quite an amount from the bank which he wanted to pay down. Dave got very close to buying 15 per cent of the club when negotiations fell down over whether JJB Sports might be merged into Manchester United prior to taking the merged group public.

So Martin was still looking for some sort of a deal when he was approached by one Michael Knighton, who was to all intents and purposes a complete unknown and mystery man. He proposed buying the entire club for £20 million thereby netting Martin just over £10 million for his shareholding. Knighton must have signed something because on around 17 August 1989 Martin allowed him to go onto the pitch at Old Trafford on a match day as the 'new owner' of Manchester United.

Embarrassingly for all concerned it emerged within days of this spectacle that Knighton either never had the £20 million purchase price or, if he had, the financial backer (who insiders believed was the dreaded 'Captain' Bob Maxwell) had deserted him so that the deal collapsed ignominiously.

More rumours then started to fly of another bid at the same price from a 'Middle Eastern source'. How prescient!

At this point I could contain myself no longer and called Martin to invite him into the office for a chat. He came in a matter of hours later and we sat in my boardroom. I told Martin that I believed he would be very ill advised to sell the club for as little as £20 million. In my view he should take the club public and only sell as many shares as he needed to pay down his bank debt and provide any working capital the club needed to expand. Martin's first reaction was that it was very difficult to take a football club public and furthermore he wasn't sure that he was cut out to be chairman with all the attention of 'the City' focused on him.

I told him that this wasn't just any old football club, this was Manchester United, one of the most iconic brands on the planet with huge potential for future growth based on merchandising around the world. I also suggested that Professor Sir Roland Smith, a former marketing lecturer from Manchester who had forged a major career as a professional company chairman (his most famous chairmanship was that of the House of Fraser, which included Harrods, leading to a four-year battle with Tiny Rowland of Lonrho who wanted to buy the group), would be an ideal chairman for Manchester United. Both Martin and I knew Roland and Martin felt very comfortable with that suggestion. I convinced Martin that he should kick all other offers into the long grass and concentrate on taking the club public.

I thought this was good advice to Martin and also acting on the IPO would be good business for AW.

Immediately we telephoned Maurice Watkins, a solicitor who sat on the board of Manchester United, from the speakerphone in my boardroom. We got through to Maurice and Martin explained that he was with me (I thought I could feel Maurice wince in consternation at the mention of my name!) and explained the plan.

Maurice said, 'Well, what do you want to do, Martin?'

Martin replied, 'This is what I want to do.'

'All right', said Maurice, 'then that's what we will do.'

I told Maurice I would be in touch with him in a few days to carry the process forward and we left things at that. I dropped Maurice a line and also confirmed all my advice to Martin in writing. After two to three weeks I had heard nothing from Maurice, so I called him.

'Oh yes,' said Maurice, 'it's all under consideration. I'll be in touch.'

I never heard from Maurice again and within months the IPO of Manchester United went ahead, Sir Roland Smith was appointed chairman to Martin's chief executive, and they never looked back. All told Martin probably made £130 million to £150 million out of his shares and the law firm acting on the IPO was Addleshaws – where one of Maurice Watkins' partners Elizabeth Lee was married to the head of corporate, Paul Lee.

C'est la vie!

At least Martin and I are still friends today and I can reflect that I changed the course of history, though whether some of the more strident Manchester United fans would thank me is, I suppose, debatable!

Recently I told Dave Whelan this story again.

He said that shortly after the Michael Knighton debacle he had also had several meetings with Martin Edwards about buying out his 51 per cent stake entirely.

He told me he had sat in meetings attended by other directors including Bobby Charlton. He had offered Martin £12.5 million in cash for his 51 per cent stake and Martin had shaken hands on the deal.

Dave told me that when he got home that night he said to his wife Pat, 'I've just bought Manchester United.'

Pat said (with typical female intuition), 'Really, that will go down well with all the supporters of Liverpool, Arsenal, Chelsea and Manchester City who buy replica shirts in their hundreds of thousands from JJB!'

Dave had to think this through.

He told me that he went back to Martin and told him that he would stick to the deal to buy the shares for £12.5 million, but he felt that Martin would get best value by taking Manchester United public.

I never knew that at the time. Great minds!

CHAPTER 24

Legal Resources

About this time I got a phone call from Martin Shaw, who was the managing partner of the prominent Leeds firm Simpson Curtis. Martin told me that they had a 'club' of prominent firms that they called the 'Information Club' and the members of it were Simpson Curtis, Pinsent & Co. in Birmingham and Addleshaws in Manchester. Addleshaws had resigned as they were starting something called the Norton Rose M5 Group with competing firms but headed up by Norton Rose in London.

Was AW interested in taking over from Addleshaws? Of course Martin knew that apart from Manchester we were also in Liverpool as well as London.

The whole idea at that point seemed to be to put together loosely the 'cream' of the solicitor profession outside London, but to what specific purpose was not entirely clear, other than to share information to see how the members were doing and what they might learn from each other. At that stage there didn't seem a lot to lose and my executive committee agreed that we get on board to see how it went. About that time Dickinson Dees, the top firm in Newcastle-on-Tyne, and Osborne Clark in Bristol were also joining and fairly soon afterwards McGrigor Donald from Scotland also joined.

One of the Liverpool partners, Michael Pinfold, joined me on the Information Club committee and we kicked off. We were, I suppose, a group of similar firms and, in truth, we were all a little self-satisfied, believing ourselves to be the top firm in each of our cities, obviously excluding London. After two or three meetings I got rather frustrated with what seemed to me to be a bit of a talking shop and so I asked whether the group really had any sort of business plan and said that I could see that without some sort of aim and ambition we would just drift around rather aimlessly. I'm afraid that I have always had a habit of speaking my mind and overall it has served me well, though not always!

The approach worked here. We formalised the structure and formed a company called The Legal Resources Group ('LRG') and decided that quite apart from sharing financial information we would create a national training organisation, a national library service and a joint approach to professional indemnity insurance, and together we would create an international referral panel.

We soon had a chief executive, a national training director and we were off and running! It was a good bunch of firms and overall a good bunch of people to work with. It served us well for the next five or so years until we made the 'Great Leap Forward'!

At around the same time I was introduced to someone who was to loom quite large in my life for a few years, an American lawyer called Rod Hills. To this day I can't quite remember how we met but I think it was around 1990. Rod was a big hitter. He was married to Carla Hills who was at the time the US trade secretary in the government of President George Bush Sr. He had originally been a partner in the firm of Munger Tolles in Los Angeles which was headed up by the legendary Charlie Munger, a lawyer and right-hand man to Warren Buffett, even then one of the world's greatest investors.

From there Rod had gone on to be the chairman of the Securities and Exchange Commission and, by the time that we met, he was a partner at an old-time US law firm called Donovan Leisure which had offices in New York, Washington DC and Los Angeles as well as a small office in Paris.

Donovan had been founded shortly after the Second World War by General William 'Wild Bill' Donovan, a very influential figure who was generally accepted as being the founder of the Central Intelligence Agency (CIA). By the 1960s Donovan Leisure were recognised as one of the greatest 'white shoe' law firms in New York alongside firms like Cravath Swaine & Moore, Sherman & Sterling, White & Case and Latham & Watkins, with a client base to match. At some point disaster had struck when a partner, who was representing Rank Xerox in a major anti-trust competition case, allegedly 'destroyed' some documentary evidence that would have been prejudicial to the client's case. Whether or not it was ever proved was incidental, because things such as this in the legal profession are enough to cause a 'sniff' when it simply cannot do to have any sort of question mark over the integrity of a partner which quickly then reflects on the firm.

Rod had been brought in as a partner to seek to restore Donovan to its former eminence. He and I thought the same thoughts and dreamt the same dreams. Rod was adamant that the best law firms would always be selective as to the work and clients they took on and would pride themselves on the sheer quality, inventiveness and intellectual capability of their lawyers who would be completely dedicated to getting the best result for their clients.

We foresaw the creation of a 'brand' that would be known throughout the world for its integrity, wisdom and sheer clout and we thought we had the makings of such a firm. Alsops went back almost 170 years in the United Kingdom and acted for some great clients. Donovan had been, and could be again, one of the top firms in America. We could together fashion one of the world's great law firms.

We talked endlessly of our plans to create Alsop Donovan and we made a small start shortly after the first Gulf War in Kuwait. Through his Washington connections, Rod had been introduced to a lawyer in Kuwait called Al-Ayoub, who believed that he was in prime position to pitch to the government of Kuwait in representing the country in its claim for reparations against Iraq. If we could win this mandate it would be a tremendous instruction which would get global recognition. Rod had a lawyer of Palestinian descent called Reema Ali who was based in their Washington office. She was a very bright lady. In London we had an associate barrister called Percy Marchant, an exceptional lawyer of Indian descent whose father was the senior in-house lawyer to the Hinduja family.

Reema and Percy went out to Kuwait as the advance guard, just three weeks or so after the end of the Gulf War. I had enlisted the support of Deloitte on forensic accounting through my acquaintance with John Connolly, the rising star of Deloitte. John and I went back together to our Manchester days. We rehearsed our presentations to the Kuwaiti government in London before finally taking off for Kuwait City via Bahrain.

It was an eerie feeling flying into Kuwait City in the early evening and looking out over the oil fields where almost all the oil wells had been set alight by the retreating Iraqi forces. The whole scene was like something from a sci-fi movie. We installed ourselves in the only hotel that seemed operational. We were warned not to walk out of the hotel by more than a few yards since there were land mines everywhere.

Inevitably Rod Hills knew quite a few people, including one very wealthy Kuwaiti who invited us to his palatial house which up to a month before had been occupied by an Iraqi general. He told me they had managed to hide all their valuables in an underground safe before evacuating. It was truly a very strange feeling in Kuwait City where only a matter of a few weeks before it had been a war zone and under Iraqi occupation. We finally got our slot for a presentation typically at some extremely unsociable hour – I think about 11.00pm.

An hour or so into our presentation the panel of seven, all in their white flowing robes, all stood up to retire for prayer for an hour or so.

I thought we gave a really good account of ourselves and we were told we would hear in two to three weeks' time. In the meantime our new joint venture law firm of Al-Ayoub Alsop Donovan had come to life despite resistance from my executive committee!

The whole Rod Hills/Donovan Leisure experience served to broaden my mind and strengthen my conviction that my enduring and burning ambition of creating the biggest and best law firm in the world was actually possible if I totally believed in it and just kept pushing every single day to achieve it. After I got back from Kuwait I took out two to three days to reflect on our progress over the last few years.

Alsop Wilkinson was the first substantial North/South law firm and through the Legal Resources Group we had offices in every major city in the United Kingdom. Through LRG we had also started a small representative office/lobbying facility in Brussels and we at Alsop had our nascent office in Hong Kong as well as our close association with Donovan covering New York, Washington, Los Angeles and Paris. If I could pull all this together I would certainly have the makings of my world-class law firm.

Pooling our client base, intellectual know-how, geographical spread and financial resource would definitely have the makings of everything I had been working for. The only problem I could foresee was to convince a number of my partners, not least my own executive committee, that all this was possible.

In going through my old papers to research for this book I came across a written record of an executive committee meeting in the London office in June 1991. The committee then included Peter Wayte and David Cooke, both formerly of Wilkinson Kimbers, David Edmundson and David Mawdsley, both from the Liverpool office and Richard Parker, a lateral hire partner in commercial real estate whom I had brought in about five years earlier and who had quickly risen through the ranks.

David Cooke was a good man, albeit quite conservative, but generally prepared to back my judgement as was Richard Parker. David Edmundson and David Mawdsley, commercial property and shipping respectively, were much more conservative and were being pulled in by the magnet of Peter Wayte who as always was the 'ubermeister Prophet of Doom'.

I had proposed that we should construct a proper three- to five-year business plan which would lay out our growth targets, financial performance criteria and rationale for creating a truly top-class law firm. I also wanted to create a small central unit that would coordinate all these plans including relations with Donovan, Legal Resources Group and our expansion projects.

All this seemed entirely logical to me but it sparked a not untypical tirade from Peter Wayte backed up by David Edmundson of which I noted the following remarks and comments:

Peter Wayte:

We should *not* have a business plan

We should not cooperate with LRG to form a small business unit

I do not want to support any more speculative ventures

If we win the Kuwaiti reparations contract it could mean big problems

A central secretariat has a cost without any tangible benefit

We should be much less grandiose in our thinking

David Edmundson:

We are walking a financial tightrope – Peter's comments are a source of great worry and concern

[NB – We had no bank debt as I always insisted on keeping a seven-figure office account credit balance!]

Richard Parker:

We are getting a lot of quality work referred from Donovan.

David Edmundson:

They might swallow us up.

Peter Wayte:

Roger has acquisition mania. He has time on his hands

and therefore is likely to continue on the acquisition trail. He is doing too many things, Hong Kong is a perfect example, it's not properly controlled.
[Totally without foundation.]

David Edmundson:
You [me] are hiring too many people.
[They were all bringing in good clients.]

We are going to have to have a big IT spend and we need strong financial control.
[We had no bank debt.]

The other LRG Firms are way ahead of us in the UK domestic market.
[We ended up as the strongest of the lot!]

David Mawdsley:
Are Donovan the right people?

Jesus wept!

I walked away from this meeting, as happened many times, in almost complete despair. How could I ever move this thing forward when a number of my fellow board members had such a totally negative attitude?

I sometimes felt as though there was a small group of partners who were marching steadfastly and purposefully down the highway of ambition and growth but behind us we were dragging along a huge sack of infighting, writhing and wrestling partners who were in constant denial and always complaining and hand-wringing.

Were all big commercial enterprises like this? Or was it just law firms? Well, I wasn't going to give up or be pushed off course. We were going down the road despite this bunch.

At around this time I was out in Hong Kong on one of my then frequent visits. We were starting to get some real traction in Hong Kong although the former Barry Driver partners were really not up to the game and I had to remove two of them.

A day or so after my arrival I got a call from Derek Morris, the senior partner. Alan Greenough who was managing partner of the Manchester office had been to see him to say he wanted to retire from the firm to go into business with some clients.

Would I return to the UK immediately to sort it out? Panic stations!

I was furious. Alan had made a solemn promise to me that he would run the Manchester office for at least five years after my departure for London. He had recruited too many people jeopardising the profitability of the office and now wanted to leave without even having the grace to call me directly.

I told Derek that there was only one response to Alan, which was, 'Will you change your mind, and if so, how much money do you want?'

Derek called me back. Alan didn't want to change his mind.

Will Holt, whom I had brought in from British Vita, then called me. Either I appointed him managing partner in Manchester or he would leave!

Terrific!

In fact, I knew that the best partner to lead Manchester would be my protégé, Nigel Kissack, but he was still in his mid-thirties. I called some other members of the executive committee and agreed we should go with Will Holt. He was going to inherit a difficult situation, with the first job being to remove some of the people that Alan had hired at the end of the 1980s boom. Talk about Snakes and Ladders!

CHAPTER 25

Russian Land Reform

B ack in London I had been getting close to a client called
Carroll Group, a property development and investment
group which we had started representing in about 1987. The
group was headed up by Gerald Carroll who had become
a good friend of Lord Jermyn, now the Marquess of Bristol
after the death of his father. I met Gerald through John and
we started to undertake a lot of work for them, taking the
work off Slaughter and May, which was very satisfying!

The early 1990s had seen another great property crash
and this had caught out a lot of commercial property entre-
preneurs including Carroll. However, Gerald had some great
foresight, particularly regarding the newly created Russian
Federation.

Following the collapse of the old Soviet Union in 1989
there was a whole swathe of change going through Russia.
Boris Yeltsin was now the president of the Russian Federation
and his vice president was Alexander Rutskoi. Gerald had,
through whatever contacts, got a deal to build a new office
block in Moscow and I had found a Russian-speaking lawyer
to help him. Through these contacts Gerald had been introduced to Alexander Rutskoi. Rutskoi came from Kursk in
southern Russia which was a major agricultural region where

one of the staple crops was sugar beet. Unfortunately in the years of communism production had fallen dramatically and desperately needed capital investment and know-how.

Gerald had also been introduced to a region in Siberia which supposedly had a surplus of oil but desperately needed sugar. Gerald had been in contact with the British Sugar Corporation (BSC) and had hatched up a rough tripartite deal. In essence the Siberian region would agree to sell two or three tankers full of oil to Kursk in exchange for sugar to be delivered at a fixed price at a later date.

Kursk would, through Carroll, assign that oil contract. We would sell their oil on the open market and use the cash so raised to buy capital equipment and human resources through BSC which would be transferred out to Kursk and invested in dramatically increased sugar beet production, and that sugar would in due course be sent to Siberia to pay for the original oil delivery.

Such was the deal as presented to me by Gerald. He wanted me to go with him to Russia together with a group of consultants from BSC and a couple of ex-Foreign Office/ Diplomatic Service guys including the former British ambassador to Moscow.

So started one of the most interesting adventures of my life.

We flew out on British Airways to Moscow in September 1992 in a plane that was virtually empty. Not too many people wanted to go to Moscow at the time. When we arrived we were transferred into central Moscow and checked into a huge Soviet-style hotel close to Red Square and the Kremlin. The airport terminal had seemed to me to be dark and threatening and the city of Moscow itself a dour and uninviting place.

That evening we wandered into Red Square and I was

surprised to find that behind the edifices giving onto the massive square there was virtually nothing. It was like a film set where everything was a facade with no substance at all behind it. Back at the hotel the rooms were grim, without towels and with old newspaper serving as toilet rolls. On each floor was located an old lady who was some sort of supposed 'manager'. Her job seemed to be to dispense towels to guests. Why the towels weren't put directly in the rooms seemed unclear, and the towels themselves were ragged articles that must have been through the laundry a thousand times. She also served tea 24 hours a day – a good thing apart from the fact that the tea itself was repulsive.

We were pleased to leave the hotel the following morning and make our way to the 'government' airport. This airport was much nearer the centre of Moscow and as we pulled in I started to look round for what might be our plane. I had imagined that given we were a party of eight or so there would be a smallish propeller plane on the tarmac, but I saw nothing that looked likely. I mused to our (English-speaking) driver as to which plane might be the one destined to fly us down to Kursk. He pointed out two large airliners parked up: 'One of those is Yeltsin's and the other is Rutskoi's, it'll be one or the other!'

We were dropped at a very comfortable small departure building and fairly soon a red carpet was being rolled out from the main door of the departure lounge to the steps of one of the airliners. Soon we were summoned to board the plane, picking our way along the red carpet across the tarmac and up the stairs onto the plane. On board the first impression was of very comfortable leather seats and at the rear half was a boardroom. We were told that Rutskoi and his entourage were already on board in the rear.

Gerald, as the principal guest, was invited to go back to

sit with Rutskoi. The rest of us made ourselves comfortable (not difficult) up at the front half. After a couple of hours of fairly pampered service we arrived at Kursk airport not only to another very long red carpet but also this time to the refrain of a quite large brass band and several hundred people waiting and then cheering on the tarmac. In true Russian fashion a line of Zil limousines awaited our disembarkment. In no time at all we were in the back of a large black limo heading into town, and almost before I had gathered my thoughts and impressions we were all pulling up in the centre of town at what appeared to be a cenotaph or war memorial.

The next thing I knew I was walking up to the memorial, laying a wreath of red poppies and bowing. It felt very much like a royal visit. Not much later and we were attending the first of what seemed like a great number of banquets. The main feature was that there seemed to be hundreds of people invited and a great number of them seemed intent on making a speech. At every table setting was placed a half bottle of vodka. This was required to toast the speakers and everyone was fairly soon completely legless.

Gerald gave a speech in English which was one of the better ones (Gerald only drank Coca-Cola so was always sober). I doubt many there understood a word of English but that didn't seem to matter very much and everyone seemed to be thoroughly enjoying themselves – in a Russian way. I say 'in a Russian way' for a reason because I very quickly learnt that your average Russian is pretty philosophical and also prone to frequent bouts of melancholy brought on in large part, I should think, by the consumption of copious amounts of vodka.

So after a very liquid lunch we went back to our limos as I understood that our meetings were to be held at some out-of-town location. Our line of limos was preceded by outriders of police on motorbikes who swept ahead of our cavalcade, clearing the roadway in front of us so we could travel at very great speed untroubled by oncoming traffic. Motor cars, cyclists, trucks and buses were all forced to the side of the road, sometimes into the ditch, to allow us to thunder away.

Amazingly, at every intersection stood a uniformed soldier who smartly saluted as we hurtled by. After a couple of hours of this we swept into a very grand driveway at the end of which was a huge country house, I assume from the days of the Tsars, which I understood served as a retreat for the main Politburo members in the days of Brezhnev.

We were ushered to our bedrooms and disconcertingly discovered that we were sharing. My room-mate was a decent guy from the British Sugar Corporation but it felt odd to be sharing. After settling in we assembled for our first plenary session. If there were about eight in our party there must have been at least 80 of them. Delegates from Kursk, Moscow, Siberia and God knows where else, all sat down around a massive table in an equally massive room.

After two or three introductory speeches, and no progress at all, I decided it was time for me to speak through an interpreter. I basically said that we were very pleased to be there and it would no doubt be a momentous occasion but we could only make progress if they would select a maximum of ten of their number to join us in detailed negotiations. Suddenly the room was full of mixed feelings. There was joy from most that they could be excused the drudgery of negotiations around a complex 'oil for sugar for cash' deal, tinged with concern that they individually may lose some face and prestige by not being part of the smaller group.

We eventually got down to our small(er) negotiating committee which included two representatives of the all-important Siberian delegation. Without their oil to kick-start the process there was no deal. I stressed to them how important they were. I also told them that we would want total control of the tankers of oil the minute they were on the high seas as we would be selling the oil for cash to buy tractors and all manner of other agricultural equipment. They both stressed that they fully understood the vital role they were playing. We negotiated for several hours until the evening's banquet and speech/vodka quaffing sessions began.

The following morning with thick heads we resumed until we had hammered out the bones of an 'Accord' which the diplomats and civil servants had turned into draft agreements. At this point most of our crew disappeared to go and look at the farmland and the basic state of the current equipment. I was left alone and wandered around the campus. Finally I found what seemed to be a very large canteen serving lunch. I wandered in. Not a soul spoke English so I simply sat in a spare chair and waited to see what would happen. Lunch arrived and after three or four courses, and not a word to a soul, I got up again and walked out. I later found out that this dining establishment was nothing at all to do with our party!

Back at the plenary session I found Gerald in conversation with Alexander Rutskoi through an excellent KGB interpreter. Rutskoi felt like doing some fishing while the scientists were beavering about. Did we want to join him? We did and, in no time, I was in the back of a Volkswagen van with Gerald, Alexander Rutskoi and four ex-KGB men. It felt pretty surreal to be bumping along a forest track going deeper and deeper into the forest in a VW camper van sitting next to the vice president of the Russian Federation. Rutskoi was a very interesting guy. He had been in the Russian air force and was shot down over Afghanistan where he was tortured. He showed us where his fingernails had been ripped out by his Afghan hosts.

We eventually came out to a clearing by a large river where was located what looked like a fairly modest but large dacha. This was Leonid Brezhnev's getaway dacha. As we went inside it was like entering a Tardis. What looked modest on the outside was palatial inside with every luxury.

Rutskoi decided we would barbeque and had his men set up a long trestle table outside. A bit of fishing went on but soon we were sitting at the table mob-handed and involved in the national sport of talking and drinking vodka. Around us in the woods were armed soldiers and maybe a dozen people at our table. The vodka bottle had obviously been passed around the guards as one by one they lay down and fell asleep. The same thing happened on our table until at last was left only Rutskoi, Gerald (non-drinker), the KGB interpreter and me.

By this stage the conversation was pretty forthright. I asked Rutskoi what stuff he was working on and he told me that he was in charge of the Russian land reform programme. All land and buildings were owned by the state and he told me that out in the countryside he proposed to give everyone the house they lived in but then the huge fields would be split up into designated individual parcels and given to the local residents. I told him that this was a bad idea. It would be almost impossible to operate since every attempt to farm the huge fields could be held up by quarrelling between the multitude of owners.

He said, 'If you're so smart, what would you do?'

I told him I agreed of course that everyone should have their own house, but that all the land should go into a joint stock company and then the shares in the company be handed out to the local residents. That way the board of the company could put deals together on behalf of the residents without one or more difficult people holding the others to ransom.

Rutskoi thought this was a grand idea. 'That's what I'm going to do,' he said. We shook hands and had another slug of vodka!

When we got back the civil servants and the technicians had done their stuff and the Grand Agreement was ready to sign. I got hold of the Siberians one last time to make sure they understood that their oil was vital to the entire venture. In front of Alexander Rutskoi they assured me they did. By the time everyone surfaced the following morning we were finally ready to sign up. To great applause Rutskoi signed for Kursk with the mayor of Kursk. Rutskoi the local boy had delivered. We drove in convoy back into Kursk to yet another reception at the town hall. Rutskoi and the mayor insisted that we must have our pick of any building in the city for our joint venture office.

We took a car and driver and went round with the mayor. Gerald picked one very impressive building; it was the city library. We could have anything but that. He picked another which turned out to be the local Parliament building. Apologetically they said it wasn't possible for us to have that either.

Someone had a bright idea. We drove to the outskirts of town and through a magnificent pair of huge stone gates into parkland where eventually we came across a large rambling mansion next to a lake. This looked very impressive. We walked around and it seemed to be full of people who looked desperately ill. We said that we liked the building and the setting but wondered what they would do with all the occupants.

'Oh, we'll just throw them out,' said the mayor cheerfully.

We said we'd sleep on it, thinking what a great start it would be if our new joint venture emptied a hospital and sanatorium as its first move in town! Back at the town hall the reception was now in full flow. Rutskoi was giving televised interviews and everyone was in great spirits (almost exclusively vodka!). I was clock-watching. We were booked on the 9.00pm British Airways flight from Moscow to Heathrow. It was already 5.00pm and no one seemed remotely ready to leave Kursk for the two-hour flight to Moscow.

Eventually I pressed my point on the KGB interpreter who had been by Rutskoi's side throughout. 'Oh, don't worry, the British Airways flight will leave only when we decide it can – relax!'

Sure enough we arrived back to land at the main international airport at 10.30pm to find the British Airways flight waiting on the tarmac. We pulled up next to it in the Rutskoi airliner and after very cheery and heartfelt goodbyes we went straight up the steps of the BA aircraft with our baggage and took off for London.

What a trip!

There were two sequels to the story. First, within a couple of weeks the much heralded joint venture was unravelling. It turned out that the Siberians had already sold the same oil cargo three times over! I called the group in Siberia to ask why on earth they had gone through such a charade and wasted everyone's time.

'Well,' they explained as if addressing a child, 'Rutskoi would have been upset if we had told him that it was already sold. We didn't want that!'

About six months later I picked up my *Times* over breakfast and found an article headlined 'Rutskoi announces Russia Land Reform Programme'.

I was amazed, and very flattered, to see that he had

incorporated my proposals in full. I should have sent him a bill for my services rendered!

On 5 October 1993 there was an attempt to depose Boris Yeltsin and the insurgents picked Alexander Rutskoi as their choice to succeed him. Rutskoi was declared president of the Russian Federation and holed up in the White House in Moscow which was then put under siege by the supporters of Yeltsin.

Rutskoi lost, and spent the next years in Lefortovo prison from where he was eventually released on 26 February 1994.

I never returned to Russia.

CHAPTER 26

More Frustration

Back in the real world I was again in review mode. I was in truth frustrated that the plan was proceeding less quickly than I wanted. We were continuing to attract some good new people in London, Hong Kong was starting to build well under Camille and Stewart Crowther and the Liverpool office continued on its serene and stately path. Manchester had gone from the wildly profitable star in the firmament to a somewhat troubled child.

Will Holt as managing partner was fiercely protective and also seemed to believe that there was a secret plot to get Alan Greenough back into the fold to replace him. Alan had, as so often happens when very successful corporate lawyers believe they can run companies better than their clients, found that it really wasn't all beer and skittles and was now looking to return to private practice. I certainly had no intention of bringing Alan back over Will's head but he seemed to continue to believe I might.

The Legal Resources Group had done well, up to a point. We had made great strides in setting up a joint training and education programme which was getting recognition as one of the very best across the profession. The librarians were working well nationally to combine resources so that we need not have to buy new books across every one of the ten or so large libraries across the country.

We had hired a chief executive out of industry, Peter Rodney, who was doing a good job of pulling all the financial data together and reviewing how we could learn from each other on financial disciplines, practice management, KPIs (Key Performance Indicators) and a whole range of MI (Management Information).

Our relationship with Donovan Leisure was doing well, in truth because Rod Hills and I worked so hard on it, but often it felt like pushing water uphill.

In an effort to get Peter Wayte involved as a believer in the benefits of international practice I suggested that he join me in my upcoming regular USA visit to review progress with Donovan and to set a clear path forward which may lead to some form of future integration. Despite the best will of Rod and me the trip was not a success. The managing partner of Donovan seemed to share an affinity of scepticism and negativity with Peter. He was also called Peter – Peter Coll Jr. About 30 minutes into our first day-long session Peter Coll said he had to take a client call (he was a litigator) and, leaving his jacket on the back of his chair, left the conference room for he thought no more than fifteen minutes. We saw nothing of him for the next six hours or so.

Stephen Blair, who was our main reinsurance partner in London and a close buddy of mine who had moved to New York to focus on his USA reinsurance practice and was based in Donovan's New York office, was with me (and Peter Wayte) in the meeting.

Peter Wayte said he was very concerned about what everything was costing and eventually in a private meeting with the other Peter (he of the hanging jacket and complete absence) agreed to cancel the 'lawyer secondment exchange 'program' at a saving of about £40,000 per annum which together they seemed to regard as a great leap forward.

Within a year, despite the best efforts of Rod Hills and some of his partners, our relationship began to wither on the vine.

Peter Coll Jr. was the managing partner in 1994/95. On 20 April 1998 the firm folded. Sixty lawyers left, 40 went to Orrick, Herrington & Sutcliffe.

The contemporaneous quotes were:

'We had difficulty competing.'

'There is a perception that a firm needs to be of a certain size to be a player.' (Told you so!)

The *New York Times* reflected that the demise of Donovan shows what happens to law firms that continue to practise law as the gentlemanly profession of the past rather than as a competitive business. Apart from Rod Hills, notable alumni of the firm included Lloyd Blankfein, the current chairman and CEO of Goldman Sachs, as well as Bill Colby (whom I knew well), who was the director of the CIA from 1973–6. A great US, formerly 'white shoe' practice had gone to the wall through poor management and my ambition to create the makings of a global firm, Alsop Donovan, disappeared with it.

It was time for a big shake-up. I persuaded the executive committee that we really had to have some third-party validation of the strategy I was intent on pursuing. We had used a number of consultants including Alan Hodgart and David Andrews but the one who was our current putative guru was Professor Stephen Mayson.

Stephen was, and is, a good and sensible guy. He interviewed every partner, reviewed every practice area and, after about four months, came up with a report which I could have sub-titled 'A Statement of the Blindingly Obvious'! We had to have clear leadership. I should be appointed (elected) to the new role of chairman of the firm, David Cooke should become London managing partner and there should be many other fairly obvious moves. At least it felt as though we might be setting the stage for another real push forward.

The usual suspects objected to the report but despite that it got voted through and so I became chairman of the firm in 1994.

Despite everything we were a quality law firm with some great clients and a number of very good partners and the makings of a plan, which in my head had never changed since 1977, to be one of the best and better still THE best law firm in the world. From offices in London, Manchester, Liverpool, Hong Kong and New York, we clearly had a very long way to go but it was equally a long way on from a small one-man office in Kennedy Street, Manchester just seventeen years earlier.

Will Holt left the firm shortly after this, having apparently refused to believe that there was not some great conspiracy to replace him as managing partner in Manchester. I felt Will's departure was to prove to be yet another major fork in the road; he would re-enter the story two years later as one of the architects of the concept of creating the present DLA.

Back then we immediately stepped in and appointed my top choice, Nigel Kissack, as managing partner in Manchester. Nigel was a natural leader and a man in whom I had total confidence after sixteen years of working very closely together.

Then, during one executive committee meeting in early summer 1994, David Cooke told us all that he had had an approach from Jim Edmundson, the managing partner of Turner Kenneth Brown in London. TKB were a combination of two or three good, long-established London practices, including Turner Peacock, Kenneth Brown and

Baker Baker, and had some excellent clients. However, due to poor management (prior to Jim) and a completely uncontrolled IT budget they had got into financial difficulty and needed to be rescued.

David suggested I lead the negotiations. TKB were represented by an accountant from Binder Hamlyn called Christopher Honeyman-Brown. Over the next two to three months I put a huge amount of work into putting a deal together that would ringfence the debts of TKB, set a deal with their bankers and give them every hope of paying the bank off and becoming full partners in AW within two to three years.

TKB had some great partners and some wonderful clients, but already good partners had started to leave. Catherine Usher, a leading real estate partner, had gone to upcoming Dibb Lupton Broomhead's new London office, quickly followed by Karen Friebe, a top leisure and hotels partner, also to Dibb Lupton Broomhead.

Honeyman-Brown and I got on well and although it was something of a gamble it was very much a calculated gamble, and Jim Edmundson was a very decent man who was doing his best for all his partners. All the final terms were thrashed out and were due to be signed at our executive committee meeting to be held in the Manchester office one day in late summer.

At the last minute Peter Wayte advised that he wasn't coming to the meeting and furthermore was voting against the TKB deal. This spooked the faint-hearted members of the executive committee so by a small majority the deal was voted down. Three months' work down the pan and I had to make the difficult phone call to Jim Edmundson to give him the news.[1]

---

[1] Within a year or so TKB's practice was acquired by Nabarro Nathanson where it flourished.

The Hong Kong office was in 1995 still a joint venture rather than an integrated brand or subsidiary. Barry Driver had moved on a year or so before resuming his practice over the harbour in Kowloon. Camille Jojo was the managing partner and other key partners included Stewart Crowther and Claudio de Bedin. The reader will recall that Stewart had joined from World Wide Shipping. Claudio, who was Hong Kong born and bred, was half Italian and acted for just about any Italian company doing business in Hong Kong or mainland China, of which there were very many.

Camille had built the litigation and restructuring practice and Stewart had hired some good people on the shipping side including Satpal Gobindpuri whom he had found in the London office. The office, which had been set up with a very small budget, had grown and grown and now had about twenty lawyers and an excellent support staff team.

The executive committee, particularly Peter Wayte, loved to goad me about Hong Kong. They knew it was my baby and as much as I wanted to integrate the office fully into the firm, constantly the committee found reasons to object. David Edmundson from Liverpool seemed to be particularly concerned that communist Chinese would overrun our office in 1997 and nationalise all our assets so therefore why should we build it up any more?

In the end the committee decided that Peter Wayte should be given the job of agreeing terms for integration with the Hong Kong partners. Talk about putting King Herod in charge of an infants' school!

A meeting was arranged in London which Camille flew in specially to attend with Peter Wayte. Peter forgot about the meeting so Camille had to return to Hong Kong. More delay.

Eventually a meeting was arranged and I quickly found

out from Camille that Wayte had kicked off the meeting by complaining that he had never wanted the office there and so tried to sell it to the Hong Kong partners! He eventually proposed some completely unrealistic terms for integration which the Hong Kong partners rejected out of hand.

Two weeks later while sitting in a restaurant in Beaune in Burgundy I got a call from Camille. They had had enough and most of them were leaving to start a Hong Kong office for Barlow Lyde & Gilbert, an old-time London insurance practice. While I completely sympathised with the Hong Kong partners I was quite beside myself with anger. This typified the problems I faced with a small minority of awkward partners. I had this constant vision of building castles which were then trampled on by the thuggish behaviour of a small gang who could not come up with an original thought, plan or idea to save their life!

I went ballistic and it took me a week or so to calm down.

Stewart Crowther decided to stay, Hong Kong was immediately integrated into the UK (the hard way) and we virtually started again in Hong Kong.

God – how frustrating!

CHAPTER 27

Dibb Lupton

Back in Manchester, Will Holt had ended up at a very interesting firm, Dibb Lupton Broomhead, based in their Manchester office. While Alsops traced its roots back to 1821 in Liverpool, the history of Dibb Lupton Broomhead went back even further. In 1764 two lawyers, Mr Barnard and Mr Bolland, started a law firm in Leeds. It seems to have pottered along quite quietly for the next 69 years until, in 1833, one Thomas Dibb became a partner and immediately the firm became Atkinson Dibb and Bolland. Thomas Dibb was clearly a thrusting and ambitious young lawyer but it was another 53 years before the name of the firm changed again to Dibb and Co. Shortly after that, in the early 1890s, a few miles further south in Sheffield (Steel City), Henry Shelley Barker and Edward Pye-Smith got together to form Pye-Smith and Barker.

It seems that, after Pye-Smith's death in 1924, Henry Shelley Barker carried on a sole practice until his son Tony joined and the firm became H. Shelley Barker & Son in 1932. Sheffield was growing at an incredible rate on the back of its global reputation as Steel City and Shelley Barker became the pre-eminent firm in the city over the next few years, representing just about every company of note in Sheffield and

South Yorkshire. In 1960 a young man called Chris Barker joined the firm. He went on to be the guiding light and main thrusting force of the firm for the next few decades.

In 1970 Shelley Barker merged with Neal, Scorah & Siddons to form Neals, Shelley & Barkers and in 1977 another merger with local rival, Broomhead, Wightman & Reed, formed the then dominant regional player of Broomheads & Neals. By 1988, under the leadership and guidance of Chris Barker, the Sheffield practice merged with the then Dibb Lupton & Co. from Leeds to create Dibb Lupton Broomhead (DLB). At this time Robin Smith was leading Dibb Lupton in Leeds. He was a pillar of the Leeds business community and a major cricket fan and leading light at Yorkshire County Cricket Club.

Between Chris Barker and Robin Smith they had promoted one Paul Rhodes as managing partner of the merged firm. Paul Rhodes was a man with a reputation. That was of a dynamic, driven, thrusting northerner who called a spade a shovel and kicked filing cabinets demanding that the contents be converted from work-in-progress to client bills to cash, preferably as quickly as possible. Under Paul Rhodes in 1990 DLB took over the London and Manchester specialist insolvency practice, William Prior & Co., which gave DLB its first foothold in those two cities. Shortly after that DLB took over an old-line practice called Needham & James in Birmingham and openly declared itself to be the regional firm to be reckoned with. It still had a great determination to make major headway in the Mecca of legal marketplaces, London. By 1995 Paul Rhodes had burnt himself out and had selected a young corporate partner from Sheffield, Nigel Knowles, to succeed him as managing partner.

I bumped into Will Holt at a drinks event in Manchester and he told me he was enjoying his new firm. He had proceeded quickly through the management ranks and was now on the board at DLB. He told me that he thought the two firms of DLB and AW could make very suitable merger partners. Instinctively I was not so sure. Will had never really settled at AW and I suppose that in truth I questioned Will's judgement.

Back in London in spring 1995 one of my headhunting men, John Grimwade, said that he had a new target for me, Lawrence Graham. LG was yet another very traditional London firm with its history in part in insurance and shipping but also with a strong real estate practice and a reasonable corporate department.

John arranged for me to meet one of their senior partners and we quickly figured out that potentially there was some quite good synergy between the two. I got my board broadly on side but then, having spent a couple of months weighing up the possibilities, the deal came off the rails because my counterpart was apparently ploughing his own furrow without any significant partner support behind him. The deal cratered.

During the process the inevitable rumours had got out and one day Christopher Honeyman-Brown (of TKB fame) called me and asked if it was true that I was talking to LG. I told him I was and he asked me how I was going to manage a much bigger merged firm. I hadn't thought of that, simply assuming that I would step up to the plate and just get on with it. I agreed to see Chris for lunch. As we talked things through I realised I needed help and support to get to the next level. Fighting people on my own board like Wayte was frankly very tiring and extremely frustrating. Chris and I had worked well together on TKB and the idea of him joining as a CEO to my chairman role at AW suddenly seemed to feel appealing.

I was just coming up to 50 and in reality had been going flat out for nearly twenty years, balancing management while still having a lot of client interface. I was still very involved with some of my favourite clients like Timpson, JJB Sports, which we had floated very successfully the previous year, Mining Supplies (MS) International and also increasingly the Bank of Scotland – a friendship back in Manchester with the local manager, Mike Murray, had spread to London when Mike's assistant, Stuart Middleton, had moved south a year or two earlier. The Bank of Scotland was fast becoming one of our biggest clients and was about to push into major expansion mode taking us with it.

I still liked the challenge of management and strategy but I knew now I needed a like-minded right-hand man. The board agreed, as did the partners, and within a couple of months Chris joined us as CEO. We were one of the few large law firms to have a chartered accountant as CEO. Chris and I got on well despite Peter Wayte being clearly anxious that there should not develop too cosy a relationship between the chairman and CEO.

We really tried ever harder to focus on effective financial controls, with a good deal of success, and how we were going to push forward on the grand master plan of creating the world's biggest and best firm. A few months went by as we looked at one or two target firms but nothing really of interest came up.

Another of my headhunter buddies, and probably the most successful of his generation in the legal market, was Gareth Quarry.

I saw Gareth quite frequently and we had hired some good people through his introduction. One day he called me; he had got a great merger idea and he needed to come up and see me soonest. I told Christopher of the meeting so he could sit in with me at the Dowgate Hill building just next to Cannon Street station. Gareth arrived with one of his sidekicks and without much of a preliminary said, 'The firm you should merge with is Dibb Lupton Broomhead.'

Christopher went a strange pale colour, said to me: 'We need to talk,' and dragged me from the room.

In an adjoining meeting room Chris told me that via Will Holt, Peter Wayte had been approached (Will apparently thought I would be unreceptive) and Peter had told Chris, plus one other partner, Paul Gordon-Saker, our head of restructuring, to see how he thought the two (very large) insolvency departments might fit together. I was furious with Chris that he would involve himself, as he and Peter had done, in preliminary meetings with DLB without first telling me as chairman.

We apologised to Gareth and then they left and Chris told me the whole story. Peter Wayte had sworn him to secrecy and I immediately suspected that Peter was keen to find a prime slot for himself in the negotiations. Our board was intrigued but wary. DLB was in Leeds and Sheffield as well as Birmingham, London and a smallish Manchester office, plus a volume debt recovery and remortgage business in Bradford. We were pretty dominant in Manchester and Liverpool and we had a big London office as well as our Hong Kong and New York offices. Putting the two together would create by far the biggest regional player in the UK with a much larger combined London operation and the beginnings of an international practice. Our strengths across the departments were largely complementary and, in principle, the combination made sense.

I had met the senior partner of DLB, Robin Smith, at the Grand National at Aintree in 1993 (the year of the first and only false start which completed and hence became the 'race that never was'). Also Sir Roland Smith was their chairman; I knew Roland fairly well through the Manchester United/Martin Edwards episode and had had dealings with him when he was chairman of House of Fraser (Harrods).

Dibb Lupton Broomhead had their new managing partner, Nigel Knowles, who had been appointed the previous year. We arranged a 'get to know you' dinner in London when, for the first time, I met Nigel, the man who was to become my soul mate, business partner, close confidant and friend for the remaining and most dramatic stage of my career.

That evening really was a fork in the road.

The next few weeks were pretty hectic. Because DLB had a reputation for being somewhat aggressive a decision was made to put a 'dove' onto our negotiating team. The dove was Philip Rooney, a commercial real estate partner from the Liverpool office who was bright and savvy but also seen as very fair-minded and unselfish. In these sorts of deals there is always a scramble for position. It was clear from the outset that both sides were happy to retain Sir Roland Smith as chairman of the merged firm. Ironically two or three years earlier, before the Mayson report, I had pushed the idea of bringing in a non-lawyer chairman and specifically listed Roland as a candidate. My then executive committee turned the idea down.

I was chairman of AW and Robin Smith was senior partner of DLB. Robin was a little older than I was so I suggested that I would take the role of deputy senior partner. Peter Wayte got a position on the merged board but seemed keen that Philip Rooney, rather than me, took another board position. Our executive committee were having none of that and graciously Philip declared that he was happy for me to take the slot, a typically selfless act on Philip's part.

We did some numbers and worked out that our combined fee income in the first full year should top £100 million and we could also improve profitability. Christopher Honeyman-Brown would be the chief operating officer and their finance director, David Liddle, would be the CFO with our finance director, the excellent Stephen Churchill, his deputy.

Another key board member was to be Andrew Chappell, a litigator who now ran the volume Bradford business as well as Will Holt who rightly took the credit for pushing the proposed merger in the first place.

The Legal Resources Group was still just about going despite the fact that two members, Pinsent and Simpson Curtis, had carved a secret deal to merge to form Pinsent Curtis without involving any of the other members in the discussion. That had created bad feelings at LRG.

The creation of Dibb Lupton Alsop (DLA) pretty much sounded the final death knell of LRG, in many ways a shame, since if those firms had agreed to merge together two to three years earlier they would have formed a pretty powerful, albeit UK practice, law firm. Equally I'm glad now that we didn't since, absent that deal, the opportunity to create what is now DLA came about.

The first months post-merger passed relatively smoothly other than a couple of DLB partners who took what seemed to be a very obscure, typical lawyers', issue and blow it up. It was a shame as they were good and valuable partners. They left to join Linklaters & Paines. In truth the merger had been about the creation of a very strong national law firm with a good-sized London office. We had a very good market position in the north-west, Yorkshire and a reasonably strong office in Birmingham, based on the acquired Needham & James firm, a reasonably diverse London office and our two offshore offices in Hong Kong and New York.

There was a lot of work to do but fairly soon problems emerged at board level from the most unexpected source. Will Holt was, I think quite wrongly, getting the blame for the departure of the two partners to Linklaters. Will could be explosive – I likened working with Will to living in a tent pitched next to a volcano! – but he was scrupulously honest and fair-minded.

It soon became clear that there was an issue between Robin Smith, Nigel and Andrew Chappell. I think Robin resented Nigel's ability to command a situation quickly and to articulate his position. Andrew Chappell believed himself to be a 'numbers' man who took an entirely dispassionate view of life and felt he spoke from a position of power because the volume business in Bradford appeared to produce a stream of consistent profits. Robin was a fan of Andrew and Andrew believed he was the man best placed to run the numbers and therefore the firm.

They both misjudged Nigel and, I have to say, me. In truth we had little of an international strategy and that was an area I passionately believed in. The reason was fairly simple. Looking forward, the law firms that would prosper in the decades to come would be those which could distinguish themselves by the type of work they undertook. There would be a role for the 'volume' players in insurance or litigation work and equally there would be a role for dedicated 'niche' players in areas like high net worth private clients and entertainment work.

What we had to do was represent the best companies, as well as ultra-high net worth individuals, who generated work which required a very high level of sector knowledge combined with lawyers at the very top of their game both intellectually and commercially, who could see how to get a deal done in a way that ultimately was not susceptible to 'nickel and diming' on fees. The two were incompatible. It was just not possible to provide a top service at a bargain-basement price.

It was that upper echelon where we needed to be and it was those clients who would expect a service that could be delivered consistently through an international platform and, as importantly, expect their law firm to open doors and make contacts and opportunities for them around the globe. It was that which would ultimately differentiate us from the pack.

We would outperform all our regional competitors if we had such a global practice but, as importantly, we would have as good, if not better, international offices as our Magic Circle competitors in London and New York. However, those firms would lack the massive outreach that we were accumulating in the regions.

That was in my view how we had to differentiate ourselves. To put all my thoughts down for an international strategy I needed two days uninterrupted, which I managed to grab in the unlikely setting of a hotel in Doncaster in the two days before a board meeting of MS International plc to be held there. I got it all down on paper and then shared it with Nigel. We tweaked it together in readiness for a strategy meeting of the board at a country house hotel near Bath.

I laid out the plan at the meeting. Probably not surprisingly, Peter was unenthusiastic, describing it as 'grandiose'.

The reader might think from time to time that I have been unduly hard on Peter Wayte. I have to make it clear that Peter is nothing if not a highly intelligent and committed individual. He did many good things for the firm and almost certainly he would say that he was the seat of realism on the seesaw to my other seat of unbridled optimism. He succeeded me as Senior Partner of DLA Piper after I stepped down and he continues his close relationship with the firm today as a consultant, as I do.

Peter was supported by Andrew Chappell and, to an extent, Robin. Of course, Nigel was strongly supportive and Roland Smith made a long speech about world economics and 'seismic shifts' which I think nobody really understood, thus enabling all sides to claim that Roland's 'world view' supported their position!

The bottom line was a fairly lukewarm commitment to progress the international plan. Within the next twelve months there would be one or two events that would (happily) set a clear way forward for the firm.

CHAPTER 28

Wheels and Deals

In New York Stephen Blair had established a small office
that specialised in reinsurance and this generated work in
New York and London. We had to decide how we might
grow our presence in the United States, arguably the world's
biggest and most profitable legal market. Nigel and I had
planned a trip to New York and beyond where we would
meet various law firms and pitch the DLA story to see if
we could find quality US firms who might be interested in
teaming up. At the same time Stephen and I knew a small
practice in New York run by an Englishman, Keith Berman.
Keith's practice was around very high value debt recovery. He
wanted to explore moving his practice into our New York
office where we had some surplus space.

Nigel and I visited a few firms in New York, then
Chicago and Minneapolis, before swinging back to New
York. The evening that we got back to New York we had
arranged to meet up for dinner at one of my favourite restaurants in New York, The Monkey Club. When I arrived,
Nigel and Stephen were there as was Keith Berman and
everyone was very jolly. I must say the notion of putting
Keith's office into ours seemed like a 'no brainer' to me. We
would sublet some surplus space and have the possibility

of getting other work out of Keith's clients where he only handled his specialist area. Keith acted for many of the large casino operators in Las Vegas. I remember that Keith was to become a consultant to DLA based on him getting a very small retainer and a percentage of business he introduced, a pretty simple and straightforward arrangement.

A day or two later Nigel and I returned to London. At an upcoming board meeting we were due to report on our visit to the States and also would report on the arrangement with Keith Berman, which seemed like a very minor matter. Before the board meeting Peter Wayte, Robin Smith and Andrew Chappell heard about the Berman 'deal' and immediately went into overdrive. They believed that Nigel and I had exceeded our powers and committed the firm to the acquisition of a business without the board's approval.

At the board meeting there was a massive row with the three of them demanding an 'investigation' and a full report. Robin took the position that all this proved he had been right and that Nigel should not lead the firm. We organised an 'off site' meeting at King's Cross station (don't ask me why there!) in some board meeting facility there. It was like *High Noon*. Robin proposed that Nigel stand down as managing partner and that Andrew replace him. Clearly at that point Andrew was supposed to step forward and confirm that he was ready, willing and able to step up to the plate.

He hesitated and then backed off, and we ended up with some woolly compromise where Andrew would shadow Nigel in a sort of deputy CEO role. This was totally unworkable nonsense. This meeting, though unpleasant, was actually very cathartic. It strengthened Nigel's hand as he had survived intact and had weakened Robin because he had lost. Within the next few months I had persuaded Robin to stand down to allow an election for the role of chairman, which would combine the role of chairman and senior partner. Sir Roland would remain on the board as a non-executive director, Christopher Honeyman-Brown would leave, and Andrew Chappell would take the role of chief operating officer. In all truth I had not enjoyed the role of deputy senior partner, in fact I loathed it. I've never liked being 'deputy' anything!

For a few days there was some jockeying as to who else might stand for the combined role of chairman and senior partner. Robin was trying to line up people that he thought might beat me. He approached two or three of the 'usual suspects' but in the end they decided not to stand. John Winkworth-Smith was a litigator from Yorkshire who had gone in to run the Birmingham office on the acquisition of Needham & James. John was a good sensible guy and he put himself up to run in the election in a two-horse race with me.

I thought that John would carry a lot of the Yorkshire vote, some Birmingham and part of London. I thought I would carry the north-west, a good part of London and also pick a few votes out of Yorkshire and Birmingham. John and I agreed that whoever lost would leave the firm so as not to make the job of the victor more difficult. I really didn't want to forecast the result and Andrew Chappell was doing his best to push John's candidature since he saw me as Nigel's ally.

In a secret national ballot the final draw was made in the Sheffield office by finance director David Liddle. John and I were in separate rooms. David walked in and announced to me that I had won – roughly by two thirds to one third. I walked through to John Winkworth-Smith and we shook hands and he wished me well. John left shortly afterwards to become a very successful mediator and also to write a novel. This left me on the bridge ready to steer the ship on the journey ahead.

During the senior partner election I had been working pretty hard for JJB Sports and my old friend and client Dave Whelan. JJB had gone public in 1994 and had been a roaring success, the share price having doubled and trebled. As ever when it is obvious that any area of activity is very profitable, others gather to join in the feast. That had happened with JJB and one particular company called Sports Division was becoming a major competitor.

Sports Division had started off in Scotland with Tom Hunter selling sports trainers from the back of a van. Tom had moved into the high street and teamed up with another entrepreneur, Philip Green. Philip had had mixed fortunes in his retailing career up to that point but had managed to acquire, at a knockdown price, the Olympus sports retail chain from Sears plc (of which more later). Tom and Philip had teamed up to create Sports Division which was now a serious rival to JJB and was actively considering its own IPO. It was clear that this would be a great fit with JJB, giving Olympus extra representation in Scotland as well as around London and the south-east. Dave had got the bit between his teeth and was keen to buy Sports Division. He had an initial meeting with Tom Hunter in Scotland and it seemed that a deal could be done, but only for cash. The price would have to be at or around £300 million.

JJB was debt free and generating lots of cash and the combined business would be very profitable. UBS Warburg, our investment bankers, could raise a £150 million bank loan and a further £150 million could be raised by placing some new JJB shares.

Dave and I flew up to Prestwich Airport where Tom picked us up and took us to his house in Troon. Tom Hunter was, and is, a very decent man as well as being a canny Scot. We went through the deal in great detail and finally agreed a price of £295 million in cash. Of this Tom would receive about £250 million and Philip Green, or rather Philip's wife Tina, in whose name their shares were, would pick up around £45 million. Tina had already moved to live in Monaco – good planning! Robert Glennie of McGrigor Donald was the lawyer representing Tom and Philip.

As corporate deals go it proceeded fairly smoothly with my usual corporate right-hand man, Jonathan Watkins, working by my side on the paperwork, plus Andrew Sherratt, a great corporate lawyer in London. Through the deal I spent a good deal of time with Robert Glennie and Tom Hunter and met Philip Green on a couple of occasions. Philip was, and is, a very different personality from Tom. His *modus operandi* could best be described as 'thrusting' but I got on pretty well with him, given that Dave Whelan had decided that he didn't want any direct negotiations with Philip. He would only deal with Tom. Within a few short years afterwards both Tom and Philip were honoured with knighthoods. Dave is still waiting!

When the deal was announced it was met in the City with cries that JJB was overpaying for the business. Within three years JJB's profits would soar to over £110 million and its market capitalisation would top £1 billion. The City got it wrong, at least on that occasion.

Sears plc was the retail group which had sold Olympus to Philip Green. Sears was a conglomerate that had been put together by the late Sir Charles Clore and included the British Shoe Corporation, many retail chains in shoes and clothing, Selfridges department store plus, importantly, a great number of freehold properties mainly in central London but also throughout the UK. In the mid-1990s it was run by a CEO called Liam Strong, whose background had been in marketing with British Airways. I had spent months studying the numbers for Sears and working out the breakup value of the huge collection of assets. The price of the shares was 'always £1' in City folklore. The price hovered around 100p a share for months and years on end. My estimate of the breakup value of the business was around twice that figure. Sears had little or no debt, good cash flow and some terrific assets not least of which was Selfridges.

My plan was to bid for Sears, using a mixture of cash and shares in a newly quoted listed company, with the intention that a Sears shareholder would get 50p in cash for each share, funded by a loan, and one new share in the new plc. The existing shareholders would end up with 90–95 per cent of the new plc with me and my team getting 5–10 per cent dependent on how we did in terms of asset realisations.

Through my old friend Victor Blank, I hired Charterhouse as our investment bank. I secured in principle a loan of about £450 million to cover the cash element of the bid from a major Japanese bank and I had John Timpson and Patrick Farmer lined up to sort out the British Shoe Corporation business. I would sell or spin Selfridges off as a first move and then sell all the retail business leaving the core real estate portfolio behind. Through an old friend I lined up Sir Patrick Sheehy, who was the former CEO and then chairman of British American Tobacco, to head up our bid. I also got hold of Stuart Rose (another one now knighted!) who was on holiday in the south of France and expressed himself to be very interested in running the retail businesses and selling them off. I even lined up one institutional share-holder who had a big stake in Sears to sell. Everything was ready to go and then, typically, the Japanese bank lost its bottle and we had to back off.

Philip Green, or rather Mrs Green in Monaco, took the £45 million we paid him for his shares in Sports Division, teamed up with the Barclay brothers, and launched a hostile bid for (guess what) Sears plc! After a bit of haggling a price was agreed for a recommended bid. Philip sold off all the retail businesses and got all his, and the Barclay brothers', money back, paid off the loan he had secured from the Bank of Scotland, and was left, for nothing, with the real estate. I calculated he had quickly turned his £45 million into about £200 million.

He then used that £200 million to take out British Home Stores (BHS) from the Storehouse Group and knock some sense into that, with much help from Richard Caring and, not long after that, secured a deal to bid for Arcadia where, by then, Stuart Rose was in charge.

Small world!

Philip managed to parlay £45 million into well over £1 billion in about three smart moves, kicked off by the Sears deal which I had so narrowly missed myself.

Good for him!

Back at the law firm, my election was followed up with the inevitable board 'retreat' where we bunked up in a smart country hotel in York for two nights to figure out how we would move the strategy forward. We made some progress in that we agreed that henceforth the senior partner (me) would chair the board and that Sir Roland Smith would become a non-executive director. I started pushing for the separation and then disposal of the volume debt collection and remortgaging business branch in Bradford, much to Andrew Chappell's annoyance. I simply couldn't see that on the one hand, we wanted to advise top companies in major deals, while on the other hand, the CEO was finding that his brother-in-law was also being represented by the firm in claiming back £100, being the excess on his motor insurance policy. It just didn't feel right.

At least we came away from that retreat with a strapline for our three-year plan – 'Top ten in the City. Dominant in the regions with a presence in Asia.'

By now Nigel was well and truly getting back into his stride following the departure of Robin Smith. Stewart Crowther had been mandated to grow the office in Hong Kong based around our strong marine and insurance practice. Unfortunately Andrew Chappell had annoyed Stephen Blair, who was running the New York office, so much that Stephen had decided to leave – a great loss. Nigel and I were getting to know each other better and better. To me it was vital that he and I worked as a team and that I played my role as chairman to his role of CEO. It had to be clear that Nigel as CEO ran the firm and that there was no chance of putting so much as a tissue paper between him and me. That would only work if Nigel discussed his planned moves with me and that we totally agreed on the strategy being pursued.

It was around this time that we had a particular piece of good fortune that was to stand us in good stead for many years afterwards.

CHAPTER 29

International Push

O ne of our national rival firms, Eversheds, had a Brussels
office which was run by David Church and his right-
hand man, Mike Pullen. David didn't feel that Eversheds had
the right strategy for him and his team and Nigel got into
talks with David to switch over to us. Nigel in full flow is
fairly hard to resist and I reckon that I can be fairly persuasive myself. David, Mike Pullen and the team came across
to us and as a result we had at least the makings of some sort
of European reputation. Five or six lawyers in Brussels was
hardly massive, but at least it was a start, and in David Church
we acquired a man who in my view was to do more than
almost anyone to help build our international firm.

Mike Pullen worked in the Brussels office with David and
specialised in what is probably best described as 'public law'.

Mike's background is unusual but in my view it typifies
why DLA Piper stands apart from its global peer group. Mike
was brought up in a travelling showground and circus – constantly moving from place to place – a nomadic lifestyle of
'Travellers'.

To this day I find it amazing that Mike put himself
through school and university and then qualified as a solicitor in England before moving over to Brussels to practise

international public law, regulatory issues on a global scale, advice to sovereign states; the list goes on and on.

Some time after 2000 Mike came to me to say that he thought it might be helpful to him and the firm if he took his New York Bar examinations so he could be dual qualified. I told him that these were quite difficult examinations and I wondered how he would ever have time to study. Mike said he had thought of this.

He normally finished in the office at about 10.00pm. He could then fit in four or five hours a night in distance learning for the New York Bar and still manage four hours' sleep – and the odd beer!

I told him to go for it. He did and qualified at the first attempt.

Short, stocky, rumbustious, pugnacious, gregarious, intensely bright and definitely a good man to have a beer with.

As I write these words Mike has just been advising one of the wealthiest countries in the world on their migrant worker and human rights record.

Through David we worked hard to put together some sort of European office strategy. We found law firms in Madrid, Barcelona, Paris and Germany, all of whom agreed to work together on a virtually exclusive basis, and the idea was that this would form the nucleus of our wider international practice. We intended to launch this new offensive at the International Bar Association, a major convention of law firms to be held in Barcelona where we took over one of the iconic Antoni Gaudí buildings for our launch cocktail party.

As a keen student of history I was keen that the new arrangement be given some sort of grand title. So was born the name for our 'groundbreaking' international strategy

– 'The Barcelona Accord' – which we announced to great fanfares at our launch event.

We thought we had invited about 100 or so people to our launch but it felt like the whole of the International Bar in Barcelona turned up and the building was overflowing, as was the champagne! People obviously knew a good thing when they saw it. Now, as well as the Hong Kong and Brussels offices (which were truly our own) we had 'affiliates' in Paris, Barcelona, Madrid and Cologne.

We were off!

Nigel and Andrew Chappell had a difficult relationship after Robin Smith left. I hardly felt close to Andrew since he had fairly openly opposed me for the position of senior partner. Quite why was not clear. Andrew was supposed to have taken over the role of chief operating officer from Christopher Honeyman-Brown but quite where the line was drawn between CEO and COO was less than clear. At about the same time, we got the chance to consolidate all our London operations under one roof at a brand new eleven-storey office building at 3 Noble Street, very close to our main London office at 125 London Wall. JP Morgan Chase, who were the main tenant of 125 London Wall, were expanding and wanted our floors. They were prepared to pay a hefty premium to get us to vacate the prestigious top floors which we occupied. At the same time, the landlord of 3 Noble Street wanted to give us an equally large premium to move in there and the combination of the two meant that there was more than enough cash to fit out the new office. Getting everybody in London under one roof would be a big boost and it would be a great statement to have our own prestigious office block in the heart of the City.

One day Nigel called me to say that Andrew Chappell had been to see him and wanted to leave. In truth I was not surprised. Andrew needed to be completely in control and that just was not going to happen so long as Nigel and I were around. We had an annual partners' conference upcoming and that was taken as the event at which Andrew announced he was going. He wanted to make a farewell speech to all the partners, which he did, although it was a rather strange and rambling affair with one or two fairly 'off-colour' observations and a particularly biting reference to a management (presumably Nigel and me) 'who seemed to prioritise Shanghai over Sheffield'. It was better for all that Andrew pursued his goals elsewhere.

Altogether we were building a stronger and stronger team.

Andrew Darwin, a first-class corporate lawyer who had started as Nigel's trainee in Sheffield, now headed up the corporate practice nationally. Philip Rooney in Liverpool headed up the national real estate practice, Neil Micklethwaite litigation, David Bradley human resources and there were many other good and strong partners.

Following the untimely demise of our London managing partner, Paul Nichols, to a massive stroke, Nigel and I picked real estate partner Catherine Usher to head up the London office. Catherine was a first-rate lawyer, as well as a no-nonsense pragmatist who had a knack for carrying the troops along with her. She was to remain in that role successfully for many years.

In Hong Kong Stewart Crowther was continuing to make good progress and had hired some excellent new partners, as well as expanding the office to the extent that we now had wonderful space in the upper floors of the Bank of China Tower in Central. I was still a very regular visitor to Hong Kong and was working closely with Stewart on the Asia strategy. The 'handover' to mainland China had gone smoothly since 1997 and the fears of my old executive committee at

AW of the early 1990s of the communists overrunning the former colony, stealing our clients' accounts and holding everyone hostage had not materialised! Stephen Pan of World Wide Shipping continued to be a great friend of the firm and a sound advisor.

At last, despite concerns from Peter Wayte, we got our Singapore office going, sending a good shipping partner, Mike Melwood Smith, down there to team up with a good local practice headed up by one Desmond Ong, a great lawyer and an even greater character! Stewart had also brought another great insurance and marine lawyer, Roy Chan, into Hong Kong and among Roy's clients were mainland China's second largest insurance company, a behemoth called Ping An Insurance, headed up by a dynamic entrepreneur called Peter Ma whom I had met and got on with well.

Ping An were about to move into Shanghai in a big way and wanted Roy to open an office for us there to head up our own expansion into the mainland. We applied for a licence to practise in Shanghai and I went up to Beijing with Stewart and one of our Hong Kong Chinese Mandarin-speaking partners. We met at the Ministry of Justice in Beijing. The official dealing with our application was amazing. He knew more about the firm than I did. He told me that he thought we would be a very good addition to the legal scene in Shanghai because not only did we have offices in London (like all the others, he said) but also Manchester, Liverpool, Leeds, Birmingham and Sheffield. He wanted to see representation in Shanghai for the industrial heartlands of the UK. He would make sure that our application was shuffled up to the very top of an extremely high pile of applications.

Result!

We also realised that in Hong Kong we must have more 'local' partners. Most of the other London firms were rotating

London partners on three-year tours of duty. Of course the clients in Hong Kong and Asia saw straight through that. Why bother getting to know a partner if in a couple of years' time they would be heading back to the UK?

Stewart had brought in another shipping partner, Nick Mallard, who was an old China hand and a generally great guy. Our really great coup was to bring in Mabel Lui, a very feisty, and fun, Hong Kong Chinese partner, and her two fellow Chinese partners, Horace Wen and Ivan Ng, who had all been part of the Coudert office in Hong Kong. Coudert was an old-line US firm which had done very well as Coudert Brothers in the US and Paris and had also built a good practice in Asia which was beginning to crumble. We capitalised on that by hiring partners not only in Hong Kong but also in Bangkok and Beijing.

Mabel is a great lawyer and also a very strong character and she made sure that the Hong Kong office, which by now was growing very rapidly, was a very healthy mix of Chinese and European lawyers. After a lot of hard work our Asia strategy was really starting to pay off with a large Hong Kong office and growing offices in Shanghai, Singapore and Bangkok and later added to by a very significant office in Beijing.

CHAPTER 30

DLA is Born

After our 1996 merger we carried on with the name Dibb Lupton Alsop for three or four years but in truth neither Nigel nor I liked the name. It was awkward to pronounce for non-UK clients and lawyers and, in any event, now we were becoming increasingly international it was just an encumbrance as a brand. We started to refer to the firm as 'DLA' and got people internally comfortable with using that name. One Tuesday afternoon sitting in the office in London I started doodling (obviously I must have been 'between' large corporate assignments to have had the time to doodle!). I played around with a few ideas which then morphed into a square with DLA in the corner as follows:

And so our new name and logo were finally born.

This was a fairly unusual move for a law firm then but there were precedents in the world of the Big Five – soon to become Big Four – accountants like KPMG, PWC, E&Y, so there was space for a law firm to do the same. It would work so much better internationally where in a given country we could use the brand together with local branding, so DLA Nordic or DLA International, and it was so much easier for everyone from around the world to associate with, let alone pronounce. Adopting it also gave us a good opportunity to respond when people asked 'What does DLA stand for?'. The answer, of course, was and is that it stands for 'quality, assurance and a brand that speaks on a global platform'!

So Dibb Lupton Alsop disappeared and we became DLA.

In Europe the 'Barcelona Accord' firms were a mixed success. For example, in Paris we had a very good firm called Ginestie where the senior partner, Philippe Ginestie, was an excellent corporate lawyer and, at partnership conferences, pronounced in presentations to all partners in true Gallic fashion that his association with DLA was 'a love affair' and that he was quite wedded to the union. However, our experience was that 'associations' never really quite work. The office must be a true DLA office and there has to be a single brand portraying the firm and its values throughout the world.

Much as Philippe believed that we had a 'love affair', whenever Nigel or I tried to persuade him to fold his business into DLA fully, Philippe pronounced either that he wasn't ready, or that his wife wouldn't let him do it! Likewise in Germany we had a very good firm called Görg but the partners as a whole couldn't bring themselves to go the whole hog and become DLA Germany. Ulrich Jüngst was the main mover and shaker at the firm and he could see the future very clearly. We all tried to convince his other partners but in the end they didn't want to give up their independence and so we agreed terms with Ulrich to join us and build DLA Germany from scratch.

In reality the 'buy and build' strategy in Europe seemed to be a good way to go. We adopted a similar approach in Milan with Federico Sutti and Madrid with Kenneth Bonavia, while, at the same time, bringing in good local firms in Brussels and then Amsterdam and Antwerp. Our main message was important. We were not an Anglo-Saxon London-centric British firm out to colonise the rest of the world like many of our rivals. We truly believed that what we were creating was a new international law firm unlike any other where our partners from all over the world would join together in the adventure of creation. Our country offices would include as far as possible the cultural values of the region, while the office looked like any other DLA office whether in Birmingham or Bangkok, Shanghai or Sheffield. In Scandinavia we were very fortunate to meet up with Henning Øglænd from Oslo. He is another very far-sighted man in the same mould as Ulrich Jüngst and Federico Sutti. Through Henning we put together DLA Nordic.

I suppose it's true of any business that the really hard part is the early years when there is everything to prove. With disciples like David Church relentlessly travelling around Europe and the rest of the world from about 2000 onwards, the snowball effect was remarkable.

Sir Roland Smith, who continued as a senior consultant advisor to the firm, summed up our approach in this extract from our 2001 annual report (note the corporate analogy!):

The key to DLA's rapid growth has been the ability of the management to delineate a clearly achievable vision and, more importantly, to take the incremental day to day steps required in order to deliver on that vision. The strength of purpose among everybody I have encountered at DLA not only at Board level but throughout the Firm, indicates that DLA will continue to be at the forefront of the professional service market.

The phrase 'strength of purpose' to me sums it up.

I don't think a day ever went by without us, mainly Nigel and me, constantly piling on the momentum in a relentless drive forward to get to our very clear goal – to be the world's foremost law firm. I was still trying to keep up with my client work. Increasingly that meant focusing on client relationships and supervising transactions rather than actually drafting the documents myself.

JJB Sports, where I had been on the board since 1998, had been going from strength to strength although, as we shall see, that was slowly getting into choppy waters.

Timpson as a private company was also powering ahead and again, I retained my non-executive directorship there. We had absorbed one of our main competitors, Automagic, where we had bought their substantial business out of administration and soon would acquire the biggest of our competitors, Mister Minit, which by then gave us truly national coverage as the nation's service provider in shoe repairs, key cutting, dry cleaning, watch repairs and increasingly, locksmiths and other ancillary businesses.

MS International, where I had been a non-executive director since 1983, had been through mixed times after we sold the coal mining equipment business to Dobson Park. If ever there was immaculate timing that was it! To be honest, some of the companies we had bought with the cash received from Dobson Park had been less than exciting and we were now back to focusing on our strengths of supplying the navies of the world with 30-millimetre deck mounted guns using our world breaking 'optical fire director' technology (in short, keeping the gun on target in the very heaviest of seas) as well as 'arms' for forklift trucks, where we were and are world number two, and forecourt structures for filling stations across Europe.

My original private client practice, including the landed estates of the Cholmondeley family, the Longleat estate and the Bristol estates, had passed over to Glenn Hurstfield and in 1997 we had, much against my better judgement, decided to exit private client work entirely. Glenn, together with Andrew Young and the rest of the team, had moved with our blessing to Lawrence Graham in London, though I still maintained my relationship with Glenn and Lord Cholmondeley.

Sadly John, the seventh Marquess of Bristol, had died in 1999, having lived in his 45 years at least two if not three lifetimes.

Glenn had also taken over the trust work for the Mostyn estates in north Wales, which included the ownership of the coastal town of Llandudno, although I remained, and am still today, a trustee and director of Mostyn Estates.

CHAPTER 31

Banking

A fairly certain way to grow a commercial law firm is to act for at least one major bank and preferably two, three or more.

Banks are terrific clients who produce a large amount of (normally) high quality legal work. They lend money (sometimes) and when they do any significant loan needs to be documented, normally at the borrower's cost.

If the loan runs into choppy waters it normally moves into 'intensive care' or whatever other soothing and helpful description ('business support') masks the true summary that the bankers in this section are hard as nails, charging their struggling clients substantial fees for advice, big fees for renewed facilities (even if only short term) and if they have to move to administration then the bank's lawyers move in and sell off all the assets and/or 'restructure' the banking facilities.

Many a great law firm has been built on a strong banking relationship.

In England one of the best and earliest examples has been the 'magic circle' firm Freshfields. James Freshfield joined the firm around the turn of the 18th century and thereafter the firm became called Freshfields. As far back as 1743 Freshfields became the solicitor to the recently created Bank of England and one Samuel Dodd secured the instruction.

Freshfields were in at the start of the global banking industry through their connection (which continues today) with the Bank. Through that relationship Freshfields took on countless other quality clients introduced by the Bank.

Coward Chance (later to merge with Clifford Turner to create Clifford Chance) had been the solicitors for the Midland Bank for decades. For a long time Midland Bank was the biggest bank in the world and through that had representative banking relationships across the globe.

As each of those overseas banks realised it was essential to have their own representative office in the financial centre of the world, London, they asked Midland to recommend lawyers, and so more often than not Coward Chance was put in the frame and as a result built a massive banking practice.

Cameron Kemm Norden (now CMS Cameron McKenna) were the 'house' solicitors for Lloyds Bank and literally had one or more partners who walked around the head office of Lloyds talking to each manager and picking up instructions as they went along.

In my early days in Manchester my bank was the National Westminster, and my constant efforts to get instructions from NatWest were met with a fairly standard response which was that the bank's lawyers were Wilde Sapte in London, and locally in Manchester Slater Heelis. Interesting to note that now Wilde Sapte has ceased to exist as an independent practice having merged some time ago into Dentons, and Slater Heelis (despite my attempts to woo it) disappeared into the welcoming arms of Addleshaw Goddard.

Fortunately I had started to court Royal Bank of Scotland in Manchester with much more success and so another lasting bank relationship commenced for my growing firm. Ken

Duncombe was the northern chief of RBS and became a good friend and ally. When Ken moved to London (about the same time as me) to head up corporate banking there, again Ken made sure that we were well and truly in the frame.

Later, of course, NatWest was acquired by Royal Bank of Scotland and instructions then started to flow from the much-enlarged client.

From my early years in Manchester I had got to know the Bank of Scotland. There was a manager back in the early 1980s called Mike Murray based in Manchester who was a Scot, with a very broad accent when sober and almost totally indecipherable after a few drinks. Nevertheless, or perhaps because of this, he and I got on famously and when Paul Webster joined us back in 1986 with Tony Neary, Paul worked hard in developing a thriving banking practice. As well as the Bank of Scotland I had, as I say, got to know Royal Bank of Scotland and Paul had developed the Irish banks, Bank of Ireland and Allied Irish. We had represented Barclays for decades so our banking client base was pretty compelling. Mike Murray's number two was a very able young banker called Stuart Middleton and we worked closely with Stuart in the early days of leveraged buyouts, a lot of which had been built on our experience with Timpson, Norwest Holst and other large MBOs.

When I moved to the London office in 1989 Paul moved with me and teamed up with Mark Vickers of Wilkinson Kimbers to create a London-based banking practice which was to go on to become one of our great success stories.

Mark had the Clydesdale Bank in his portfolio and Mike Collins, who had left the firm in 1989 because of his 'shafting' by some of his former partners, had joined the Canadian Royal Trust Bank but then rejoined DLA later, eventually to head up the banking practice in London.

In the Manchester office a very bright young banking partner called Simon Woolley had joined in the late 1980s and also had built a close relationship with the Bank of Scotland as well as other long-standing clients (through Alsops and Brett Ackerley and Cooke), like Barclays. During the 1990s the banking department flourished and I continued my relationship with the prime movers, particularly at the Bank of Scotland. Two emerging leaders in London were Graeme Shankland and Craig Wilson. Craig and Graeme were very focused on supporting the private equity market where the bank would provide the senior debt in acquisitions mainly by the big private equity houses like Permira, Candover and a host of others.

It was the private equity players who were of course making the big killings in this marketplace. The bank would get a good fee for agreeing to provide the senior debt but normally they were lending at very tight margins and had no share of the upside when the company was eventually sold on. I spoke often to Graeme and Craig about this and I basically felt that it was unfair to the bank that they were not getting their share of the equity profits for the risk that they were taking.

Through Graeme and Craig I met Peter Cummins who was based in Edinburgh but who was rapidly becoming one of the main leaders in the bank. Peter felt the same way about the leveraged acquisition market and he had decided to set up the 'principal finance' division of the bank, where the bank would not only put up the debt but also all or part of the equity and so get a bigger share of the rewards for the large deals.

The principal finance division kicked off with a team get-together and dinner at the Cameron House Hotel in Loch Lomond and Peter and Graeme invited me up to be a dinner guest and then give the main after-dinner speech at their inaugural dinner. This was very flattering and I think was also a reflection of the close relationship that we enjoyed.

This relationship continued to blossom and grow, with Simon Woolley and corporate partner Jonathan Watkins becoming the lead team for the bank in some huge deals including Philip Green's acquisition of Arcadia, the Barclay brothers' takeover of the *Daily Telegraph* and dozens of others.

Within three or four years the Bank of Scotland was to become the largest client of the firm in the UK, closely followed by Barclays and Royal Bank of Scotland. The Bank of Scotland 'integrated' finance division also became hugely successful and profitable for the bank. About five years after the inauguration dinner at Cameron House in Scotland I was invited by Peter Cummins and Graeme to the celebration dinner held at The Grove near Watford. Again I gave the main after-dinner speech and everyone was in great spirits.

The team were the kings of the jungle!

Some four to five years later, in the great banking crash that was to engulf the world at the end of 2008, the Bank of Scotland was humbled and was forced into the arms of Lloyds Bank, where, by then, my old friend Sir Victor Blank was chairman. Most of the blame for the bank's woes was piled on Peter Cummins who was made the scapegoat.

I thought this was totally unfair. I knew at the time that Peter and his team were under greater and greater pressure, from the likes of Sir James Crosby and Andy Hornby, to push and push for more and more lending to up the profits of the entire group as other divisions produced mundane performances. Peter was a lateral thinker in banking and his one fault was perhaps that he regarded real estate as almost risk-free, particularly residential property where he just kept buying and lending. He will be right about that eventually!

In April 2013 James Crosby and Andy Hornby, together with former chairman Lord (Dennis) Stevenson, were all heavily censured by the Parliamentary Banking Commission who decided that they were the men behind a 'colossal failure of senior management' that left the bank needing a £20.5 billion bailout from the taxpayer.

The former risk director of the bank, who had been sacked as a Jeremiah by James Crosby, said at that time that Peter Cummins had been made a scapegoat for the risky decisions of others.

No matter how bad each crisis (in my lifetime 1975, 1990, 2000 and 2008), there is only one thing that is certain. The next generation will forget and it will happen all over again and again.

Plus ça change, plus c'est la même chose!

CHAPTER 32

Future Strategy

On 11 September 2001, which became known as 9/11 (the telephone number used for emergencies in the USA, a coincidence certainly appreciated by the perpetrators of the attack), the world was stunned when at just before 9.00am Eastern Standard Time a passenger airliner was flown into one of the Twin Towers in downtown Manhattan, New York. A few may have thought it was an accident but when, 40 minutes later, another airliner was flown into the second tower, no one was under any illusion that these were anything but deliberate attacks. This realisation was reinforced when another aircraft was flown into the Pentagon in Washington, and finally when a fourth aircraft crashed in Pennsylvania, killing all those on board.

Two and a half hours that changed the history of the world:

7.59am   Mohamed Atta departs on American Airlines flight 11, which under his control will crash into the World Trade Center

8.18am   American Airlines flight 11 is taken over by Mohamed Atta and other hijackers

8.46am	American Airlines flight 11 crashes into the World Trade Center North Tower
9.03am	United Airlines flight 175 crashes into the World Trade Center South Tower
9.37am	American Airlines flight 77 crashes into the Pentagon
9.59am	South Tower of World Trade Center collapses
10.03am	United Airlines flight 93 crashes into a farm in Shanksville, Pennsylvania
10.28am	North Tower of World Trade Center collapses

The mighty USA was under attack on its home soil, the first time since the Japanese attack on Pearl Harbor in December 1941. The president, George W. Bush, was visiting a school in Florida, and was quickly bundled into the presidential aircraft and flown around while it was ascertained how serious the situation was and whether any more attacks were likely. Needless to say, all other aircraft throughout the USA were grounded.

At about 3.00pm French time, Nigel called me on my vacation from London where I was reading by the pool. Nigel said, 'Turn on your television, the world is going mad!'

In the very short term, the effects for business were little short of calamitous. Everyone seemed to freeze. The truth was that there was a mild recession in place anyway. The so-called 'dotcom bubble' had burst the year before, after any company involved with the internet had seen its shares rise to ridiculous and, with hindsight, clearly unsustainable, heights.

Lawyers, like everyone else, had to cope with the dotcom bubble. As with the railways in the 1840s and automobiles in the 1920s, the internet in the 1990s was going to transform people's lives (and, of course, they all did, but not quite as fast, or as profitably for most speculators, as some would have the gullible believe at the time).

In 1995 Nicholas Negroponte, author of *Being Digital*, wrote that 'digital living' would reduce everyone's dependence on time and place, close the generation gap and contribute to 'world unification'. Microsoft chief Bill Gates, who did make money faster than any speculator could have predicted, wrote in his book, *The Road Ahead*: 'The information superhighway will change our culture as dramatically as Gutenberg's press did in the Middle Ages.'

The impact of internet-based shares on the stock market was startling. Yahoo!, after only one year of operation and with annual sales of less than $5 million, went to a price on the first day of dealings on the market which made the company worth $850 million.

Edward Chancellor wrote of the dotcom bubble:

> The boom in internet stocks strengthened in 1998. By the end of the year, the market values of leading internet companies competed with those of America's largest corporations; the market capitalisation of Charles Schwab, the discount broker with online trading facilities, overtook that of Merrill Lynch; eBay, a recently founded online auction house, outstripped Sotheby's; and AOL, the internet service provider, became more valuable than the Disney Corporation. The market capitalisation of Yahoo! was over 800 times its earnings and over 180 times its sales revenue, or $35 million per employee. The share price of Amazon.com, an online bookstore, multiplied 18 times during 1998 (despite the company's escalating losses). One fund manager described it as 'the most outrageously priced equity in the world', but advised buying the stock nevertheless.

Fred Hickey, the editor of *High-Tech Strategist*, called the upsurge 'the greatest investment mania since Tulip Bulbs'. In late January 1999 Alan Greenspan, chairman of the Federal reserve, observed that internet valuations were 'pie in the sky' and that investors were indulging in a lottery, since most internet companies were doomed to failure and their shares would become worthless.

On 16 March 2000, as the dotcom boom neared its peak, the Dow Jones index enjoyed its biggest one-day points rise, no less than 499.19 points to 10,630.6.

Just over a year later it suffered its biggest one-day fall, 684.81 points, when the market re-opened on 17 September 2001 after the attack on the World Trade Center six days earlier.

★

By 2003/04 I was starting to think about my future. I was 57 going on 58 and, in the previous 25 years or so, had enjoyed success in the law beyond even my wildest dreams. I had managed to save a fair amount of cash in my pension saving schemes which were invested in God knows what by two or three insurance companies. I decided to set up for my own benefit, but then also as an umbrella facility for all DLA partners, a dedicated Self Invested Pension Plan (SIPP) through my advisor David Mawson and the actuaries Barnett Waddingham. In reality I had always lived very comfortably off the law with a decent income although, with the exception of the Timpson deal, I had not made any serious capital gains and, like most of my peers, most of my capital was locked up in the house we lived in. I had a decent amount of cash in my SIPP and I wanted to find a good home for it.

I had always been interested in commercial property, and at that time it seemed to be good value and in a cycle that looked like it was more likely to go up than down. I wouldn't be able to buy much myself but I worked out that if I pooled my cash with that of a few other DLA partners and friends we could buy some decent investments. Together with one of my Manchester property partners, Roy Beckett, I started to look around the market with a local commercial property agent.

We looked at lots of stuff but eventually came across a building right in the centre of Manchester that had been renovated and had just been let on a new fifteen-year lease to US retailer Tommy Hilfiger. Based on the purchase price the yield (income) from the property was about 7 per cent plus and when I enquired from my bank, Coutts, they said they would lend 65 per cent of the price at 5 per cent interest, so cash-flow wise we would be ahead of the game from day one. I rounded up some of my partners and pals and we bought the building.

Suddenly I was inundated with calls from agents. I was the 'new buyer on the block'. I knew I needed help. Through an old friend and occasional business partner, Ron Stratton, who had built a very successful car dealership business covering Rolls-Royce, Bentley, Ferrari, Aston Martin, Land Rover and BMW, I was reintroduced to Stan Annison and Martin Schuler who had recently retired as CEO and CFO of the Orbit Group, owned by a local, extremely successful property tycoon, Peter Jones. Peter lived close to me in Alderley Edge in the 1970s and I used to play snooker at his house from time to time.

I got together with Stan and Martin and in short, together with Ron, we decided to set up a new company to arrange and manage property syndicates. I would be responsible for legal structuring and fundraising, Stan would find the deals and Martin would arrange the finance. They were both very close to Rothschild Bank in Manchester so, almost from the outset, Rothschild also became our partner as they would underwrite the equity funding for each deal while we would approach our syndicate database on a 'deal by deal' basis.

I called it Lanebridge. Our timing was perfect and soon we had bought about ten different properties, all of which looked like they had a lot of upside potential.

(Later we sold most of those properties at a very good profit. In 2007 we sold the company to Rothschild. At that time prices for commercial property were going ever upwards with the Irish buying heavily. I wanted to sell everything and move into cash and farmland – unfortunately I was outvoted!)

At the same time at JJB Sports Duncan Sharpe, Dave Whelan's son-in-law, had sadly taken his own life in tragic circumstances and we had brought in Tom Knight as CEO who had spent some time at rival JD Sports. JJB was still doing well but we had branched out by buying discount retailer TJ Hughes, in a £45-million deal that the 'market' didn't like because 'they' felt it would be a distraction for management.

At the same time one particular rival, Sports & Soccer run by one Mike Ashley, was snapping at our heels discounting even our very keen prices, so increasingly the pre-eminence that we had enjoyed in the sports retailing market was being challenged. This was not really surprising; whenever everyone sees someone else making money in a particular activity, they want to try to take a part of it. That must be the most natural instinct of the human (and animal) race!

At the annual general meetings of JJB, Dave Whelan hated going through the boring process of putting through resolutions and dealing with technical questions so he tended to leave that to me. Dave didn't particularly like dealing with 'the City' and basically thought that would be better done by me. We started talking about me taking over as non-executive chairman of JJB Sports plc.

Nigel Knowles and I were still thriving on (almost) every new day. The empire that we had built together now spanned not only the UK – Edinburgh, Glasgow, Leeds, Manchester, Sheffield, Liverpool, Birmingham and a now very large London office – but also Europe, with our own offices in pretty much every major European city, as well as Hong Kong, Singapore, Bangkok, Shanghai and Beijing and, with the acquisitions of the former Ernst & Young legal team, good-sized offices in Moscow and St Petersburg. We had close relationships with Philips Fox in Australia, Cliffe Dekker in South Africa and growing influence in the Indian subcontinent.

There was one obvious glaring hole in our 'global' firm but quite intentionally so. We did not want to seek out a partner there until we had a firm grip on the rest of the world. We knew that the stronger we got in Europe and Asia, the bigger our bargaining chip would be at the table of the biggest legal marketplace in the world.

The United States of America had to be next and now we were ready!

CHAPTER 33

The Big One

Our strategy since the DLA merger in 1996 had really been very focused on expansion in Europe and Asia. When I took over as senior partner in July 1998 from Robin Smith we had held a two-day board retreat and we felt it was important to summarise the strategy in a simple strapline so that the board and the whole firm could stay focused and concentrate on the task ahead.

Our strapline coming out of the July 1998 retreat was: 'Top ten in the City. Dominant in the Regions with a presence in Asia.'

It is interesting to look back now and think why that strategy was adopted – and to think how realistic and/or scaleable it was.

'Top ten in the City'? Realistically, at that time we were certainly outside the top ten in the City of London. We were probably, at a guess, somewhere around fifteen. However, given our strengths in banking, corporate and real estate, it was certainly conceivable that we could build and aspire to be in the top ten within three years. By 2001 I think we had made the lower ranks of the top ten, particularly on the back of our growing work for the Bank of Scotland, Barclays and RBS.

'Dominant in the Regions'? This was definitely achievable

given that in the north-west we were one of the top three firms and likewise in Yorkshire. In Birmingham and the Midlands we were outside the top three but that was to change considerably as we hired top corporate lawyers, Chris Rawstron and Russell Orme, so within three years we were in the top three.

We never strayed into the north-east or the south-west since in our view both markets were not large enough to sustain law firms of our size. We did not exist north of the border in Scotland, but that was to change within the following three years with the acquisition of Scottish firm Bird Semple in Edinburgh and Glasgow. We became the first 'English' firm to 'acquire' a Scottish firm but found the Scottish Law Society to be entirely helpful to break ground in putting the deal together.

'A presence in Asia'? This sounds like a very modest ambition but probably intentionally so. There were still a number of voices on the board that railed against international expansion but yet in my mind, and increasingly in Nigel's, the main way we were going to differentiate ourselves, particularly from the heavyweight national and regional firms, was to have a strong international practice that could offer support to business clients around the world. So our 'presence in Asia' back in 1998 was the office in Hong Kong run by Stewart Crowther which was building steadily.

By 2001 we were ready for the next ramp up and had persuaded the board that we had to be a very strong 'European', as opposed to British, law firm. It seemed to us that none of our competitors was trying to grasp that particular prize and if we could, it would be a very strong differentiation that would set us apart from our rivals.

So in 2001 we changed the strategic strapline to: 'Top five full service European law firm with a significant presence in Asia.'

It is worth dissecting that strapline for a moment.

'Top five' sounded very grand, but in fact if we could push forward through most European capitals over the next three years we could certainly be in the top five in Europe.

'Full service'? Here we were differentiating ourselves from one or two of the 'Magic Circle' firms, who were very focused on corporate work, whereas we put out full teams in litigation, real estate, competition and regulatory, human resources (employment), insurance and commercial work.

Again, it was a worthwhile differentiation.

'European' because in pushing out across Europe we had seen so many of our competitors seek to 'colonise' mainland Europe with their 'City' or 'British' culture. We were different. We were building from scratch and could offer our prospective partners a full seat at the table to be in at the beginning of the creation of a new force in the European and global legal marketplace. This was truly different.

Now we added 'significant' to our presence in Asia because we had to steal a march by getting into the key Asian markets as soon as possible. By and large our partners thought we were doing a good job in expanding the firm so would buy into this rollout plan.

By 2001 we had finally opened in Singapore by sending Mike Melwood Smith from Hong Kong and hooking up with Desmond Ong and his partners, which also brought us small offices in Bangkok and Jakarta. We soon added greatly to our strength there by bringing in Peter Shelford from Clyde & Co. on the shipping side and Peter became a very steady influence in Singapore and Bangkok over the following years. In 2002 Roy Chan moved from Hong Kong to Shanghai as our licence came through with the support of client Ping An Insurance.

By that time I was spending a good deal of time in Asia

pushing ahead with the plan. I found the whole area to be pulsing with innovation and so vibrant compared to Europe. Shanghai was like nothing I had ever experienced before. To take a huge city, of a comparable size to London, and then redevelop pretty much everything south of the Thames, sums up the approach taken in Shanghai, and was simply incredible. The more I got to understand the Chinese mind and general approach to business the more it fascinated me. So 'significant' would certainly summarise our intentions for Asia and we achieved that and much more over that three-year period from 2001–04.

In Europe over those three years we had a tremendous push to live up to our plan. Starting in Holland with Schut & Grosheide, we ramped in Belgium (Caestecker), Austria and eastern Europe (Weiss Tessbach), Italy (Federico Sutti and the team from Coudert), Germany (Ulrich Jüngst, formerly of Görg, who put together a world-class team of lawyers in all the major German cities), Henning Øglænd in Scandinavia and Kenneth Bonavia in Spain. They were all part of the single firm of DLA.

The momentum of the much-recanted plans of the Big Five accounting firms to move into legal services had come to something of a juddering halt with the quite remarkable, almost overnight, disappearance of Arthur Andersen in the wake of the Enron scandal.

This gave us a great opportunity as we made some good acquisitions from the legal arms of the Big Five (soon the Big Four) across the UK but also in Belgium and vitally, in Moscow and St Petersburg, where we managed to acquire the whole legal arm of Ernst & Young. This made us one of the largest law firms in the Russian Federation.

So by 2004 we were certainly ready for the next big step.

We had not pushed any particular relationship in the USA

since the trip Nigel and I had made over there in 1997. The New York office had been disbanded under the short-lived reign of Andrew Chappell and we had not replaced it. Donovan Leisure had imploded due to poor management and my old friend Rod Hills was by now in semi-retirement in Washington DC.

As usual, it was the ever resourceful David Church who took on the ground work for the biggest deal we had pulled off so far. I think that a former Donovan partner had moved to Piper Rudnick but, for whatever reason, David had got an introduction to the firm and he and Nigel set off to the States to follow up.

In 1887 William Marbury had started his own law firm in Baltimore. At that time Baltimore was one of the most prominent industrial cities in the United States as well as being a major port. The firm appears to have attracted new partners, hence the name changes over the following decades, and the firm ultimately became Marbury Miller & Evans.

In 1952 Marbury Miller & Evans merged with Piper, Watkins, Avirett and Egerton to create the largest law firm in Baltimore, Piper and Marbury. Piper and Marbury specialised in corporate finance, mergers and acquisitions and real estate development and financing. Over the next 50 years or so the firm developed a national reputation with major practices in corporate and securities law and litigation.

In 1927 in San Diego on the West Coast a cousin of President Woodrow Wilson, Gordon Gray, joined up with Judge William Cary to form Gray Cary. Gray Cary quickly grew to be the largest law firm in San Diego with a heavy emphasis on litigation and a glittering client list including leading San Diego headquartered companies, as well as a number of *Fortune* 500 clients.

Likewise, in 1969 Ware & Freidenrich was formed in

Palo Alto by Leo Ware and John Freidenrich and was in at the start of the Silicon Valley explosion of technology. It quickly became one of the leading corporate and intellectual property practices and later John Freidenrich chaired Mission Partners, one of Silicon Valley's most prominent venture capital firms.

In 1936 Harry Rudnick and Sydney Wolfe started their own firm in Chicago. From its early days that firm developed a speciality area around large commercial real estate developments and franchise law. The firm acted on the development of the famed Prudential Plaza in Chicago and Harry Rudnick helped to establish the International Franchise Association. In November 1999 Piper and Marbury joined forces with Rudnick and Wolfe, which, at that time, was noted as the largest domestic merger of equals in US law firm history, to create Piper Rudnick.

In 2002 Piper Rudnick brought in the major government affairs practice in Washington DC, Verner, Liipfert, Bernhard, McPherson and Hand and, in the following year, Piper created its Boston office by hiring some top partners out of Hill and Barlow. In 2004 this was followed up by adding Steinholt and Falconer in San Francisco and, at about the same time, a strategic alliance was struck with the former US secretary of defence, William S. Cohen, to bring in the Cohen Group, an international strategic business consulting firm.

Today Hugh Marbury, the great-grandson of the Baltimore office founder in 1887, is a partner in DLA Piper's Baltimore/Mount Washington office. Paul Rudnick (the son of Chicago office founder, Harry) and his son Bill Rudnick are both partners in DLA's Chicago office today. Gray Cary had by then merged with Ware & Freidenrich to create a major California law firm.

When Nigel and David returned from their visit to the USA they were very excited. So often when we had dealt with US law firms in the past we had found them to be quite blinkered and very set in their cultural belief that it was 'their way or the highway'. Nigel reported that in Piper Rudnick we had potentially found a US firm that was very similar to us in background, culture and ambition.

The publication *Legal Week* noted that other legal practices were keen on the deal. Under the headline: 'Rival firms back DLA to merge with Piper Rudnick', it wrote on 6 February 2004:

> Three quarters of respondents said that a merger with PR would be a good move for the Top 10 UK firm, according to the *Legal Week* Big Question survey of more than 100 partners ... DLA has reached the stage in its evolution where it needs a US merger to go on to the next stage ... Clive Garston of Halliwell Landau said, 'Nigel [Nigel Knowles] is very capably driving the firm forward so, if he sets his sights on a US merger, then he will do it.'

The 'Piper' part of the firm had its roots in the East Coast but, rather than, as usual, being predominantly a New York firm with offshoots as we have seen, Piper grew from Baltimore and Philadelphia and out of a similar Industrial Revolution background to us in cities like Manchester, Sheffield, Leeds and Birmingham. Piper Marbury had joined up with Rudnick which was based largely in Chicago and had a very strong real estate practice. The combined firm had grown into New York and had expanding offices on the West Coast. The twin driving forces of Piper were Frank Birch and Lee Miller who were based in Baltimore and Chicago respectively.

Another of their senior statesmen based in their Washington DC office was Senator George Mitchell, the man who, at the instigation of President Clinton, had played such a large part in arbitrating and finally bringing peace to Northern Ireland in the Good Friday Agreement in 1997. Through George Mitchell the firm had impeccable political connections, a must in the USA.

From the outset our determination was to create a single firm that was not dominated by the Americans or the British or the mainland Europeans or Asians, but rather to create a practice that no one could brand as anything other than truly international.

We got some good advice on structures from our auditors PWC and soon were making good progress with the detail behind the merger as well as the joint strategy to create a truly global practice that was focused on providing the very best solutions for our clients wherever their opportunities or issues arose. We made sure that we had a significant 'expansion pot' to fund the growth of further offices around the world as well as a 'global bonus pot' so that we could reward those partners who made a truly global effort to expand and improve the practice.

As we got closer to finalising the deal along came another great opportunity to add a third arm to the merged firm, namely Gray Cary, a pre-eminent Californian practice that would push us to the top of the pile in the USA as well as increasing our window on the Asian market from the West Coast with large offices in San Diego, Los Angeles, San Francisco and Silicon Valley. Terry O'Malley, the CEO of Gray Cary, was another man who shared the vision and we instantly and instinctively got along with him.

So now it was a three-way merger with the 'issue' of what the firm would be called from day one to give a sufficient nod to the component parts. We settled on the inevitably ponderous and extended name of 'DLA Piper Rudnick Gray Cary'. What a mouthful, but it had to be that way. We also had the understandable and inevitable jockeying for position in the merged firm.

There was never any doubt that Nigel Knowles would be at the head of the executive and so it was that to start off with we had *three* CEOs: Nigel, Frank Birch and Lee Miller. The obvious choice as global chairman had to be Senator George Mitchell. Much as I would have liked that job and title I accepted pretty much from the start, particularly after I had met and spent time with George, that he was the right choice. I would be senior partner (Europe and Asia).

All this gave me time to reflect on my own future. It was almost exactly 27 years ago to the day when I had started on my own in that little office at 20 Kennedy Street in Manchester. My dream from the outset had been to create the world's biggest and best law firm and we were now on the very threshold of achieving that dream.

I was also starting to be in demand as a non-executive director. As well as my non-executive directorships at JJB Sports, MS International, Timpson and Mostyn Estates, I had been put on the board of Pubmaster, which owned about 3,000 public houses – where stockbrokers Panmure Gordon had put me in – Civica plc, a large outsourcing public company who were clients of Andrew Darwin and the firm, as well as Paymentshield, a consolidator around the mortgage and insurance market, where the Bank of Scotland integrated finance team had put me in to look after their interest after they had taken a majority stake.

Another one of my interesting clients was a Los Angeles-based businessman called Jack Flowers who I first met in 1982 when I was representing the vendor of a specialist

valve company that made parts for the British defence industry. The company was Dynamic Controls.

I must have impressed Jack as the buyer because within
months of him completing the purchase he told me that he
wanted me to be his lawyer rather than those lawyers who
represented him on the deal, which was pretty flattering.

Over the years we became very firm friends. We get
together whenever he passes through London and I have
been deep-sea fishing with Jack off the coast of Mexico and
had some fabulous times.

We jointly own a company called Naval and Nuclear
Technologies Ltd (a very grand title!) and our ambition is
to use this as a vehicle to acquire specialist defence contractors which we can build up into a mini-conglomerate for
ultimate sale. Time will tell if we succeed.

The non-executive role suited me. I could use my
corporate law experience, give some corporate governance help and use my management experience of running
one of the biggest professional services businesses around.
Furthermore, the money would come in handy as and when
I stood down from DLA. I talked it through with a few
clients, most particularly with Dave Whelan at JJB Sports.
Dave was keen to have me take over as non-executive
chairman and the company then had a market capitalisation of about £750 million with some tough challenges
ahead. Most importantly I talked it through with the two
people whose opinions mattered most, my wife Pamela and
Nigel Knowles. Pamela was very supportive, just so long
as it didn't result in me spending any significantly greater
amount of time under her toes at home (!) and Nigel too
thought the timing was good.

I could step out at the age of 59, having achieved just
about everything I had set out to do, but, most importantly,

could remain very involved with the firm of which I was immensely proud, as the Senior Consultant. I could continue to hold my non-executive directorships and build on those while still focusing on helping the firm and on referring business into the firm wherever I could.

I announced to all the partners that I would be standing down as an equity partner from 30 April 2005 and agreed with Nigel that I could say my farewells formally at an upcoming global partners' conference, the first after the DLA Piper merger, which was to be held in Paris in the spring. Nigel also very generously wanted me to have a retirement party which we organised in July at Wentworth Golf and Country Club and to which we would invite partners, clients and friends to celebrate my 40-odd years in the law. It felt right then and it was a decision that I never regretted.

The conference in Paris was a major event with over 1,000 partners in DLA Piper attending from around the world.

In the past we had had mixed fortunes with speakers at our conference with perhaps the biggest, and in some ways funniest, being a guest appearance from the 'comedian' Bobby Davro the previous year. Despite my having vetted him on the content of his speech and entertainment as carefully as I could, he opened by offending virtually every nationality present as well as the hundreds of women partners with some sexist drivel.

I was sinking deeper and deeper into my seat when our then director of operations (I won't name him to save some blushes!), who looked as though he had spent the day not involved in the business sessions of the Conference but at a pub and bar crawl around London, got up very unsteadily from his table and started weaving his way to the front.

He waved his arms at Davro and said, 'Why don't you just fuck off?'

Half the audience realised there was a problem but the other half obviously thought this was part of the entertainment and burst into a round of applause!

Bobby Davro wasn't going down without a fight. His response to the audience was, 'I've had enough of you lot. You've made me feel about as welcome as Gary Glitter (a former glam rock pop star and convicted paedophile) in Mothercare!'

The audience loved this and clapped even harder!

Bobby then pointed at me and said, 'And you can take your cheque and stick it right up your arse!'

And with that he turned on his heel and marched off the stage.

The audience was now very confused. If this was all part of the performance, why had one of the principal actors left the stage?

I got up at my table but my microphone wasn't switched on. I walked on to the stage and addressed an audience that clearly had no idea what to expect next. In the past when similar, but far less dramatic, occurrences had happened at partners' dinners, I normally started to tell stories interspersed with Tommy Cooper jokes but somehow this just didn't seem appropriate after the Bobby Davro disaster (or triumph depending on what you believed!).

(The director of operations left the firm shortly afterwards!)

So I took a long hard look at the audience and said, 'I'm sure you all enjoyed that – and I now declare the bar well and truly open.'

I think that, up to a point, I largely got away with it on that occasion but for my last conference, particularly with so many new faces present, I wasn't about to take any risks. At that time former Tory leader William Hague was taking a rest from frontline politics and making good money by making speeches and writing history books. I succeeded in getting William and his wife Ffion along to the conference in Paris. I opened the conference by telling all the partners my brief life story and urging them to continue the dream, and that night at the black tie dinner I gave the main speech introducing William Hague, although I deliberately didn't mention his actual name and background until the very end to build the audience's anticipation. I spent most of the dinner trying to persuade William to go back into politics.

I had a lot of fun writing that final speech which Nigel always says was my best. I wrote most of it one night in bed and every time I thought of a new line or theme I started laughing my head off (much to Pamela's annoyance!) and had to jump out of bed frequently in the middle of the night to write it down.

Part of my theme was that in my new career as a non-executive director many of my fellow directors, including the late and great Sir David Frost, had knighthoods and, given my efforts with the Prince's Trust and other charitable causes, where we had raised many millions, it seemed to me (I said only half joking) a 'manifest injustice' that I had not been given the accolade that in my view I so rightly deserved, and that 'my honoured guest', who in my view should soon have his hands firmly back on the reins of power (as he soon did as Foreign Secretary) could sort this all out 'with a stroke of his pen'!

William got up to address the assembled masses and said, 'Well thank you, Lord Lane-Smith, for such an eloquent introduction.'

I shouted out, 'A peerage was more than I was expecting!'

Within a very few short years later, I was truly delighted when Nigel was knighted as Sir Nigel Knowles for services to the legal profession (and to the Prince's Trust) and clearly William Hague and others are just waiting for the right moment now to put me in the House of Lords!

My send-off at Wentworth in July was the most glorious day full of hundreds of my partners, friends and clients and after golf and cocktails we had a fabulous dinner crowned by a live appearance from Abba tribute band the 'Fabba Girls' (a great favourite of Nigel's and mine since we had first seen them at the Royal Albert Hall) which was capped off, by prior arrangement, with me joining the band to give my rendition of 'Money' and 'I Saw Her Standing There' by the Beatles.

This was a truly terrific and very much appreciated tribute from the firm and a day and night that I, and I think many others, will never forget.

As I draw to a close, DLA Piper is now acknowledged by almost every measure as the world's largest law firm with 4,200 lawyers across 30 countries.

The firm is still led by Sir Nigel Knowles who will shortly move up to the global chair role. The candidate shortlist to take the CEO role included partners from Italy, Spain and Britain. Simon Levine was chosen.

In January 2013 the firm opened its 96th office in Seoul, South Korea, as one of the first non-Korean firms to establish there following the deregulation that allowed in overseas competition. DLA Piper had been preparing for this for three to four years before with a number of Korean nationals in the partnership ready to move in. That move reminded me that around fifteen years earlier, I had travelled from Hong Kong to Seoul to address with three other DLA partners an audience of about 150 people all from the Korean conglomerate, Daewoo.

My fellow partners dealt with their specialist subjects and I asked the organiser what he would like me to talk about.

He suggested I talk for ten to fifteen minutes about the new-ish Blair administration and economic prospects in Europe. I put something together and what appeared to be a very attentive audience listened quietly and politely to my address.

When I finished and said 'thank you' there was a very encouraging round of applause.

I stepped down from the dais and said to the organiser, 'Do you think that went down all right?'

He responded, 'Oh yes. I think they thoroughly enjoyed it.' He then added, 'Mind you, only 10 per cent of them understand English!'

While the deal which would make DLA Piper the biggest legal practice in the world was going ahead, I reflected on the progress of some London-based firms that had ruled the roost when I started out.

Freshfields dates back to 1743. Freshfields Bruckhaus Deringer now has 28 offices in seventeen jurisdictions and employs 2,500 lawyers. It states on its website that it can help you in regions where it *does not* have an office such as Africa, Australia, Brazil, central and eastern Europe, the Commonwealth of Independent States, Greece, Israel, Latin America and the Caribbean, Scandinavia, South Africa, Switzerland and Turkey. (DLA largely has – and can!)

Allen & Overy, founded in 1930, has 43 offices worldwide and 500 partners.

Clifford Chance was formed by the merger of Coward Chance, founded in 1802, and Clifford Turner, founded in 1900. Clifford Chance was the global giant we had recently overtaken on our march to the top.

Herbert Smith was founded in the City of London in 1882. When it merged with the Australian firm, Freehills, in October 2012 it had thirteen offices across Europe, the Middle East and Asia and around 240 partners.

Slaughter and May was founded in 1889 by William Capel Slaughter and William May, both of whom had been partners at Ashurst Morris Crisp. In 1974 it opened an office in Hong Kong and, during the 1980s, acted on a number of UK privatisations including those of British Airways, British Gas and British Steel. After limited expansion overseas it closed its New York office in September 2004 and its Singapore office in October 2004. In December 2005 it gave its office in Paris to a French law firm. It now has a minimal overseas presence but despite that remains one of the most respected and profitable firms.

Linklaters was founded in 1838 when John Linklater entered into a partnership with Julius Dods. The firm was then known as Dods & Linklater. In 1920 the firm, by this time known as Linklater & Co., merged with Paines Plythe & Huxtable, which had been founded by a descendant of Thomas Paine. In the late 1990s it merged with a number of European firms and, in 1999, shortened its name to just Linklaters.

All these are strong and robust law firms that will survive the test of time.

It is my earnest wish that DLA Piper will also stand the test of time. The biggest enemy of continued progress is complacency. Nigel and I always believed in constant momentum, challenge and improvement. DLA Piper is constantly evolving and its determination is to remain the world's pre-eminent Global Business law firm.

There are too many lawyers in the world today and in reality far too many law firms.

The great shake-up will continue for years to come.

I count myself as fortunate to have operated between 1964 and 2014 – 50 years when the world for a lawyer was truly an oyster and there were pearls to be found.

Epilogue

On Thursday 16 May 2013 I arrived in Barcelona to attend the DLA Piper global partners' conference.

As partners arrived from all corners of the globe at the airport or train station they were met by DLA representatives and taken in dedicated transport vehicles down to the cruise ship dock.

In fact, quite a few partners arrived by bicycle, having traversed the Pyrenees mountains from France in support of some preferred DLA charities and raising about £40,000 in the process.

At the dock we were met by the *Liberty of the Seas*, an enormous cruise liner. The entire ship had been chartered by the firm for three days and four nights to host nearly 1,400 partners from around the world.

We set sail on Friday evening to cruise over to Cannes in the south of France where we moored up offshore by the islands.

Over those three days we had practice group and sector-specific sessions, technical updates, marketing services and a great speech by Senator George Mitchell, our Chairman Emeritus, which was particularly moving as George reinforced that the reputation and integrity of the firm was paramount: 'No assignment, no fee, no client matters more than the integrity of this Firm.'

I met up with old friends who I had known from the early days and made dozens of new ones from around the world.

The sense of determination and belief in the firm and its future was just incredibly moving and seemed to me to epitomise all those dreams I had had so many years ago.

Nigel rounded off the presentations to all partners with what was undoubtedly one of, if not the best, performances I had ever seen him give.

His summary of where we had come from, where we were in the world today and where we were going in the future was masterful.

We were now by any definition the world's largest law firm and now our intention was to become the world's leading business law firm as we focused all our efforts on representing clients wherever they chose to do business.

Nigel got a standing ovation.

Saturday afternoon was a time for socialising and joining social activities and pastimes. I had wavered between a talk on some of the world's leading vineyards and 'How to make the perfect dry Martini'. I opted for the latter!

Later, after some more motivational speeches and awards in the lecture theatre, over 1,350 partners sat down to a gala dinner in an enormous dining 'theatre' with tables spread over two huge levels.

I sat with Nigel, Lord (Tim) Clement-Jones the managing partner of the London office, and managing partners and senior partners from New Zealand, France, Berlin, Oslo and Qatar.

I asked Nigel and Andrew Darwin if they would mind if I got up to give a short address to the assembled company at the end of dinner.

I thought Andrew looked a little nervous – he had long memories of me speaking at partners' conferences over many years – but to his credit he agreed that I could and should and introduced me.

Here is the short speech I gave:

Back on 1 October 1977 I started my own law firm in Manchester in about 500 square feet of office space with a receptionist and secretary.

I decided on that first day that my vision and ambition was to create the world's number one law firm.

[The audience laughed and gasped so I pointed out that the definition of failure is to aim low – and miss!]

36 years later and we *are* the world's number one law firm. We have 96 offices – when will we reach 100?

[Loud applause.]

I have listened a lot to everything over the last two or three days and heard some fantastic ideas for making the firm even better.

[I had.]

But it's not *just* about the law. It's about global connectivity and market intelligence.

As a client I value commercial advice, contacts and *local* know-how.

If you want to do a deal in my home city Manchester, come to me – I know where the bodies are buried!

In this firm we have that knowledge in virtually every business location throughout the world.

From Birmingham to Brussels, from Baltimore to Beijing, from Bahrain to Brisbane – we know where the bodies are buried!

That is gold dust!

As Sir Nigel said today, we will never *follow* the market.

We will *set* the market and we will lead the market globally – BECAUSE WE CAN!

Thank you for this wonderful event. I'm brimming over with pride.

36 years ago *even I* could never have dreamt that 35 years later I would be sitting on one of the world's largest cruise liners – having chartered the entire ship! – off the coast of the south of France with over 1,350 partners from all around the globe and on Saturday afternoon my chosen activity was 'How to make the perfect dry Martini'!

You couldn't make it up!

Index